Millionaire Homeowner

Millionaire Homeowner

How to Turn Your Home into a
Real Estate Goldmine

Stuart Leland Rider

EP
Entrepreneur.
Press

Managing editor: Jere L. Calmes
Cover design: Austin Metze
Interior illustration: Larry Jost
Composition and production: Eliot House Productions

This publication is designed to provide accurate and authoritative information in regard to the subject matter covered. It is sold with the understanding that the publisher is not engaged in rendering legal, accounting, or other professional services. If legal advice or other expert assistance is required, the services of a competent professional person should be sought.

Library of Congress Cataloging-in-Publication Data
Rider, Stuart Leland.
　　Millionaire homeowner: how to turn your home into a real estate goldmine/by Stuart Leland Rider.
　　　　p.　　cm.
　　Includes index.
　　ISBN 1-932531-65-3 (alk. paper)
　　1. Real estate investment—United States. 2. Residential real estate—Purchasing—United States. 3. House buying—United States. 4. House selling—United States. I. Title.
HD259.L45 2005
332.63'243—dc22　　　　　　　　　　　　　　　　　　2005004986

Printed in Canada

11 10 09 08 07 06 05　　　　　　　　　　　　　　　　10 9 8 7 6 5 4 3 2 1

Contents

Contents

Contents

Contents

Contents

Preface

The number of people of all ages who are buying million-dollar homes continues to astound me. People who end up with million-dollar homes started with smaller, more modest ones, and worked their way up the ladder. You can, too! This book is intended to show you how you can become wealthy without undue risk. It will require hard work, diligence, perseverance, and analytical thinking. The major topics of discussion will be:

- Profiting from your personal residence
- Investing in housing
- Renovation and expansion of residential real estate
- Managing income properties for a profit
- Real estate development of raw land for houses
- Portfolio building and strategies for wealth

Along the way, we will be discussing all the basic tools you will need to accomplish these goals. You cannot neglect the basics, and there are no shortcuts. If you do not do the work, you will be disappointed in the results.

This book is about houses and homes and how to make a great deal of money by working with both. You might notice that I differentiate between the two; a home is a place where you live and raise a family, and a house is a building that you can invest in for a profit. In this book, I will show you that they can be one and the same, but must be considered differently. Starting with the house you own, you will find out how to make a lot of money over a lifetime. In addition, once you understand and have experienced that process, you will begin to consider the possibilities of working with your own home as well as other houses that you do not intend to live in. The combination of the two can make you rich enough to quit your day job. This book will show you how to:

- Make the most of your current home or your first home
- Move up in the world and increase the investment possibilities with future homes
- Buy the right properties every time
- Build your own home for a profit
- Become a land and/or housing developer

You do not have to start working on your own home with the thought of eventually becoming a developer. You can work with it throughout your lifetime and do very well.

For most Americans, the home is, and will be, their largest single asset. You can make your home the most productive asset in your economic lifetime. Start with your home and take the journey wherever you want to go. No matter how far you go, there's a lot of money to be made. Millions of people are doing just that!

Become an Entrepreneur

It's Easy to Do

CHAPTER 1

The Case for Real Estate

There are characteristics of real estate investment that are not shared by any other investment type. When added together, they create a formidable argument in favor of investing in residential and income-producing real property. There is also ample argument for investing in raw land for the long pull. There will be more on this later in the book. The characteristics that are inherent in real property investments are as follows:

- Real estate is a finite commodity; it appreciates over time due to the increasing scarcity of the commodity. The creation of new land is so costly that only governments can afford to do it. So long as people continue to immigrate to our shores and people continue to have babies, there will be a constantly increasing demand. Some areas of the country benefit more from this than others.

- Each piece of property is unique.
- Income property sells for a Cap rate on actual earnings, so you can generate a cash flow with a specific return on equity from day one.
- Your investment property may be depreciated, and the resulting write-off shelters your annual income. Properly purchased income property can produce an income where 70 percent of the cash flow is tax sheltered. This dramatically increases your annual return on investment (ROI).
- When you decide to sell a piece of real estate, you can reinvest in another property, defraying the capital gains taxes indefinitely.
- If you want to cash out, your profits are taxed as capital gain at the current federal rate of 15 percent.

I am not aware of any other single investment that shares all of these characteristics.

Unique Aspects of the Investment Itself

Another view of real property lies in its uniqueness. Other than the tract home, all real estate is unique. At first, the location is unique, and second, the buildings on the land are unique. This aspect lends a certain cachet to each and every piece of real property. The single overriding characteristic that has contributed to value in real property is location. The old saw about the three most important characteristics of a piece of real estate being "location, location, and location," is as true today as it ever was. The definition of location has, however, changed with the times. In the old days, the 100 percent location in any town was at the intersection of Central and Main. Location, however, is now defined by our mobility. The most important characteristics of location are now visibility (from vehicles) and accessibility (by vehicles). This is true of any type of real property. The better these characteristics are, the more the property is worth. The other factor that affects real property and is common to all commodities is supply and demand.

How this relates to housing is that homes are valued by their location in relation to commute corridors, amenities, natural attractions such as lakes, seashore, mountains, and views. Within the breakdown of housing, there are other factors that relate to value, but the overall location will determine a great deal of the value of a particular home.

Creating Real Estate

Real estate properties are most often created by a real estate developer. It is usually that individual's primary occupation, and he or she must do it well enough to create a profit. Sometimes it is created by the occupant and later sold to another user/investor. No matter who creates it, it is everywhere you look. The home you live in was created by a developer, and sold to you or the original occupant at a profit. The corner grocery store and the dentist's office building are other examples. Almost every structure not owned by the government can be classified as a real estate investment of one kind or another.

How Do You Fit In?

I have always worked with the theory that if someone else can do it, then I can do it. By learning as you go, and not biting off more than you can chew, you can, too. What you don't know you can find out; what you cannot do, you can hire to be done. You can find partners, consultants, employees, and experts to fill in all the gaps in your knowledge. All you need is the desire and some common sense, and you will be well on your way to becoming a real estate investor, or even a developer.

I define the business of development and/or investment as the business of taking calculated risks, and the process is one of winnowing the list of known risks to the point where the individual involved is comfortable making the go or no-go decision for the project.

You will notice considerable repetition as you progress through this book. As each topic is examined, the repetition is designed to cause you to recall the previous associations, as many topics, if not all of them, are discussed from a variety of viewpoints with different considerations in mind. The single elements of real estate investment and development can be summed up in one paragraph, but the ramifications, choices, considerations, and alternatives involved in the decision-making process must be examined and implemented from multiple viewpoints.

Housing—The Prime Mover

The single most important force behind the real estate market in the United States is the desire of all Americans to realize the traditional American Dream—to own their own homes. The single-family home has been the average family's answer to getting ahead and saving for the future. As if March 2005, Kiplinger reports that a record 69 percent of American families own their

Heads Up

You are probably thinking that you are not interested in becoming an investor or developer, but you would be wrong. If you proceed to create wealth with your home, you will be doing just that. Admittedly, you will be doing it on a somewhat limited scale, but the process is the same, and your attention to detail, the formulation of a well thought out plan, and executing it correctly and on time, will determine your level of success.

Heads Up

As you read through this book, you will be constantly changing hats, from a buyer to an owner, from an investor to a seller, from a builder to a manager. Before you're done, your hat rack will contain an amazing variety of hats, some comfortable, and some decidedly not so. Wear those that are comfortable, and hire someone to fill the ones that don't fit you.

homes, and it is anticipated to go as high as 72 percent this decade. Home ownership is considered the cornerstone of the American Dream.

After World War II, the U.S. Congress passed a series of laws enabling the ownership of housing by most citizens. The law enabling the Veterans Administration (VA) and Federal Housing Administration (FHA) loan system has been further reinforced with government-backed home mortgage securities known as Fanny Mae, Freddie Mac, and Ginny Mae loans. Without boring you with detail, these laws enable people to buy homes with as little as zero dollars down (in the case of the VA loan). The banks that make these loans bundle them together and trade these securities on the market to investors, both large and small. The sheer volume of money made available by this process is what enables the average American to own a home. The more we build, the more affordable they are, and the faster they sell. The absorption of housing is what prompts the creation of everything else in real estate. People need to eat, play, and work, and all these activities require buildings. These buildings are all real estate investments. Believe me Donald Trump does not build them all. People like you and I create them. I think that's why you're reading this book. If you don't want to build, you might like to buy. You can make money either way.

Purchasing Your Own Home

Individual home ownership has proven to be the most widely used, and popular form of savings for the average American family. Since everyone needs a place to live, and paying a mortgage is not much different than paying rent, most people find that the only obstacle is the down payment. The government-backed mortgage has solved this by lowering the down payment from the 20 percent required by a conventional loan to as little as 3 percent for an FHA loan. The benefits are many; the interest is deductible from your gross income for tax purposes, and the house appreciates in value while you live there. The mortgage payment is designed to pay off the loan balance over the life of the loan. People are then free to use the resulting equity in their homes for any purpose they wish. It has become common to use it to purchase a college education for their children or to purchase cars and boats. Sadly, a great many people use it to pay off their accumulated credit card debt.

Rentals

People who have surplus funds often find that they can look at a modest investment in another house for rental purposes. Many a real estate empire has started with the purchase of a second house for rental. The rent collected allows the landlord to pay the mortgage, thus building equity in a second house. When this is parlayed into several more, it often leads to exchanging ownership in several houses for ownership in an apartment complex or small office building. Thus, a real estate investment program can be grown into a significant real estate portfolio.

Leverage

If ownership is desirable as well as profitable, using leverage merely compounds the benefits. Leverage is the most common way to use other people's money (OPM) to make more money on your own money. This is the best characteristic of investing in real property. It makes your return even better.

A simple example, reflected in Table 1.1, of leverage occurs when people use a mortgage to buy a home. If you buy a home for $100,000, using a conventional down payment of 20 percent, you need to borrow $80,000 to complete the purchase. Simplistically, if you sell the house for $120,000, you have made a gross profit of $20,000. However, the deal is better than it appears as you have used the leverage of the borrowed $80,000 to increase the rate of return on your cash invested from 20 percent on the gross price of the house, to a 100 percent rate of return on the $20,000 cash down payment originally invested.

Table 1.1—*Rate of Return Analysis*

Item	Purchase Price	Sales Price	Cash Yield	ROI
Home	$100,000	$120,000	$20,000	20% on price
Down payment	$20,000		$20,000	100% on equity

A more realistic look at a typical home sale and the realistic impact of leverage is shown in Table 1.2.

Table 1.2—*Leverage and the Single Family Home*

Item	Cash Transaction	Leveraged Transaction
Purchasing the home	$100,000	$20,000
Debt	$0	$80,000

Table 1.2—*Leverage and the Single Family Home*, continued

Item	Cash Transaction	Leveraged Transaction
Interest for 2 years at 7% simple	$0	$11,200
Net sale price	$130,000	$130,000
Total cash invested	$100,000	$31,200
Gross profit	$30,000	$30,000
Net profit	$30,000	$18,800
Return on cash invested	30%	60%
Annual rate of return	15%	30%

There you have it, the background, the reasons the market is what it is, and the cast of characters. By the end of this book, you will have a pretty good idea of where you can fit into the picture, and how you can profit by doing so. This book deals with using your own home as a basis for building wealth. Starting with your home and expanding into the residential market and beyond, you can build an impressive portfolio. What you do with it is up to you.

Where Are We Going?

You have lived your entire life in and around other people's money-making investments. You were born in one, went to work in one, lived in one, played in one, will most likely die in one, and be buried in someone else's money-making investment. Yes, people who build cemeteries do so for a profit! It's about time you took a good look around and understood the implications of this.

Almost everyone who deals with investments of any type is involved in real estate. Over 69 percent of our country owns a private residence, and real property is an integral and essential part of everyone's daily life. The sad fact is that most people seem oblivious to the fact that every structure involved in their daily life is a money making enterprise for someone else. Even the majority of people who own their own home seldom spend any time thinking about real estate as a pure investment opportunity.

"They" say that a home is the single largest purchase that most people will make in a lifetime, and yet it is amazing how little thought to the investment aspects of the transaction goes into the decision to make such a purchase. You would think that if someone were spending that amount of money, he or she might be a touch more analytical about the purchase. If someone were buying an office building or a shopping center, I'm sure there would be a more complex analysis of the potential of the property purchase.

I believe that analytical thinking should be applied to all aspects of life, and especially to major investments. I define this as the beginning of entrepreneurship. *Webster's Dictionary* defines entrepreneurship as "the organization, management, and assumption of risk of a business enterprise"; hence, an entrepreneur is one who does exactly that. My own definition is a little more whimsical, as I define entrepreneurship, correctly applied to deal making, as trying to see around all the corners of a deal. What exactly does this mean to me? This question is the subject of this book, and the answer to this question has become the philosophy by which I try to live my life. Simplistically, I'm a professional pessimist. I attempt to identify the worst possible scenario in a transaction and evaluate whether I can live with this potential eventuality. If I can, then I proceed to the next step. The unique spin that I give to a deal is to imagine every potential direction the deal may take, and then pursue them all relentlessly. I then have the option to take the most profitable direction offered by the deal, as it evolves. In my day-to-day life, I tend to be analytical about most actions, but perhaps less sanguine than I am when looking at a purely financial transaction.

Entrepreneurship

How does this philosophy apply to a real estate investment or a real estate investment career? I look at it as a fail safe approach to all transactions. When most people buy a home, they look at where it is in relation to their work, shopping, schools, entertainment, and the area that best reinforces their self image. The entrepreneur also looks at it as a business deal with a view to maximizing the return on investment over a specific period of time. That is not to say that the decision will rest solely on the business aspects of the home, but that all factors will be taken into consideration prior to the purchase. The true entrepreneur is always looking at the ROI.

There are many ways to look at the value of an investment, and in this area, I am a purist. I have no use for the discounted rate of return, the present worth of the dollar, or after-tax rates of return, I believe that the only true measure of a deal is cash return on cash invested, aka the cash-on-cash return. If that works for you, all else is gravy.

Definition

ROI is the acronym for return on investment; also known as the rate of return or the percentage yield on cash invested.

What This Book Covers

This book is intended to show you how you can become wealthy without undue risk. It will require hard work, diligence, perseverance, and analytical thinking. The major topics of discussion will be:

- Profiting from your personal residence
- Investing in housing
- Renovation and expansion of residential real estate
- Managing income properties for a profit
- Real estate development of raw land for houses
- Portfolio building and strategies for wealth

Along the way, we will be discussing all the basic tools you will need to accomplish these goals. You cannot neglect the basics, and there are no shortcuts. If you do not do the work, you will be disappointed in the results.

Housing vs. Investment Property

Personal housing is a subject and an investment that most people have in common. If you can adjust your thinking about your personal housing then, treated properly, your new mindset can become a foundation for an investment philosophy that can carry through to other investments and other aspects of your life. You should show a profit, personal or financial, in everything you do; with a little thought and planning, you can consistently do so. A house is not just a home; it should also be a serious income producing asset. It can, and should be, a primary stepping stone for wealth building.

Once you have it made financially, you can treat your next home as a reward for a job well done, but while you are working on building a solid net worth, you cannot afford to neglect your primary financial asset. Many people, in fact, make a career out of housing in many different ways.

Investment property, by its very nature, demands analytical thinking, and it is somewhat difficult for most people, all of a sudden, to become analytical. It must be studied and practiced daily so that it becomes second nature to you, and then whenever you are called upon to be analytical, you can take your everyday mindset and ramp it up to suit the occasion.

What to Look For

If you are buying a home, you will need to examine all the usual aspects of the home as they relate to your life and your future plans. But, in addition, I want you to ask yourself some additional questions that pertain to the potential investment itself, rather than the housing aspects of the purchase.

- How long am I going to live there?
- How much can I expect to profit from this house, and where is the profit going to come from?
- Where will the area be in ten years?

- Is the house in the path of growth, or in an established neighborhood?
- Can the home be upgraded or expanded?
- Will the area support an improved and expanded house, or will doing so over-improve the home?
- How should I pay for the house?

These are the types of questions that you would ask yourself if you were buying an apartment complex, an office building, or a retail building. Why not apply a little entrepreneurial thinking to your home as well?

What's Going On

Some people make money on a home before they buy it. Normally, when a developer opens up a new tract for sale, early buyers get a better price on the homes and more freebees than later buyers; once the tract has been accepted and sales accelerate, prices rise. The normal turn-around time for a builder in a tract is six months from purchase to move in. During this time, it is not uncommon in areas that are experiencing growth, for prices to increase 10 to 15 percent or more during that start-up period. It has become increasingly common for people re-sell the home before they buy it, making a handsome profit on their initial earnest money deposit. Currently, this is an increasing trend in growth areas. In an article in the *Arizona Republic*, dated 8/1/04, by Glen Creno and Catherine Reagor Burrough, there is a discussion of the growing impact of this investment trend, and the industry's reaction to it. The developers have found that this type of investor behavior hurts their developments and significantly raises the housing price to all buyers. They now, in both the Las Vegas and Phoenix markets, are starting to require that all buyers must actually move into the home if they are purchasing it. No move in, no sale. At the very least, most housing builders are limiting the number of investor sales in their new tracts.

What can you glean from this article? My take on this is that the quick turn-around speculators have too little imagination and are trying to jump on a train that has already left the station. They are lazy and guilty of sloppy thinking. The people who started this trend have already moved on. The situation cited in the article mentioned above is symptomatic of an environment where prices are rising in the face of consistent demand. Currently, 60,000 plus homes a year are being built in this area of Arizona. When rampant speculation like this occurs, it's best to look for another area or another type of home. The very nature of a residential tract will limit your increased value to normal appreciation. Because of the uniformity of the typical tract, there are finite limits on what you can do to a home without over-improving it. You will also compete with all other homes that are the same model. If you look in areas of custom housing, your opportunities are infinitely greater.

Timing

An important aspect of entrepreneurial thinking is to be on the front end of the curve. Some specific examples from my own career that will give you an idea of how good projects evolve are discussed below.

War Stories

In 1976, for my first real estate development transaction, I optioned a piece of property from Boise Cascade Corporation in San Ramon, California. We were able to negotiate a two-year option at a specific price to give ourselves a chance to get the required governmental approvals and pull the project together. Because my financial partner had limited funds, we were very careful about our front-end expenses. Accordingly, we offered our architect a fee plus a percentage if he would defer the fee until such time as the project started construction, and our option price to Boise Cascade was paid with letters of credit rather than cash.

At the end of the two-year period, we had secured all the approvals necessary for the project, including a building permit, and had executed leases for the project for 97 percent of the leasable space. Our total investment was $13,000 in cash, and letters of credit for $50,000. It was time to build. In the meantime, another developer approached us to inquire whether we would sell him the project as-is. After several months of negotiating, we agreed on a price with the new developer assuming all outstanding obligations including the architect. Our conclusion was that we could not do better on a rate of return than the price we negotiated. Our total cash investment was $63,000. Our yield was money back and $750,000. Our entrepreneurial approach to the front end resulted in an ROI of 1190.47 percent over the two-year period; or a 595.23 percent annual ROI.

As a result of this deal, our company policy was changed to accommodate this type of marketing for every project we would undertake. Since that time, our projects have been both for lease and for sale from the moment we open the escrow. The result has been that, on projects sold before construction (approximately 50 percent of our projects), we have averaged a 300 percent plus annual ROI, and on projects actually built, we have averaged 180 percent annual ROI. Our projects' rates of return are calculated from the time we start spending money on a deal to the time when the project achieves a 95 percent occupancy or sale.

From that point on, the development phase is over, and the operating phase begins. That is another project category I refer to as *Continuous Redevelopment*©, and it is a constant condition until the project is sold. This subject is dealt with in great detail in *The Great Big Book on Real Estate Investment* (Entrepreneur Press, 2005).

Your Home

What does the above story have to do with your home? Probably nothing. I'm trying to tickle your mind into thinking about new ideas and approaches; when this happens, a host of new possibilities will open up for you. Some readers will finish this book and spend their lives buying and selling homes, perhaps even building homes and subdivisions, while others may play with housing for a while and decide to tackle something else like commercial property. The important point I want to drive home is that entrepreneurial thinking is essential to your prosperity. Good ideas abound, keep your eyes open, and take advantage of any and all opportunities you run across.

The Long-Term Mindset

What I'd like you to include in your analytical toolkit are the following concepts:

- Research your market; update your findings annually.
- Look for the best location for every home.
- Re-examine the market; test your conclusions.
- Look at every new purchase in every conceivable way.
- Work all the possibilities simultaneously.
- Do not fall in love with any particular piece of real estate.

> **Heads Up**
> Real estate is demanding painstaking work, but it can be indecently lucrative if you do it right.

- Approach every transaction as if it is the most important transaction of your investment career. It might turn out to be just that.
- Sign all your checks yourself, no exceptions, unless you have become so large and successful that it doesn't matter to you.
- Do not delegate negotiations on financial matters to others, especially attorneys. It's your wallet on the line; make your own mistakes.
- Hire good consultants, listen to them, and then make the decisions yourself.
- If you make a mistake, correct it immediately and move on. Forget about blame, there's no profit in it.

With this as a basis for your thinking, you can approach any real property transaction with a healthy mindset. I have always said that real estate investing is not rocket science; even people with an eighth grade education have become multimillionaires. One friend of mine made it big after escaping to the United States from the East German coal mines. He had a fourth grade education. He retired from the housing business as a multimillionaire.

The Process

Any real property transaction is relatively simple and impossibly complex at the same time. It is really what you make of it. The unconscious mind looks at it like this:

- *Housing.* Find what you like, buy it, move in, and live there.
- *Income property investment.* Find a property you like, arrange for the financing, buy it, and hope your tenants stay and pay rent.
- *Real estate development.* Find a piece of vacant dirt or one with a disposable building on it, buy it, design a building, build it, and fill it up.

If this is your view of the real estate investment and development process, don't bother with the rest of this book. I can't help you. If, however, you think there might be more to it than meets the eye, and want to know what it's really like; if you want to make some serious keeping money, and if you are willing to learn and work hard, real estate investment and/or development may be the vehicle most suitable for making your fortune. *At the very least, you will be able to make money consistently on your own home.*

Your Objective

This book is going to deal primarily with housing, starting with the home you already own, or if you do not own one, with your first house purchase. Using that as a foundation, we will explore a progression of strategies which will result in you profiting from your own home throughout your lifetime, and perhaps, branching out and expanding into home renovation or construction for profit.

This book will touch briefly on various commercial real estate possibilities to expose you to the other half of the business. That way, if you get bored with housing, you will have some idea of where to look for your next potential transaction. The following chapter will provide you with specific detail on what you can and cannot do and expose you to real estate markets and how they affect the value of your home and potential future investments. It will also introduce you to all the players in the real property business.

CHAPTER 2

The Nuts and Bolts of Real Estate

Every pursuit or discipline has its own particular language and methods of operation; real estate is no different. Real property, aka real estate or realty, involves the improvement, management, purchasing, and selling of land and/or land and buildings. There are many terms and actions involved in real property transactions that, while not unique to real estate, are routine in the daily control and manipulation of real estate assets.

Land Descriptions

Land is described in many ways, the most common of which, for small parcels, is called a lot. A lot is pictorially represented by a plat. An example of a plat can be seen in Figure 2.1.

Figure 2.1—*A Typical Plat*

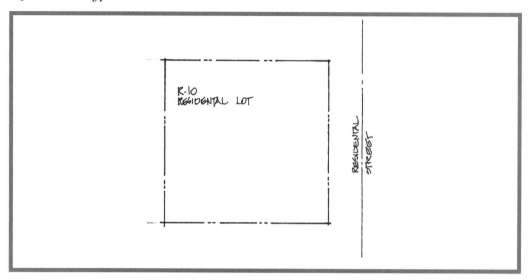

Heads Up

When you are dealing with the purchase, renovation, or construction of a house, you will encounter most of what is covered in this chapter. Breeze through it and become acquainted with the scope of the components, but do not dwell on it. You can come back to this for reference when you need it. By working with houses, you will eventually become expert in all of it.

Lots are typically small parcels of land, less than five acres in size. Larger-size lots are referred to as parcels. A square mile is 640 acres, also known as a section. A section can be broken down into 160-acre parcels; these resulting parcels are known as quarter sections.

Meets and Bounds

Today there are basically two methods of identifying property. Large parcels of land are described by meets and bounds. These are similar to the old eastern system, that used trees, rocks, and other physical features on the land to describe a parcel. Meets and bounds now use modern geometrical location points and compass headings based on the range and township principles. This method has recently been replaced by a system using Global Positioning Satellite (GPS) information. Ranges and townships are artificial lines on a map used by the government to delineate areas of land broken down into manageable sections.

Parcel numbers (tax) and local government budgets. The purpose of tax ID numbers, in addition to providing a legal description for a parcel of land, is to simplify the collection of real estate taxes for the local municipality and county governments. This enables a uniform basis for taxation and land identification. Once a large parcel of property has been broken up, i.e., subdivided, new parcel numbers are given to the newly created individual parcels of land. This enables the local government to identify and tax each individual parcel of land. This also simplifies identification of individual parcels for the purposes of buying and selling land. A typical tax parcel number is similar to a Social Security number. If you look at the tax bill in Figure 2.2 you will see how the government not only identifies each parcel but how it prorates taxes on each parcel of land. On this particular tax bill you can see not only how the parcel is identified, but also the components of the taxes and how they are allocated to this particular parcel.

Encumbrances

In addition to describing a piece of real property, there are other conditions imposed on individual pieces of property that will appear in the property title report (or abstract, if you are in the eastern part of the country). These items are known, in general, as encumbrances, and can be liens, easements, or public encumbrances, such as assessments, rights of way, and utility easements. These can also be depicted graphically such as shown in Figure 2.3 wherein a residential lot is depicted with easements and setbacks in the locations shown.

You'll notice in Figure 2.3, the platted lot drawing, that there are both easements (PUE) and setbacks. Setbacks are government-imposed requirements, as is the PUE which is a public utility easement. In addition to the above it is not uncommon to also have deed restrictions, height restrictions, and general subdivision requirements such as covenants, conditions, and restrictions (CC&Rs).

Deed Restrictions

Deed restrictions are recorded conditions, put in place against a piece of property that can restrict or impose conditions on what may be built or housed on that particular piece of land. There may be, for instance, a restriction that you can only have one horse per acre, and no farm animals. Or, there may be restrictions against the construction of two-story houses on the property or homes less than 3,000 square feet in size. The restrictions are enforceable, and are voluntarily imposed on a piece of land by the owners. These restrictions are then passed along with the land to any successor owners.

Covenants, Conditions, and Restrictions (CC&Rs)

CC&Rs are restrictions imposed upon a subdivision by the developer, to ensure its uniformity during the development and ownership periods. These generally

Figure 2.2—*Typical Tax Bill*

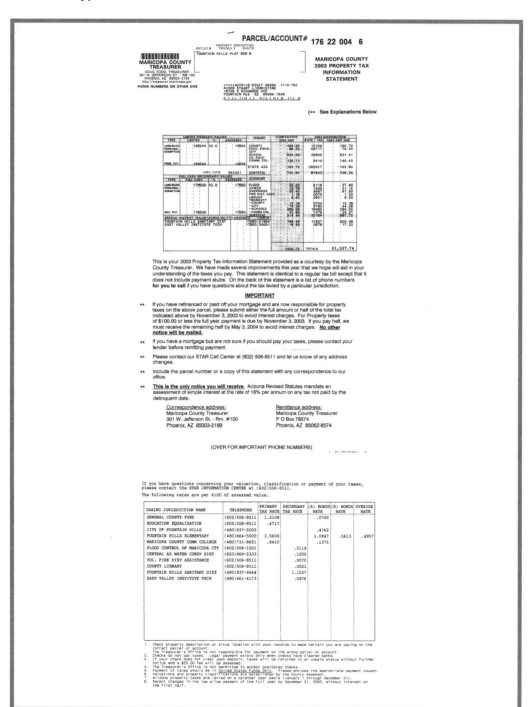

Figure 2.3—*Platted Lot with Easements*

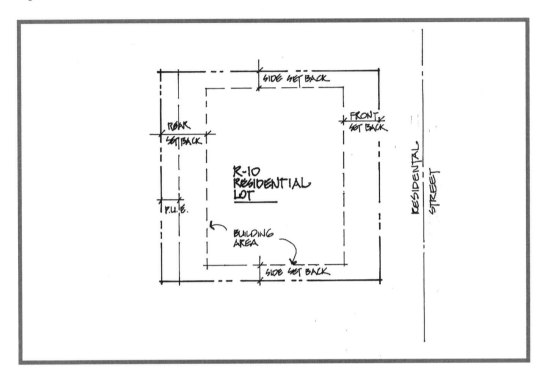

spell out minimum house sizes, exterior finishes, parking restrictions, landscaping requirements, and restrictions for pets and other animals. They may, in some instances, also restrict your ability to rent the property to an unrelated third party.

Public Restrictions

Public restrictions on private property deal primarily with the issues of zoning, and issues that deal with the uniform building code (UBC) as it is applied to each class of property.

Zoning. Zoning restrictions are those imposed by the city, town, or county, and they are imposed on classes of property rather than specific parcels of land. They spell out, among other things, height restrictions, setbacks, and allowable lot coverage.

These property classifications are relatively simple to understand and separate real property into industrial, commercial, residential, public, or governmental property classifications. Within each classification there are additional breakdowns such as R–1, R–3, and R1–43. These classifications simply outline the density of the dwelling units per acre, or, in the case of commercial and industrial property, the total square footage per acre permitted in each zoning category.

The law of eminent domain. Another right that the public holds over private property is the right of eminent domain. This right allows that, for the public good, public agencies may take private property with compensation for use for public projects. In some instances, it may take private property, reclassify it, and resell it to private individuals for development. This is the case in urban redevelopment. Condemnation of property (the actual taking) is very common in areas where highways are expanded and widened. The only control the individual property owner has over this particular process is that he or she may bring suit against the government or file an appeal for a better price on the property taken.

General plan. Uniformly, in all areas of the country, property is broken down into property classifications governed by an overall master plan for that particular area, known as a general plan. A general plan is not a fixed plan of development; rather, it is a work in progress that is periodically updated and frequently changed as the community expands. Individuals may affect changes in the general plan by making application to the local governing body such as the town council, city council, or county board of supervisors. This is a relatively straightforward process and requires a submission of plans and the payment of fees. There may be additional studies required such as traffic studies, and in the case of the state of California, an environmental impact statement (EIS) or environmental impact report (EIR). This will require input from the planning staff and hearings before the planning commission, city councils, or county boards of supervisors.

Within the general plan, property classifications are broken down into individual zoning areas.

Zoning Classifications

Zoning classifications are, as mentioned earlier, defined as industrial, commercial, residential, and public. Typical industrial zoning is I–1, or M–1. Typical commercial zoning varies from C–0, to C–1, C–2, and C–3. The C classifications shown here stand for commercial office, and commercial 1, 2, and 3. The differences in the C classifications are that C–0 provides only for the construction of office space, whereas C–1, C–2, and C–3 provide for both office and retail developments. The differences may lie in the individual uses permitted and restrictions on such design criteria as setbacks, building height, and drive-through facilities. Typical residential classifications are broken down by density. One classification, for instance, designated as R1–43 means that only one home per acre is permitted.

Designations such as R–3 or R–5 usually mean that 3,000 or 5,000 square feet of land is required per dwelling unit. Each area has different breakdowns and you should refer to your town or county zoning code to determine the specific residential classifications for your area.

Specific Zoning

The specific zoning classifications are covered in your town manual that spell out at least, but not limited to, the following criteria for development:

- Maximum building coverage
- Maximum building heights
- Maximum lot coverage
- Maximum stories
- Setback requirements
- Parking requirements
- Livestock restrictions
- Landscape restrictions
- Use restrictions
- Architectual standards
- Permitted building materials
- Slope ordinances

Uniform Building Codes (UBC) and Local Building Codes

The uniform building code (UBC) is a national code that dictates minimum standards for a variety of construction types. It spells out minimum structural standards, finish standards, and safety standards. It is also linked to OSHA, the federal Occupation, Safety, and Health Act. OSHA spells out working condition standards which must be maintained during the construction of anything. The UBC is supplemented by additional codes imposed by local municipalities. Local code enforcement takes precedence over the national code, and the municipality always has the last word. It is their responsibility to interpret the code and enforce it as they see fit. In times of dispute, the local municipality almost always wins. After having been in the business for almost 30 years I am unaware of anybody successfully challenging a municipality in court over the interpretation of the building code.

Public Utitlity Easements (PUE)

Public utility easements are most often found along the front property line (the street side) of the individual pieces of real estate. They provide room for the construction of public utilities such as water, sewer, electricity, gas, and cable TV to the individual pieces of property. Sometimes these easements will go along the side of the property line so that the utilities can access property in the rear of a particular piece of land. This situation is commonly found in subdivisions utilizing small lots, or in areas of challenging terrain.

Private Restrictions

Private restrictions imposed on individual pieces of property are primarily deed restrictions. These can be individual deed restrictions imposed by the current owner, or general deed restrictions such as CC&Rs imposed by the original developer of the property. A deed restriction can cover almost any restriction you might want to impose. They can be similar to those imposed under the zoning code. For instance, you might own several lots that are adjacent and wish to restrict construction on the lots on either side of your home so that no one can build a two-story home. This will ensure the privacy of your backyard, and the uniformity of construction in your immediate area. Deed restrictions of this nature survive the transfer of real estate and cannot be lifted without the consent of the beneficiary parcel's owner.

Easements

You may also have easements imposed on property that deal with rights rather than restrictions. For instance, you might own a piece of property that is land-locked, with no direct frontage on a street. Since this lot would be illegal if it did not have access to a street, this lot would generally have an access easement across the parcel of land that lies between it and the street. This is called an easement or access and egress. Your parcel would have the "dominant easement," and the parcel across which you have the access would have the "serviant easement." The dominant easement is the one that the easement is in favor of, or that which benefits from the service of the serviant easement.

Miscellaneous Entitlements

Two other entitlements that can be placed on the land are use permits and variances. A use permit is granted by a city, via the public hearing process outlined later in this chapter under entitlements, and permits a property owner to use his or her property for a use not specified under the property's zoning definitions. Examples of this are bed-and-breakfast businesses, day-care facilities, and nursing homes. These entitlements expire when the property changes hands or the use is discontinued. The other entitlement is a variance. Upon application, a property owner may ask for a variance from the zoning restriction, and if granted, this variance will be passed on in perpetuity with the land. A typical variance would modify a side yard setback to accommodate a roof overhang that would normally be an encroachment into the setback area. Typically, these variances require the written consent of the property owner whose rights will be encroached upon. Both these entitlements are granted by the typical public hearing process.

The Entitlement Process

All of the property rights inherent in any piece of property are known collectively and individually as entitlements. These rights are granted initially under the general plan and the specific zoning. These rights can also be acquired by the process of changing the master plan and/or changing the zoning for a specific parcel of land. This process starts with an application and specific design drawings for your proposed changes. As mentioned earlier, it may also entail studies such as traffic impact and/or an environmental impact report. The application, usually accompanied by a sizable fee, is submitted to the planning staff. After extensive staff review, and more often than not, requests by staff for modification of your designs, the application is then forwarded to the planning commission for itsreview and recommendation. The recommendation of the planning commission then goes to the city council or county board of supervisors for enactment or rejection. This is a relatively standard process and is common to most towns, cities, and/or counties in the United States.

Subdivisions

Large parcels of land are broken into smaller, more usable parcels, by the process known as subdivision. This process takes place "in the public eye." That is to say that the public, most specially, the adjacent landowners, will have a say in the process, and input into the final product. The rationale behind this is to protect the public at large and the adjacent property owners, in particular, from a use or a design that may adversely affect the property values in the area. A subdivision can be as large as a master-planned community or as small as the creation of more than five lots from the original parcel. A master-planned community generally occurs where large pieces of farmland are broken into individual parcels covered by its own master plan, comprised of parcels with many different specific zoning categories. Smaller parcels of land are broken into usable parcels—industrial, commercial, or residential—by the subdivision process.

The Process

The subdivision process is relatively standard, coast to coast, and is a two stage process. In the first stage, the applicant is required to produce an engineered drawing showing the size and location of specific parcels of land, their intended use, and the public improvements required to produce these parcels, such as streets and/or utility extensions. There may be requirements, for instance, for the developer to set aside land for public uses such as schools, fire stations, and hospitals. In addition to these plans, there may be additional requirements for traffic reports and environmental impact studies. These plans are then reviewed by the county or municipality staff, and there are always negotiations related to the particulars included in the plans. Items such as public dedication, density, lot sizes, drainage, and grading are all reviewed and negotiated with the applicant. When this process is finished, the preliminary subdivision plat is referred to the planning commission for recommendation to the city council and/or county board of supervisors. If approved, the applicant is then directed to prepare the final plat for the parcel of land. The final plat will include all civil and mechanical engineering required for the onsite and offsite improvements and parcel descriptions. When this is prepared, it is resubmitted to staff, heard again by the planning commission, and finally approved or rejected by the city council or the county board of supervisors.

The Subdivision Report or Public Report

In addition to the local process of master planning and zoning, each county requires a subdivision report for residential housing. This is a public report which must be given to each potential buyer prior to sale of any individual lot within the subdivision. No lots can be offered for sale prior to the approval of the subdivision report.

Property Condition and Title Reports

During the buying and selling process, the legal condition of any individual piece of land is ascertained and presented to potential buyers and sellers alike by a process known as "the preliminary title report" in the western part of the country, and "an abstract of title" in the eastern part of the country. This report deals with the chain of ownership, and any recorded and/or known restrictions and property rights pertaining to the individual parcel of land. In all cases, this is known as a preliminary (prelim) title or abstract.

The Prelim

The prelim, or abstract, deals with things like water rights, the restrictions, easements, mining rights, recorded leases, mineral rights, and anything else that may be recorded against the property by the individuals involved. It will also show any liens recorded against the property such as assessments, mortgages, second mortgages, third mortgages, or judgments.

A typical title report is broken into three sections. Section one, or exhibit "A," is usually the legal description of the property. Exhibit "B" is generally the deed restrictions and liens recorded against the product. Exhibit "C" generally spells out the conditions needed to be satisfied to transfer "clean" (acceptable to the buyer) title to the prospective buyer. This section usually deals with the payoff of liens or the removal of deed restrictions objected to by the buyer. This is known as a standard title report or abstract which is then converted, at the time of closing, into a standard insurance policy known as standard title insurance. In most instances, lenders and knowledgeable buyers require an extended form of title insurance known as an American Land Title Association (ALTA) policy, or extended coverage policy.

ALTA extended coverage title insurance. This extended coverage policy ensures the buyer and the lender against adverse conditions not specifically recorded against the property. These conditions might include un-recorded leases, undisclosed hazardous conditions, encroachments, or potential suits for adverse possession. Adverse possession is a legal term which denotes a potential right over a particular piece of property acquired by a third party by way of historical use and/or continuous and uninterrupted use over a specific period of time.

This can occur if someone has been cutting across a particular piece of property to go somewhere for a long enough time to have acquired the permanent right to do so. This situation may also occur when a fence has been placed inside a particular property line, and the adjacent neighbor has been using the property outside the fence for an extended period of time. The adjacent property owner might have acquired legal title to the property through the legal venue of adverse possession by a right of continuous and uninterrupted use.

Sometimes you'll notice in a large city such as New York the sidewalk in front of a building has been blocked off by barriers for a day or two. This is done to reinforce the individual building owners' rights to the sidewalk over the public's right to use the sidewalk. By interrupting the public's continuous use of the sidewalk,

> **Definition**
>
> *Assessments* are financial liens upon a parcel of land recorded to put the public on notice that the owner of that parcel of land is responsible for payment. They can be public, as when there are road improvements that are assessed against the property owners benefiting from the improvements, or they can be private, such as when a homeowner's association levies assessments to pay for improvements to its members' common property.

the building owners prevent the adverse possession possibility. This is especially crucial for areas of the building that may need to overhang the sidewalk in the future. A building's overhanging parts, such as roofs or awnings cannot, by law, encroach on another's property. If the public acquired title to the sidewalk by adverse possession, then the overhangs could become illegal.

Lot Splits

Smaller parcels of land may be broken up into even smaller pieces by an administrative process known as the lot split. This is generally done by furnishing the local planning department with an engineered plot plan showing the two new parcels formed from the single existing parcel. In some areas, parcels exceeding five acres may also be split into five or fewer parcels by this process. The law governing this process will vary from municipality to municipality, and state to state. All required engineering must be done, in the same manner as the formal subdivision, but the applicant is spared the necessity of the public hearing process.

How Property Is Bought and Sold

What is the real estate market exactly? Simply put, it is comprised of every piece of real estate in the country. It sounds rather intimidating, so how do we get a handle on it? First of all, we need to think of the marketplace as broken down into manageable segments; east and west, north and south, state by state, city by city, town by town, down to specific neighborhoods. It is not necessary to have a specific grasp of the total picture, just a general overview will serve to make you a more informed participant.

The east is the old established area of the country, first settled and industrialized. The central part of the country, with the exception of Chicago, is the rural breadbasket of the country, and the west is the frontier. Sounds simple, but it's not quite that simple. You need to understand the implications of these facts and what they mean to the marketplace. Over 50 percent of the country's population lives within a 500-mile radius of the city of Cincinnati, Ohio. That is a staggering fact, and that demographic fact has a dramatic impact within that circle on supply and demand for real estate.

Where to Live

The choice of where to buy a home is a relatively simple one. You should look where you want to live and work. Once that is settled, you need to examine the area for neighborhoods that meet your criteria for day-to-day living. Then there is your budget to consider, and, finally, what you want to accomplish by purchasing a home. We will deal with this in more detail in the residential portion of this book. Sounds like a good place to start, doesn't it? It's not really the whole answer. Read on.

Where to Invest

This is yet another type of question, and the answer may well be at odds with where you are looking to buy a home. How can this be? If you are living in an area that has little or no growth, and declining demand, the odds are that this will not be a great place to invest your money, as the potential for profit will be limited by the lack of demand. Housing may be affordable, but prospects for appreciation and future profit may be quite dim. So how do you go about deciding where to make your play, not only in the housing market, but also when the time comes to make an investment separate from your own home? You need to look at the country's real estate markets and decide where you are the most comfortable living, working, and investing.

Real Property Transfers

Who are the players in the real property market? They include, but are not limited to, the following people:

- Buyers and sellers
- Real estate brokers
- Attorneys
- Title companies
- Construction companies
- Consultants
- Architects and engineers
- Managers
- City planning departments
- Public utility companies

The Professionals

The professionals listed above make their living in and around the creation of, transfer of, and ownership of real property. Some specialties within this business matrix are held by people who have highly specialized and responsible tasks.

County recorders. County recorders' offices, coast to coast, record every transfer of property within their individual jurisdiction. In addition, your local recorder's office records any new liens and deed restrictions placed on any individual piece of property within its jurisdiction. These documents are generally prepared by attorneys and/or title companies and are given to the recorder's office to record. The chain of title, assessments, easements, and deed restrictions comprise a property's history and legal entitlements as well as its financial encumbrances. There's usually a nominal fee; in my area it costs $8 to record a document. In the past, because there were so many documents recorded that are today almost illegible, most recorders' offices have now set standards for documents to be recordable. In my county the document must be prepared on 8.5-by-11-inch paper with minimum margins of one-and-a-half inches. The typeface must be a minimum of 12 points in size. The document must have a cover sheet for the recorder's information. This ensures that, after recordation, copies will always remain legible.

Real Estate Brokers

Real estate brokers are, in reality, companies comprised of a managing broker who manages the company, salespeople who work under the broker's license, and a staff that prepares and processes the paperwork. Salespeople can be either licensed salespeople or other brokers doing business with and for the managing broker. They take a commission on each transaction that actually closes. Brokerage commissions, by law, are not standard, and are supposed to be negotiable. However, if you ask anybody what real estate commissions are in a certain area, you will be quoted a specific percentage that all brokerage houses seem to adhere to. In reality, you can most likely negotiate a reduction from the prevailing rate. Your success in negotiating a reduction will most likely depend upon your giving up some of the services included by most brokerage companies in their standard sales packages.

Heads Up

The law of agency provides that any sales agent must disclose to a buyer or seller in writing who he or she is working for. In the instance where a sales agent wants to represent both sides of the transaction, he or she must get written permission form both buyer and seller.

Sales. Most real estate sales are handled by two separate brokerage houses. This is not always true, in as much as brokerage houses can handle both the listing and sale of any property. It is most common, however, that one company will list the property for sale, and another company will bring a buyer to the transaction. This process is known as "co-brokerage," or cooperation. At closing, the two brokerage houses split the sales commission 50/50. In residential brokerage, the marketplace is generally composed of the regional or area multiple listing service (MLS). Activity within the multiple listing service is governed by rules and regulations that the members must follow. They cover such items as agency, commission splits, ethics, and duties and obligations of the agents involved in the MLS service.

Commercial properties, however, do not have an established multiple listing system. There are several making an attempt to provide this service, but most commercial brokerage houses seem to resist participating in a multiple listing service. Commercial property markets are considerably smaller than residential markets, and in most areas and regions buyers and sellers are known to most commercial brokerage houses. In their minds there still are no advantages to a multiple listing service. Hopefully, this will change in the future, as it is demonstrated that an effective multiple listing service accelerates all real estate transactions.

Leasing. Another function of real estate brokers is leasing of properties. While some landlords put a sign on the property to attract tenants, most investment properties are leased by real estate brokers.

Lawyers

Another big player in the commercial real estate market is the real estate attorney. Attorneys are, in my mind, a necessary evil. A property owner buying, selling, or managing a piece of property can best benefit from the use of an attorney by confining the attorney's activity to specific chores related to the legality of what is going on, rather than delegating negotiating rights to the attorney, or allowing the attorney to make business decisions. An attorney is deemed an expert in the law, and is not necessarily a competent businessperson. To advocate negotiating rights or business decision rights to an attorney is like handing your wallet to a stranger and hoping for the best!

Contracts and the law. All enforceable rights related to real property are governed by contracts. Under United States contract law, specifically "The Statute of Frauds," to be legal and enforceable, contracts need to meet certain tests:

- They must be of legal intent.
- They must involve competent parties.
- Consideration must pass between the parties.
- They must be in writing and fully executed.

While oral contracts, in general, are not enforceable in real property transactions, there are some minor exceptions, pertaining to leases, especially in residential properties. All major issues, to be enforceable, must be dealt with by contracts in writing.

Recording contracts. Written contracts regarding real property may be recorded against the property in question. Every part of the country has different requirements that must be met for recordation, and you need to check with your attorney for the rules in your area. The effect of recording is twofold: first it puts the public on notice that there is an agreement involving that specific parcel of land, and second, it clouds the title and makes transferring that parcel of land a problem for any third party.

Property Transfers

When a real estate property changes hands, it is handled, in the eastern United States, by real estate attorneys who specialize in this practice. In the western part of the United States real property transfers are expedited by title companies. In the eastern United States, property contracts are drawn up by attorneys, and in the west, purchase-and-sale contracts are done uniformly by real estate agents and/or title companies. Both systems seem to work quite well.

Title companies. When real estate changes hands, the buyer is furnished, at the seller's expense, with a standard form of title insurance. This is true primarily in the western United States, and in the eastern part of the country the attorney's abstract of title is underwritten by similar insurance companies. In either case, buyers are assured, via the vehicle of title insurance, that they can enjoy quiet title and use of the property they have purchased. United States title companies have also recently branched out and are doing business in Mexico. Americans who purchase property in Mexico can, in some instances, purchase United States title insurance. This has led to an increased amount of second home purchases in northern and western Mexico by United States citizens.

What Affects the Real Estate Market?

Before embarking on your quest for real estate investments of any kind, I recommend that you look at all potential choices available to you regarding where to invest, and what to invest in. Today's real estate market is such that you can choose from available sites anywhere in the United States and overseas. Wherever you decide to invest, it is prudent that you know the marketplace in which your potential development will need to compete. The most obvious location to examine first is the geographical area you are most familiar with. If you live in a small town, chances are that you are part of a larger SMSA or MSA.

Any MSA can be divided into quadrants that can be charted almost uniformly throughout the United States.

Definition

SMSA or MSA is an acronym for standard metropolitan statistical area or metropolitan statistical area. The terms are interchangeable.

The NE quadrant usually contains the most expensive residential areas; the SE quadrant, the medium-priced homes; and the NW quadrant, the "starter" or "blue-collar" homes (see Figure 2.4). The remaining SW quadrant is comprised of the old core city area and/or the industrial area of the SMSA. Why is this and why is it consistent throughout the country? The simple answer is that wealthy people do not drive to and from work with the sun glaring in their faces through the windshield. This rule seems to hold true all across America unless there is some natural or historic barrier such as a mountain, ocean, or river to prevent it. Obviously, there are exceptions, and your community may be one of them. The important thing is that if you intend to invest your hard-earned cash in any community, you had better know what is where, and how and why the area is prospering, stagnating, or declining.

If you live in a rural farming community, there will be little or no opportunity for investment and you will have to compete with the established local movers and shakers for what limited opportunities there are. You are better off searching in

Figure 2.4—*The City Quadrant Map*

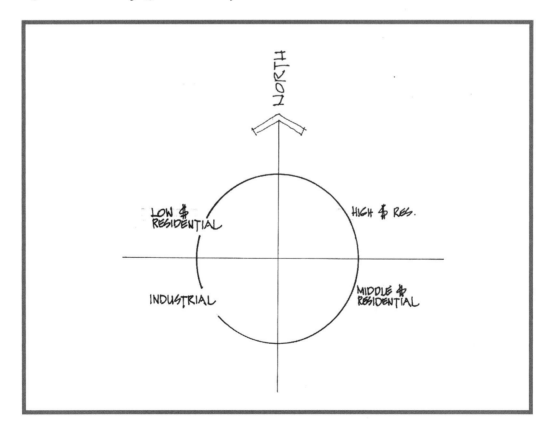

areas of growth and consistent demand. The best examples of this type of area are found in the "Sun Belt" states, which are experiencing consistent, annual, net in-migration. The demand stimulated by a steadily increasing population is the most reliable and consistent indicator of possible profit or opportunity.

Some specific areas of additional opportunity lie in states that experience high rates of population turnover. Transient areas such as Arizona, Nevada, and Florida breed demand for diverse real estate products that cater to this facet of the population demographic. An example of this would be a higher-than-average demand for rental housing.

Economic Cycles

Another factor that affects real property and its market is the national economy's cycles of growth, stagnation, and recession. Since the early 1990s, the United States economy has achieved a new pattern of growth that has perhaps put our old cycles to bed for good. The effect of the Reagan-Bush presidencies and the "supply side economics" of that era caused a sustained prosperity and economic boom that lasted over ten years, putting to bed the traditional three-year cycle theory. In the past, our economy had grown and retreated in three-year cycles. Real estate markets had gone from scarce to overbuilt, in a fairly predictable pattern. Smart money purchased land and buildings during the down cycles and sold at the top of the growth curve or built new properties into an improving market. This is still good practice, but our traditional cyclical pattern may have changed forever.

My Crystal Ball

Anyone who is an observer is entitled to an opinion about what the future holds, and I am no exception; therefore, let me say that I believe, as far as the United States is concerned:

- Sustained population growth is here to stay, fueled by natural population increase and immigration. Immigration to the United States will flourish as the country continues to dominate this new technological era.
- The United States will become the focal point of innovation and growth for the near future.
- Third-world countries will take over the manufacturing of almost all consumer goods, and their standard of living will escalate rapidly, providing an ever-increasing market for U.S. high-tech goods and services.

- The United States will become a better place to live with an international presence beyond our greatest expectations.
- Our sunshine states will continue to evolve into meccas of living and recreation for the world's moneyed elite.
- What effect will the rest of the world have on our economy? My prognostication continues. When China, Africa, Asia, and the rest of the third world start their inevitable growth spiral, the United States will accelerate the wholesale importing of educated people from all over the world to fill the insatiable demand for technologically educated people.

What Does this Mean to You?

This is not a light question. Everything in this chapter will have an effect, positive or negative, on you, your home, and your future. You need to pay attention to what's going on around you, in your country and the world. You can be sure that September 11 had a dramatic effect on everyone. It sure affected us here in Arizona.

What you do for a living, how you invest, where you live, are all pivotal facets of your economic lifetime. Experts agree that the average person born today will have three to four careers in a lifetime, necessitating retraining and education for each new venture. Increased savings and astute investment will become an economic necessity for all those who aspire to economic independence. You can no longer start out without a plan and hope for the best, or you might find yourself washed up and out of work at thirty. The one constant in our life is change, and if you act and plan with that as a given, then you will have the required mindset for the future.

Examine your investment pattern as part of your career and you should be able to make some clear, easily defined, and flexible plans for your future. Real estate should be an important part of your financial plan. Start with your home, make it work for you, and then expand your thinking.

CHAPTER 3

Get Ready to Invest

Before you launch a new venture, you should take the time to organize yourself, your finances, and your plans. It makes sense to decide what you're going to do before you do it. Plans are such that you can always alter them at any time. To launch an investment program without a plan is an invitation to disaster. This chapter is a look at the progression from maximizing your own home to committing to an investment plan based on your own financial picture. It is not a specific plan, but a look at what a reasonable determined investor like you can look forward to over a reasonable period of time. The nuts and bolts will come later. It is important that you see the potential size and complexity of a long-term endeavor.

The Rationale

Perhaps the first step you should take is to evaluate where you are today, both personally and financially. Using these facts as a given, you should be able to formulate a rational plan of attack. The first step in establishing any plan is to look at the desired end result. What exactly are you trying to accomplish? What is your goal? This may sound somewhat simplistic, but it is absolutely vital that your goals are reasonable and obtainable. You could, for instance, say that in 10 years you would like to have made $10 million after taxes. This is a pretty good goal, but if your liquid resources are a total of $5,000, it may not be reasonable to assume that this is an obtainable goal within this time frame. You must seek to strike a balance between what you have to work with and where you'd like to go. Most people who are contemplating an investment program, whether it's in real estate or any other venue, have at least a modest asset base and a viable amount of discretionary cash. The trick is to look at what you have to work with, and decide realistically how best to put it to work.

The Plan

Getting there from here is the essence of a reasonable plan. Things you need to look at involve your personal and financial resources. For the sake of this exercise, we will need to make some assumptions about who you are, what you're doing, and where you'd like to go. The following is not a blueprint, it is merely an example of how to go through the process and come out the other side with what might be a reasonable plan of attack.

Heads Up

There is no such thing as the right plan. My plan will not be your plan, and even though your plan might be brilliant, it most likely will not work for someone else. The trick is to make a plan that works for you, work the plan, and stay flexible.

What Have You Got to Work With?

Take a look at the mythical you and make some assumptions, and at the same time, let's look at some questions that you should ask and answer as part of this process. Let's say that you are 30 years old, married, with one child. You and your spouse together make approximately $120,000 per year. Like most people, you have a mortgage and a car payment. Unlike most people, you are not in debt up to your eyeballs with credit cards. You and your spouse have a plan to become financially independent by the time your children are grown and gone. This alone will set you apart from the herd, as most people seem to spend money they don't have, and, therefore, are unlikely to accumulate wealth for the future.

Financial

After analyzing your financial situation, you discover that you have the following resources:

- $30,000 cash in the bank
- $50,000 equity in your home
- $25,000 per year of discretionary income
- Prospects for increased disposable earnings of another $10,000 per year in the short-term.

Table 3.1—*Projected Cash Resources*

Year	Cash Available	Cumulative Total
Today	$30,000	$30,000
Year 1	$25,000	$55,000
Year 2	$35,000	$80,000
Year 3	$35,000	$115,000
Year 4	$35,000	$150,000
Year 5	$35,000	$185,000

After looking at Table 3.1 you can reasonably assume that you have enough financial resources to start looking at investment properties. The question is, do you wait until the end of year five when you have a more substantial cash reserve than you do today, or do you start looking around now, with a program to invest cash at regular intervals? The only way to answer this question with any degree of accuracy is to examine it in the context of your plan. Since your plan should reasonably be based on your personal background, education, and experience, what you decide to invest in, together with your available resources, will determine the logical place to start.

Personal Considerations

Now that you have examined and cataloged your financial potential, take a long hard look at the personal. In our assumption, you are married with one child. Do you plan to have another child? In what kind of shape is your marriage? You must remember that in today's world, 50 percent of all marriages fail. Is your spouse going to be supportive of your plans for financial independence? Will he or she continue to work if another child enters the picture? Will that affect your disposable income? You bet it will!

Heads Up

Making money in real estate does not have to cost you your family. Setting realistic goals, agreed to by both parties in the marriage, will allow both of you to participate in the plan without creating undue stress in your relationship. This is probably the most crucial part of the plan that you should examine, as the financial part will most generally take care of itself. This exercise is a critical step you need to take before launching your investment program.

These are tough questions; the answers may be even tougher. It would seem pointless to launch the quest for financial independence only to lose it all in a ruinous divorce. In reality, serious wealth-building can be stressful, and potentially hazardous to your marriage. We have all seen the articles written about highly successful individuals who lost their families along the way.

Establishing a Reasonable Plan

Now that you and your spouse are on a solid footing, and agree totally on your mutual plans for becoming indecently rich, it is time to take a look at your financial resources. One of the basic necessities for launching into an investment program involving real estate and real estate loans is good credit. You must review your credit situation and maximize it for the coming investment program.

The following eight steps are necessary in putting together a program that is reasonable and attainable, and they should be performed in this order.

1. Put your personal house in order (i.e., make sure you and your spouse are in agreement about what you plan to do).
2. Clean up your credit; get a credit report and remedy the problem areas.
3. Diagram your finances.
4. Perform a market survey.
5. Analyze your locale, your region, and any cities that are available to you within reasonable travel time.
6. Diagram your target area so that you fully understand what is where and what the dollar value of everything is.
7. Create and finalize a ten-year (Phase 1) plan.
8. Outline your transition (Phase 2) and long-term (Phase 3) plans.

Establishing Your Comfort Zone

Another more difficult aspect of real estate investment is deciding where to invest and what to invest in. Since we have decided to start with housing and your own home in particular, this decision is made. While you may choose to branch out at a later date, you can commit to starting with your own home. We are a very mobile society, and, therefore, can pick and choose where we live and where we invest our money. I live in the state of Arizona, and in this state, we have many investors who live elsewhere. I'm not suggesting that you immediately take to the road and look for another place to invest, simply be aware that you are not limited to investing where you live. The key to deciding where to invest will lie in your marketplace analysis. Unless you live in a very rural area or in an area with stagnant or decreasing population, you will find that there are investment opportunities in your immediate area or in cities and towns that are readily available to you. The market will be comprised of everything from residential to the entire spectrum of commercial.

You should find a good Realtor® and start the process of analyzing the marketplace. You'll notice that I use the trademarked term Realtor®. This is a specialized real estate agent dealing primarily with residential properties. Realtors are people who belong to the local multiple listing service and to the National Association of Realtors (NAR).

While items one through eight are, in fact, generic advice, it is, however, a safe place from which to launch a long-term program. By the end of this chapter you will see exactly how a long-term progression can be started with the acquisition of one modest residential rental property.

National real estate markets are vital to our economy, and housing is the engine that drives the entire market. The increase in the housing supply is directly related to an increase in population.

It is very easy to find out what cities are growing faster than others. As a general rule, I favor locations that

Heads Up

Since you are inexperienced in real estate investment, and your resources, while impressive, are limited, I would suggest that you look at a program of residential investment, starting with your own home, as the beginning of a long-term investment strategy.

have built-in, reliable, and historic population growth. Investing in places like this gives you an edge that you will not find in areas of stagnant or low population growth. The only problem with this approach is that your current job may not be in this type of area. This is a very personal decision that you will have to make early on in your investing career. You may decide that your job has a bright future, and that you are unlikely to be able to replace it in a new locale. If, where you work, the market does not provide a built-in population increase, you might want to seriously consider investing in an area other than where you live and work.

Regional diversity is also an option. One alternative to going elsewhere with your investment money is to invest in your area, and diversify your investments by location and type. This will avoid putting all of your eggs in one basket. In any investment program, you must consider safety as well as rate of return. As a general rule, the riskier the investment is, the greater the profit potential involved in that investment.

The Local Market

For the sake of this example, let's assume that you live in an area that is experiencing reasonable growth and good economic stability, and you choose to stay there and invest there. You and your local realtor decide to take apart the local real estate market so that you can understand what's where. In Figure 3.1 you can see a simple diagram charting a city. The purpose of charting this city is to start understanding why certain parts of the town grow faster, and why properties in these areas are worth more money and seem to maintain their values better.

Diagrams cannot tell the entire story; they merely point you to areas that you should examine further. If you have made the decision to launch your investment program by investing in housing, you need to decide where to invest your money so that your investment is secure, the properties are, and will remain desirable, and the prospects for these properties' long-term appreciation are more than reasonable. Your own home may be in the right place, and it may not. This will be

Figure 3.1—*City Diagram*

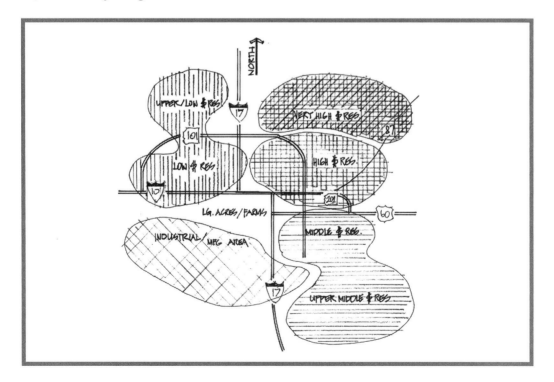

your first decision: keep your home for a while, renovate and/or expand it, or sell it and use the money to invest in a better area.

Residential Opportunities

This is not that difficult a chore. Using your diagram of the city, you can zero in on areas that have the desired potential. What you are looking for is *not* the area that is the hottest and most expensive new area. What you need is an area that is established, in a great location for commuting, and has all the necessary services to support a prosperous residential community. In addition, it would be most desirable if this area were composed of housing that was not built as a tract. If you are not dealing in tract homes, your investment will have the added potential of upgrading by way of remodeling. Remodeling and adding on to housing are discussed in Chapters 7 and 8. Assume that you have made a decision to invest in a second home for lease, and that you have determined that the area you're interested in has homes valued at around $150,000.

The dollar implications of this neighborhood are that to purchase a home of this size, utilizing a conventional mortgage of 80 percent of the purchase price, you'll need a down payment of $30,000, and approximately $3,000 to $5,000 for closing costs. Refer back to Table 3.1, and see that you will have the desired resources to purchase a home of this size in year one. If the table is restructured to allow for periodic investment in homes of this size, it will look something like Table 3.2.

Table 3.2—*Investment Projections*

Year	Cash Available	Cumulative Total
Today	$30,000	$30,000
Year 1	$25,000	$55,000
Investment	($35,000)	$20,000
Year 2	$35,000	$55,000
Investment	($40,000)	$15,000
Year 3	$35,000	$50,000
Investment	($45,000)	$5,000
Year 4	$35,000	$40,000
Year 5	$35,000	$75,000
Investment	($50,000)	$25,000

Reflecting on Table 3.2, you'll see that based on your available cash, you will be able to make four investments over the coming five-year period, and you will have $25,000 cash in the bank. You may have noticed that I have withdrawn from your available cash the original $35,000 to purchase the mythical $150,000 home, and then, subsequently, increased the deduction to 40, 45, and $50,000. This is because values in that area are increasing annually, and, therefore, the required down payments would be more and more as time progresses.

No time will be spent in this chapter discussing exactly how these investments are affecting your bottom line. It is sufficient to say that with the givens you started with, and your continuing ability to furnish additional capital, it is reasonable to assume that at the end of a five-year period you could be the proud owner of four investment properties totaling at least $600,000 in value. The effect of all this will be analyzed in later chapters when the impact of specific investments are analyzed. At this point in the game, it is sufficient to know that your initial plan is feasible.

Strategy

Strategy is the guts of a plan. It tells you how to get from here to there and then on to the next item and so on until you reach your final goal.

Phase one. This approach to the plan will get you started, but it is not sufficient to get you all the way to wealth. Starting out in this matter, I would recommend that you pursue the buy-and-lease program for a period of up to ten years. At the end of the ten-year period you should have accomplished several things; you should have increased your net worth substantially, you should have gained experience in buying and managing income property, and hopefully by then, you should have gotten a good handle on your chosen real estate market, not only the residential market, but the commercial market as well. What about your own home? This is a separate type of investment, and can be used to provide additional capital while adding dramatically to your net worth.

Phase two. Here is where the second phase of your investment plan should kick in. By now it should become apparent that managing multiple, individual properties is somewhat time consuming and unwieldy. The time is right to parlay your increased capital into a larger and more manageable piece of income-producing real estate. If you have made spectacular decisions, you may need more than one piece of real estate to absorb the capital you have been able to amass to date. Your choices when making this move are residential (e.g., multifamily apartment complexes) and commercial. Due to their sheer size, these types of properties will provide ample funds for professional management. In addition, the ongoing appreciation, through the venue of the periodic refinancing, coupled with your continuing savings plan, should provide ample funds to continue to invest. From here on, you are in the mature stage (phase two) of your investment plan.

Phase three. The ongoing assignment is to manage well, increase the cash flow and your portfolio. Have a good time, remember, it's only money.

The One Man Band vs. the Team Approach

By now you have seen the potential of what you and your spouse can do. Is this going to be enough for you? Are you going to be prepared to make the transition from managing residential renters to managing large numbers of commercial tenants? Do you have the background and training to do your own accounting, management, and long-term planning? Is this program taking up too much of your time? Is it taking you away from your family at a time when you feel your children need more of your time? In general, do you feel like you could use a little help?

There is no specific reason why you and your spouse should go it alone, as there are many different ways you can join with others in your same circumstance to share the load, increase your diversity, and afford more professional management. There are pros and cons to taking on partners, but in my opinion, the pluses outweigh the minuses.

While you are involved with a small number of properties, there should be no problem with the time involved in management, but once you start dealing with more substantial properties, the day-to-day demands of management and forward planning start to pile up. A larger portfolio will demand a more formalized approach to management, as well as involvement by a number of professionals. At this point, at the inception of phase two and three of your investment plan, you will be faced with the decision of quitting your day job, contracting out these chores to professionals, or joining with others to create an operation that can handle the professional management of a growing income property portfolio.

A logical outgrowth of the situation is to form a partnership with someone in the same situation. By combining portfolios, management skills, acquisition chores, and long-term planning, you can accomplish several different objectives.

First of all, you can share the workload; secondly, through diversification, you can strengthen your portfolio's position; and thirdly, the combined income from your portfolio and your partner's should enable you both to afford professional management, accounting, and long-term planning. Typical management fees for income properties are about 4 percent of rents collected. A gross income of one million dollars would produce a management fee of $40,000 per year.

Real property working arrangements can take different legal forms. They can be corporations, partnerships, or limited liability companies. Take a look at the differences between the three potential entities.

Types of Ownership

This section will deal with the various forms of ownership, the requirements of the paperwork as it relates to that ownership, and the resulting relationships between the parties. Why look at this? The reason is simple. Once your portfolio grows to a certain size, you will want diversity and backup for your own expertise and time. You might want to establish with your spouse that, in the event of a separation, you can both continue in the business of ownership rather than destroying what you have built. Co-ownership planned in advance will preserve your net worth and allow both of you to look to the future with confidence.

Heads Up

Some couples even start their investing career with a formal partnership that is independent of their marital status.

Except for individual ownership, all other forms of ownership are evidenced by a written agreement between the parties, and a notice, filed with the public recorder (usually the Corporation Commissioner), for the purpose of notifying the public of the relationship between the parties. In essence, the recordation of the relationship provides constructive notice to the public regarding the following facts:

- The names and addresses of the owners
- The name and address of the agent for service
- The names and addresses of the managers of the entity
- A statement of the legal life of the entity

Each form of ownership will have a variation on this requirement, and if a corporation does business out of state, most states will require that that corporation or entity register with the secretary of state as a "foreign" corporation.

Corporations

Corporations are comprised of stockholders who own the company. The company is created by incorporators who gather together to form the company, and, once formed, select the managing executives (corporate officers) and the board of directors. Its capitalization will likely be confined to capital donated by the original incorporators. The original board will authorize the issuance of stock, and the allocation of part of the authorized stock will be assigned to the original incorporators and investors in exchange for their capital or other equity contribution. There may be two classes of stock: "common" and "preferred." Preferred stock is generally non-voting stock issued to investors who may have a priority over the net earnings of the company. Sometimes this stock will have the right to be converted to common stock under specific circumstances.

Common stock is the voting stock, and these stockholders annually elect the board of directors and the corporate officers. The officers manage the day-to-day business of the corporation under the guidance of the board of directors. The initial statement of incorporation is filed with the state's corporation commission, listing:

- The name of the company and the address of its principal place of business
- The names and addresses of the incorporators
- The date of incorporation
- The names, titles, and addresses of the initial corporate officers
- The names and addresses of the initial stockholders of record holding stock in excess of 20 percent ownership
- The name and address of the agent for service

Relationships between the stockholders, the board of directors, and corporate officers are contained in a document called a stockholders' agreement. This document will be modified as the corporation grows and its dealings and management will become more structured and diverse. This will eventually be filed with the SEC when the company goes public, offering its shares for sale to the general public. This document can then be modified by the board of directors with the concurrence of its stockholders at the annual stockholders' meeting.

Close corporations. Corporations, like all legal entities, evolve from formation to grow or die as the case may be. As they grow, they issue more stock to attract more capital, and the ownership becomes more diluted. Few very large corporations are closely held. A corporation with ten or less stockholders is referred to as a "close corporation." Frequently, when close corporations borrow money, the corporate officers and/or the stockholders are required to jointly and severally guarantee the loans. The reason behind this is that with so few individuals involved, the

> ## Definition
>
> *Joint and several guarantees* mean that each guarantor assumes responsibility for the entire amount of the loan guaranteed.

officers do not have any watchdogs looking over their shoulders. This is not a hard and fast rule, but most banks seem to require this added protection.

Sub S corporations. The sub S corporation is a hybrid corporation whose tax situation is treated like a partnership. Unlike a regular corporation whose net income is taxable before dividends are paid to the shareholders, the sub S corporation is treated as a partnership with the gains and losses taxed only in the stockholders' tax returns. In all other aspects, the sub S corporation is treated as any other corporation.

Partnerships

Until the late 1990s, partnerships were the dominant form of ownership of investment real estate. The reason for this was the absence of double taxation present in the corporate form of ownership, and the flexibility of capitalization and management. With profit and loss taxable at the individual partner level, the depreciation aspects of real estate ownership became a prime motivation factor in choosing real estate as an investment. The tax reform act of 1986 changed the depreciation allowance, and made real estate less viable as a tax-loss investment, but it left straight-line depreciation to shelter annual cash flow. The new schedule, based on a term of approximately 31 years, allows most projects to provide their investors with some cash flow shelter. The depreciation is then added back to the profit on resale in a tax maneuver known as recapture. The effect of this is to lower the basis (paid in capital) of your investment by the accumulated tax deductions, to determine the amount of your taxable gain. The taxes on income are, therefore, not avoided, merely deferred.

The major tax benefit is that if you do not sell, or if you exchange one property for another, you can defer the tax consequences indefinitely.

When partnerships are formed, the states require that an "Articles of Organization" be filed with the Secretary of State.

As a general rule, it would include, at a minimum, the following:
- The names and addresses of the general partners
- The date of formation and the expiration date
- The principal place of business
- The name and address of the agent for service
- A statement of purpose
- A termination date

Unlike corporations which have no finite life, partnerships must have a termination date. The date may be extended by action of the partners and a filing of the extension, but they must have a definite termination date.

Partnership relationships are governed by a document known as a Partnership Agreement. This document sets forth the arrangement between the partners and is not a document intended for public record. It spells out the capital contributions, the profit and loss allocations, dissolution procedures, assignment rights, and management rights and responsibilities. This document may only be modified by agreement of all the partners.

General partnerships. Partnerships are self managed. By definition, the general partners are responsible for the day-to-day business of the partnership, and they assume personal liability for all debts and obligations of the partnership. If there is more than one general partner, all the partners have the same joint and several liabilities. Management is distributed between them as agreed. Most partnerships have a provision that allows the general partner to act with a vote of the majority-in-interest of the partnership. If, however, the last remaining general partner elects to exit the partnership, the partnership must be dissolved and the asset(s) disposed of. Where voluntary dissolution is concerned, the individual partners assume any lingering obligations of the partnership upon dissolution.

Limited partnerships. Limited partnerships are managed the same way as general partnerships, with one important exception. There are two classes of partners: general as in general partnerships, and "limited," as in partners whose sole liability is their investment in the partnership. Since the limited partners will not be assuming any liabilities, they are not required to be identified on the Articles of Organization. The relationship between the partners in any partnership is called a fiduciary relationship, and it is a legal obligation imposed on the partners by the law enabling the formation of the partnership.

Whenever you find yourself dealing on behalf of anyone else's investment, I recommend that you adhere to scrupulous routines that become second nature to you over time. In this, I also include lenders' funds.

You should always do the following:

- Create a new partnership or limited liability company (LLC) for every transaction regardless of common ownership.

Definition

A *fiduciary duty* obligates the general partners to treat the other partners' interest above their own interests. It mandates honest dealing and timely reporting. This is especially true in the case of limited partners. When a general partner is dealing on behalf of passive limited partners, the regulations are even more stringent.

Heads Up

If you get into the habit of administering every transaction the same way, you will not go wrong.

- Open a separate checking account for each operating entity.
- Never mingle cash from one entity with another.
- Put all reports and notices in writing. Every time!
- Respond in writing to all queries, however routine, from limited partners.
- Write and distribute a monthly status report (every month!), including anything of interest.
- Deliberately highlight any bad news in the status report.
- Send a copy of the status report to your lenders.
- Distribute your partners' earnings regularly and on time.
- Pay yourself last, and if you are taking fees, such as leasing fees as part of your arrangement, report them monthly.

Another piece of advice is also a simple one. Whenever you are in negotiations or working on a dispute, put your position and responses in writing. Most people are lazy, and when confronted with your position will tend to pick up the phone to resolve an issue. Fine, resolve it. Put your version of the resolution in a memo or e-mail, keep a printed copy, and send it off. If the dispute should ever go to court, you will find that the one with the most thorough, methodical, and complete paper trail will prevail.

The paperwork and the proper treatment of your partners will become second nature to you and there will be few surprises that can disrupt the partnership. If you follow the guidelines above, you can never be faulted for your treatment of your partners' interests.

Limited Liability Company (LLC)

The limited liability company (LLC) is a recent arrival on the real estate investment scene, and it is gaining popularity in almost all forms of business. Since its advent, I have not considered forming a partnership for a new transaction. 100 percent of my business and that of all of my contemporaries, of whom I am aware, are now conducted in the limited liability company format. Since its inception, almost all of the states, as of this writing, have adopted one form or another of the LLC.

Its popularity is not confined to real estate development or investment. It seems to have invaded all endeavors, with the possible exception of the professional partnerships between attorneys and doctors. They seem to prefer the LLP version. Since I am not familiar with the structure and rationale behind professional partnerships, I will refrain from comment and comparison.

Heads Up

Why follow such scrupulous routines? The answer is simple. If the project goes according to plan, and everyone makes money, no one will ever read the paperwork. If, however, something goes wrong, you will never have a partner or lender who can say "You never told us."

What is an LLC? An LLC is a hybrid entity combining the best features of the corporation and the partnership. The LLC offers its owners, referred to as Members, the limitation of liability of the corporation, and the tax benefit of a partnership. It is, in practical terms, a streamlined version of the sub chapter S corporation. The variation in regulation and rules for formation will differ from state to state, but the essence is as outlined below. Some states require two or more members to form an LLC, and some now require only one.

Heads Up

The limited liability company is relatively new and the best way to own investment real estate.

LLCs are either member-managed, or managed by an appointed manager. Member management comes in two forms: by consensus of a majority in interest or by a designated managing member. The most common arrangement is for the members to designate a managing member. The members do not assume the liabilities of the LLC as do the general partners in a partnership. All guarantees of loans etc. are voluntary. It is only when an LLC is voluntarily terminated that the members assume any residual obligations. This rule seems to be consistent for all artificially created legal entities.

The paperwork for the LLC, at a minimum, involves two documents: The Articles of Organization, and The Operating Agreement. The Articles of Organization require, at least, the following recitals for recordation with the state:

- The name and principal place of business of the LLC.
- The date of formation and the expiration date.
- The purpose of formation.
- The names and addresses of all of the members.
- The members' election as to how the LLC will be managed.
- The name and address of the manager.
- The name and address of the agent for service.

Other requirements may vary from state to state.

The operating agreement is similar in scope to the stockholders' agreement and the partnership agreement. It must contain the operating rules, rights, and privileges of the members, as well as capital contributions, profit and loss allocations, and dissolution and assignment clauses. Upon death or resignation of the last member, the LLC will be dissolved and the assets disposed of. The LLC is also required to have a definite termination date.

Benefits and limitations. In as much as the LLC is a new entity, there is a lack of established case law. It is impossible, therefore, to know with any certainty how disputes and differences will affect the investment vehicle. In general, it seems to be working quite well. In my experience, the LLC feels like a partnership on a day-to-day basis. I have not yet run into an LLC that has employees like a corporation, but as far as I know, there is no reason why an LLC cannot have employees. The problems, if any, endemic in the LLC will evolve over the next 20 years or so, as disputes between members make their way into our court system. The areas of conflict that I can foresee will be in the areas of assignment, profits and losses, and management rights. There might also be some issues with member liability. These problems are similar to those encountered in partnerships.

The LLC is similar to a partnership in the area of assignment of interest and membership. A member may assign his or her rights of ownership, but not the membership rights. For an assignee or a successor in interest to become a member, all of the other members must approve in writing. This does not diminish the assignee's rights to income or profits and losses, it merely restricts the assignee's right of management input. There is no provision in the LLC for a member to have a role similar to that of a limited partner. There is, however, provision within the LLC structure, wherein a member may have a specific allocation of profit and loss that bears no relation to the member's capital contribution.

Now that you know what a plan is like, and you know what the possibilities are for partnerships and sharing the investment and work, you should be able to launch your new program with an intelligent and well thought out plan.

CHAPTER 4

Why Residential Instead of Commercial?

Before getting into the specifics of how to analyze projects for purchase or development, we need to delve into the differences between investing in residential and commercial properties. In this chapter, I will highlight the differences between residential and commercial investments, and underline the similarities, to provide you with some insight into the more subtle aspects of these investment alternatives. Besides the obvious difference in scale, there are substantive differences in planning, management, and financing.

There are at least four major investment approaches when looking at potential real estate projects, and they are, but are not limited to, the following:

1. The quick turnaround cash-flow project.
2. The long-term cash generator.
3. The income-producing project.
4. The long-term capital gain approach.

In addition to the above there are two other considerations—exchanges and taxes—to be considered when dealing with real property.

Project Categories

The four approaches listed above may sound alike on the surface as they are all about making money. The differences in the four types of approach lie in how you make the money, and how you pay taxes on the monies earned. These differences will color your judgment when deciding on how to approach making money in real estate.

Quick Turnaround Cash-Flow Project

This type of project lends itself to a fast in-and-out approach. In the residential investment field, this would be what we call the "lipstick" type project. This occurs when you buy a piece of rundown property and simply rejuvenate the finishes (décor) such as paint, wallpaper, and carpet. This quick fix takes little or no time and can result in a quick sale and a quick profit. There are opportunities for this type of approach to real estate investment in residential as well as commercial. Keep in mind that 100 percent of the income from this type of project is taxable as ordinary income, and each individual project is a one-time, one-of-a-kind, project. This type of project will find you reinventing the wheel in every single deal. That isn't to say that I'm against this type of project, just that you should know what you are in for before you approach projects of this nature.

Long-Term Cash Generator

There are projects that you can tackle that will generate cash flow over a sustained period of time. Examples of these would be land subdivision, tract home construction, or merchant-builder commercial projects.

This second project type implies a need for a long-term business organization. The creation of real property projects/products for sale puts you squarely in the dealer category as far as taxation is concerned. The tax implications of this type of project are that all income generated is forever ordinary income. Companies that engage in this

Definition

A *merchant builder* is one who builds and sells rather than builds and holds his or her projects.

type of project are commonly corporations rather than partnerships, as there is little or no tax benefit generated during the build-and-sell process. The long-term view here is to consistently generate good earnings by the corporation and dividends to the stockholders. This will enhance the value of stock and provide a long-term capital gain when the stock or the company is sold.

Income-Producing Project

Investment in, and/or the development of, income-producing property is a distinctly different approach than the two above. When you buy/build, own, operate, and resell investment property, you create a scenario after 12 months whereby you create more than just cash flow; you generate long-term profit or capital gain. It is this type of project that actually allows real estate to produce the best possible interim and long-term results for the investor/developer.

Short-term benefits. The immediate benefit from building an income-producing property is potential fee income, ordinary losses, and capital gain. Since 23 to 25 percent of the actual cost of a development project is fees, the developer has the potential for some early-on income and tax write-off against ordinary income. When the project is completed, the increase in value over cost is a capital gain or profit that is not taxed until the project is sold. In the interim, between completion and the sale of the property, this profit goes directly into the investor/developer's net worth.

Medium-term benefits. During the period between the end of the development process and the eventual sale of the property, the owner/developer/investor has the benefit of cash flow and income as well as depreciation. This combination of income and depreciation effectively improves the ROI on any project. A quick example of this would be as follows: If you are in the 30 percent tax bracket, every dollar that you shelter from your project actually produces $1.30 in real income. On average, my experience has been that between 50 and 70 percent of the cash flow on a development project is totally tax sheltered. This makes the ownership of income-producing property a desirable financial endeavor.

Long-term implications. Income property, over the long-term, is also a very attractive investment vehicle beyond that outlined above. When you go to sell a piece of real property that you have held in excess of 12 months, your gain is taxable at the federal capital gain rate of 15 percent. In addition, if you prefer not to pay the taxes immediately, under the U.S. tax laws, you can defer payment of capital gain by opting to affect a 1031 tax-deferred exchange. The 1031 exchange allows owners of property to swap the property for one of "like kind" and of "equal or greater value." This triggers the start of your income and depreciation cycle again, putting off the payment of capital gain until you sell the new property. You can choose to exchange from property to property ad infinitum, rather than pay the capital gain at all. If you like, your heirs worry about the taxes when they sell.

Long-Term Capital Gain Approach

The 1031 tax-deferred exchange is very common in the commercial income property and development business. It can, however, be applied to any investment property. You can sell one investment home and exchange into another of equal or greater value. A brief look at this phenomenon is in order. The way it works is relatively simple, but, that having been said, I strongly advise that before you commit to a 1031 exchange you involve an attorney who specializes in this form of tax-deferred exchange.

Fundamentally the way it works is that you arrange to sell your property to a second party. You then assign the proceeds of the sale to an individual/business, known as a facilitator. From the date of sale, you have six months (180 days) to locate a suitable property for the exchange. You then select the property and set up the purchase so that the facilitator can buy the property on your behalf. The facilitator then "exchanges" the proceeds (in the facilitator's custody) from the prior sale, for the property you have selected for your exchange. This sounds relatively simple, but it must be done very carefully to preserve the tax-deferred status of the exchange itself. Property may only be exchanged "like kind for like kind." Meeting the government's definition for like kind is important to preserve the tax-deferred status of this action. This is why I strongly urge you to involve the use of experts, an attorney, and a competent facilitator. There are other issues involving the money that come into play with the 1031 exchange. If you do not spend all the money, the residual is known as "boot," and it is taxable. This is where expert guidance from an experienced 1032 tax accountant is vital. You don't want to go through the expense of the exchange process only to wind up paying taxes anyway.

Tax discussion. I do not pretend to have any expertise whatsoever in the matter of real estate taxation; rather, I urge you at the outset to engage the services of a competent real estate tax accountant. The proper time to discuss the tax implications of a transaction is before you start the transaction. When you are buying or developing a piece of income property, the accountant can give you the potential tax treatment of every component of the deal. While this will not necessarily improve the ROI on your transaction, it will at least give you a good idea as to the financial effect of each and every action you take in the transaction.

While different styles of approach to any project can be true for residential as well as commercial, some projects lend themselves to one form of investment more than others. So let's look at, first of all, residential projects and put them in the light of the breakdown of project types above, factor in the tax implications, and see which approach makes the most sense for you.

Residential Projects

While it is true that the majority of American families own their own homes, very few of them have actually sat down and analyzed precisely what the home is doing for them financially. Those people are somewhat aware of the rising values of housing in their neck of the woods, but very few have actually put on paper the real impact of owning the home.

Your Personal Residence

This will be discussed in detail later in this book but for now, below, you will find a quick list of the benefits of individual homeownership.

- All interest payments, on mortgages and second mortgages are tax deductible.
- If you live in the home as your primary residence for 24 months or more, all profits on the sale of the home are tax-free.
- If you maintain the home in good condition, it will continue to appreciate, keeping pace with the local market as long as you live there.
- You may borrow against your equity in the home anytime to finance other purchases. The interest on this loan is also tax deductible.

The Second Home

In addition to a personal residence, many people purchase a vacation home, or a second home for rental purposes. These two different types of second properties share many attributes, but where they differ from your personal residence is in the tax treatment. Both types of homes will appreciate, when properly maintained, with the local market. The interest on both properties is tax-deductible. A bonus with the rental home is that it can be depreciated like any other income asset. The schedule for this depreciation is slightly different than it is for commercial properties, and you should check with your accountant to verify the annual write-off. When these properties are sold, the gain, in the case of the vacation property, is taxable as ordinary income, and in the case of the rental property, as capital gain.

A Cash Flow Project—Renovation for Profit

Another form of residential investment is renovation for profit. This type of project is a cash-flow project and will be taxable as ordinary loss or gain. There are a growing number of people in the country who tackle this type of project for a living. This will be dealt with in detail in Chapter 9, the section on renovation for profit. Another form of investment in residential property is building a new home for your use or for resale. This process is, in reality, acquiring a home at a wholesale price. The effect of acting as your own developer, buying the land, hiring the contractor, and supervising the construction, will save you the markup normally charged by the real estate developer. This entrepreneurial profit is yours in exchange for your effort in designing and building your own home. The ultimate result of this will be in increased profit at the time of sale.

The thing to keep in mind when dealing and investing in residential property is that capital gain will take in properties held in excess of 12 months. You may also exchange any of the investment properties for like kind under the 1031 exchange rules.

Commercial Real Estate Investment

Commercial properties are, in general, larger than their residential counterparts. Obviously there are homes that cost as much or more than many commercial properties. The difference is that very few people invest in these larger properties on speculation. Most of the people involved in the larger residential properties are either involved as the original developer of the property, or tackle them as renovation projects.

There are two main categories of commercial properties. They are land, and land and buildings combined. We will look at the basics of dealing with both types of investment.

Land

The basics of land development have been discussed briefly in previous chapters, but I would like to review the different choices that are involved in land projects in a little more detail. Basic land projects break down into the following categories:

- Speculation
  - Purchase and long-term hold
  - The leveraged purchase and long-term hold
- The rollover
- The flip

- The cash-flow project
- Subdivision

Speculation. Pure land speculation is the purchasing of land and holding it for a period of time for profit. There are two ways to do this, either pay cash, or leverage the purchase with a seller carry-back loan. Depending upon the time of sale, the leveraged version of this deal can be more profitable based on the return on investment. Below you will see an example of how the dollars invested in the rate of return vary between a cash deal and a leveraged deal. Use the following assumptions:

- The land purchased is 200 acres.
- The purchase price is $5,000/acre.
- The holding time is seven years.
- The sale price is $40,000/acre.
- The land sale commission is 5 percent.
- Leverage available is 25 percent down and 10 percent interest only, paid semi-annually, with a balloon in ten years.

If you read Table 4.1 carefully you'll see that the rate of return is much better on a leveraged deal. The down side, however, is that if you do not have the cash at the time the balloon payment is called, you will lose your investment. This is not to say that leveraging this type of transaction is a bad idea, merely that you need to plan ahead and price the land so that it will sell within the timeframe your leverage has purchased for you.

Table 4.1—*Land Speculation Leverage Analysis*

Item	Notes	Cost	Cash (Out)/In
Land (cash deal)	200 acres for $5K/acre	$1,000,000	($1,000,000)
Closing costs	Nominal	10,000	(10,000)
Holding costs	Taxes and insurance at $5K per year for 7 years	35,000	(35,000)
Total investment			($1,045,000.00)
Sale price	$40K per acre	$8,000,000	$8,000,000
Less commission	5%		(400,000)
Gross cash in			$7,600,000.00
Net profit	Proceeds less cash out		$6,555,000
ROI	**627% or 89% per year**		

Table 4.1—*Land Speculation Leverage Analysis,* continued

Leveraged

Item	Notes	Cost	Cash (Out)/In
Land (cash deal)	200 acres for $5K/acre	$1,000,000	($250,000)
Closing costs	Nominal	10,000	(10,000)
Holding costs	Taxes and insurance at	35,000	(35,000)
	$5K per year for 7 years		
	plus interest		(525,000)
Total investment			($820,000)
Sale price	$40K per acre	$8,000,000	$8,000,000
Less commission	5%		(400,000)
Gross cash in	Less balance land cost		$6,850,000
Net profit	Proceeds less cash out		$6,030,000
ROI	**735% or 105% per year**		
Difference	**108% or 15.42% per year**		

The flip. The flip is a truncated version of land speculation without any improvements to the land. The steps are very simple.

- Locate a viable market.
- Locate a developable piece of property in the path of growth, but not too far out!
- Negotiate a purchase agreement with a long fuse, preferably one with a seller carry-back financing option.
- Open the escrow and put the land up for sale.
- Review and approve the title.
- Hope a buyer comes along before you have to purchase the land.

The rollover. Previously the rollover deal was touched on, and I would like to expand on the process. The process of accomplishing a rollover is the first step in making improvements to a property, and, contrary to the flip, which relies on timing and the bigger fool theory, the steps taken in a rollover transaction add real value to the property. In a rollover you pursue the following steps, in the following order:

- Locate a suitable market.
- Select a developable piece of land.

- Negotiate the purchase with enough time to do the entitlements, generally 24 months.
- Open the escrow.
- Review and approve the title.
- Contract for a survey and title.
- Create a preliminary development plan.
- Put the property up for sale and for lease.
- Apply to the governing municipality/county for the entitlements:
  - Master plan change
  - Rezoning
  - Site plan approval
  - Preliminary plat approval
  - Architectural approval
  - Final plat
- Finalize all required approvals.
- Sell the property to a developer prior to your scheduled close of escrow.

The cash flow project. This approach involves actually producing some saleable product for an end user. It involves all of the steps of the rollover and continues with the following additional steps:

- Hire a contractor to build the improvements.
- Close the escrow.
- Build out the improvements.
- Sell the product to the users.

This project is a cash generator, and produces ordinary income. The subdivided lots, whether residential or commercial, are the end products, and your buyers/users are either builders or homeowners wanting to build their own homes or commercial buildings.

Buying Versus Developing

Real estate investment that involves buildings is broken into two separate categories: the purchase of existing property and the development of new property from raw land. The difference between the two approaches is that the purchase of existing property (buying at retail prices) and development of new buildings (buying at wholesale prices) involve two different time frames and acquisition costs. The purchase of an existing income-producing property, when properly handled, should take between four and six months to complete. Development of new property should take an average of two years from the time the property is placed in escrow to the time the first tenants occupy the premises. These are general estimates; the actual timeframes and costs can vary dramatically depending upon the type of project purchased or developed.

Existing Property

Buying an existing building involves a fairly straightforward process, and is usually accomplished in this order:

- Locate a suitable market.
- Locate a viable property within that market.
- Negotiate a price.
- Open the escrow.
- Evaluate the title.
- Analyze the leases, loan documents, and contracts.
- Negotiate a new loan.
- Complete the financial analysis.
- Remove all the contingencies.
- Close the escrow and a new loan.

While this process may vary slightly from purchase to purchase, the timeframes are hard to manipulate. Every process involved in this endeavor takes time to complete and only your own actions in the process are under your control. It is difficult to accelerate the timeframe involving other people whose actions and schedules you do not control.

Investment. Once you have purchased a property, you enter a period of holding, and this period is known as the period of "continuous redevelopment." The process of redevelopment involves cleaning up the project paper-wise and improving the gross income and cash flow, while at the same time maintaining the property's physical condition to consolidate your investment and maximize your profit at the time of resale.

Holding periods for this type of an investment can be as short as a year and as long as forever. During the time you own the property, your taxable cash flow will be largely offset by your allowable depreciation; if you hold the property in excess of 12 months, your gain will be taxable at the 15 percent federal capital gain rate. There will be an additional tax based on the recapture of the depreciation. To learn more about this and the actual tax impact of owning and selling income property, you need to consult a tax accountant.

Development

The wholesale version of acquiring investment property is known as real estate development. And within the development field, there are two types of developers, the merchant developer and the portfolio developer.

Merchant developer. A merchant developer builds properties for sale to investors. The average holding time for a piece of property for a merchant developer is 12 to 36 months from the time of first tenant occupancy. The goal of the merchant developer is to maximize the cash flow prior to the sale to the investors. Generally, most merchant developers will hold a property long enough to make sure that everything in the building and in the landscaping is properly completed and firmly established. During that time the developer will concentrate on completing the lease-up or presales so that the property's cash flow is maximized. The property is then sold on the basis of the net income before debt service (NIBDS) and the higher the net income, the higher the price this property will bring at the time of sale.

Portfolio developer. The portfolio developer's goals are very simple; build it, fill it, hold it, and enjoy as much tax-free cash flow as possible. As properties mature, rent increases kick in, and cash flow increases during the period of ownership. The astute portfolio developer treats this property in the same manner as the investor who buys the property and treats it is a redevelopment project. The developer/owner strives annually to improve the paperwork, and maximize the cash flow. Once the development portion has been completed, his primary preoccupation becomes the care and feeding of the tenants. They are the sole source of cash flow. The happy tenant pays rent on time and does not complain about routine rent increases.

Leveraging Your Holdings

Whether you are buying or building, you need to take advantage of leverage. Leverage will not only increase the rate of return on your cash invested, but it will also provide cash for future deals. As your net income before debt service increases over the years, so does the value of your property. Periodically during the life of a property you can refinance it, and use the money to modernize the property to keep it competitive in the local market, and use the excess funds for the acquisition or development of new properties.

Properly managed properties are not only a source of income and tax shelter, but future funds for future deals. Once the property is purchased, or when the development phase is completed, it boils down to managing the property. The skills involved in development are totally different than those involved in management. While both types of operation require entrepreneurial functions, development and management are not necessarily compatible entrepreneurial skills. Most portfolio developers, as part of their team, maintain a separate management operation solely dedicated to the care and feeding of the properties involved. These differences will be discussed in detail later in Chapter 9 where the functions and responsibilities involved in the income property real estate industry.

Market Potential—Normal Appreciation vs. Capitalized Income Gain

The entrepreneurial aspects of real estate investment lie in the difference between normal appreciation and capitalized income gain. It does not matter whether you are dealing in residential real estate or commercial real estate, as in time, all well-maintained properties in decent locations will increase in value. The additional increment of value, over and above that ascribed to inflation, is generated by the entrepreneur.

Heads Up

It is your sole mission as an investor/developer/owner to increase the value of your holdings during your tenure. That is what this book is all about.

Houses and Homes

CHAPTER 5

Money and Houses

T he most basic place to start when dealing with real estate investment is your own home. Perhaps, up to now, you have not given much thought to your house as an investment. In this chapter I will deal with housing in several different ways. First will be a look at your current home, secondly, a look into a home that you may buy when you sell the one you are living in, and finally, the possibility of buying another house purely as an investment.

In the real estate industry there is a different connotation to the words "house" and "home." Throughout this book when I speak of a home I think of it as a place where you or I live. When I speak of a house, I think of it as a building project, a structure, a rental unit, or an investment. You need to, in your own head, start thinking of your home as also a house; in addition, your home is a bank account that you may draw upon at any time. If you have lived there for over two years, you may sell the house without paying any taxes whatsoever on your profits. The equity in your current home as of today is a given. What can you do to increase that prior to a sale? We will touch on some of these strategies later in this section of the book. For now, let's just outline what the potential can be:

- You can clean the place up, giving it a new coat of paint, wallpaper, and carpet, making sure that all items of deferred maintenance are caught up. This will make the house as presentable, and, therefore, as saleable as possible.
- You can embark upon a renovation program, adding features desirable in today's market that your home does not currently incorporate. This would be an upgrade, increasing the value of your home when completed. A word of caution: not all upgrades are profitable. Look at the relative value chart in Figure 6.2 on page 92.
- You can totally revamp your home through the venue of demolition and new construction, taking your home to a whole new category of house. Before you embark on a program like this, however, you need to do some serious market research. This step is the largest and most potentially profitable step in house investment, as it pertains to your personal home or investment property.

A Financial Snapshot

If you have not done an in-depth analysis of your home as a financial investment, perhaps now is an appropriate time to do so. Take a hypothetical home, owned by the average American today, and make some basic assumptions:

- The home was purchased five years ago for $160,000.
- It was purchased with a conventional loan with a 20 percent down payment. The terms were 8 percent for a period of 30 years.
- In the last five years, houses in the immediate area have increased on the average of 10 percent per year.

Table 5.1 outlines the basic financial facts of this hypothetical home. When you examine Table 5.1, you will realize that over a five-year period, you have made a profit of $94,000, totally tax-free. In addition, you actually made an investment that produced 53 percent per year absolutely tax-free. When was the last time you made such a good investment? Hopefully this puts your personal

Table 5.1—*Personal Residence/Economic Profile*

Item		Dollar Value
Purchase price		$160,000
Down payment (20%)	Conventional loan	32,000
Closing costs	Estimate	3,500
Mortgage amount	80%	128,000
Mortgage(PI) 8%/30years (APR = 8.81)	(PI)= Principal + Interest on $128K	$11,276.80/year $939.73/month
Appreciation 10% x 5 years	Compounded—Year 1	$176,000
	Compounded—Year 2	193,600
	Compounded—Year 3	212,960
	Compounded—Year 4	234,256
	Compounded—Year 5	257,682
Initial investment	Down + Closing cost	$35,500
Gross appreciation/profit	End of Year 5 New value less cost	$94,182
ROI	On $35,500	265% or 53%/year
Annual tax benefit during ownership	Estimated tax write-off	$10,240/year

residence in a new light. Having done this already, who knows what the future might hold for you if you actually planned to make money on a house before you bought it.

How to Buy a Home

Before you buy your next home, you need to decide on the most important components of your house purchasing rationale. Considerations for buying a home are, but are not limited to, the following:

- The need for shelter for you and your family.
- The home's location as it relates to your work.
- Services convenient to the home's location.
- The area's characteristics, social as well as economical.
- The financial investment.
- The potential future appreciation of the house.

- Is it upgradeable?
- Is it expandable?
- Can the neighborhood/area absorb the upgrade for the expansion?
- Where is the top of the market?
- How long do you plan to keep the house?
- Is the size of your family going to remain constant?
- How does the investment in this new home fit into your long-term financial planning?
- How much of your available financial resources are you willing to commit to this purchase/investment?

The list above can be expanded based on the details of your personal situation. Whether added to or not, you need to go through this list before you purchase a new home. I recommend that before you buy a new home, you incorporate formal investment analysis into your long-term financial planning. As you have learned, you are able to profit tax-free on the house you're currently living in. Can you find another type of investment that will be as advantageous? I doubt it.

The implication of this potential increase in your net worth as it relates to your housing is that your personal residence is, and should always be, a cornerstone of your long-term financial planning. Unless you're working with an unusually large amount of money, rotating your family home every two to three years, taking advantage of the tax-free nature of the investment might very well prove to be the single most profitable investment you are likely to make. All other investments will be taxable, either annually, or at the time of sale.

Market Research

Now that you have a clearer financial picture of your home and its current and potential impact on your wallet, you need to figure out how to go about maximizing the value and the return on investment of your next home.

Heads Up

The universal truth in real estate is that you make your money when you buy. Buy it right and you can't lose. Overpay, and you cannot recoup.

How about your area? How much thought have you given to the area you currently live in? Has the area appreciated in sync with your general economic area in the past ten years? Has the appreciation of housing values in your immediate area exceeded that of other homes and other neighborhoods in your region? If not, why not? If your neighborhood has outperformed other comparable neighborhoods, why has it? What does your realtor think about the short-term future in your area versus other areas in your municipality/region? More importantly, what do you think, and, why do you think what you think? Have you taken a good look at the market, discussed it with your realtor, with your banker, or with the local appraiser?

Comparables. Home valuation, or appraisal, is done in two separate ways; by comparable sales price, and replacement cost. In addition, the land is and can be valued as a separate item. When the land size and location exceed that of your neighbors, the land can be given a premium value that adds to the home's overall value. Your local realtor and the local appraiser utilize recent sales of comparable homes as a basis for establishing value for a specific home. In today's industry, the Multiple Listing Service or MLS®, for short, is in most areas electronic, and data retrieval and analysis of data is more sophisticated than ever before. Both realtor and appraiser have at their fingertips all current property listings, past sales, and county tax records. Over the last several years, computerization of the MLS data base has made data correlation and analysis almost instantaneous.

Are comparables accurate? One of the logical questions that people ask is: Are houses truly comparable? The answer is twofold. For tract homes yes, but for custom homes not exactly. Appraisals for tract housing are relatively simple due to the repetitive nature of tract home construction. The average tract comprised of 1 to 300 homes generally has less than eight models. Even with the variations of trim and finish that are available, appraisals for this type of home are a relatively straightforward proposition. Even extra features that are available such as additional garages, exercise rooms, swimming pools, additional bedrooms, etc., are all priced in a standard way by the original builder, and these items appreciate in a uniform manner over the years.

Tweaking the values. Custom homes, however, are a different proposition. A rule of thumb comparison can be used based on square footage values. For example, in my neck of the woods, in 2004, custom homes are selling for about $200 per square foot. Using this as a starting point, most appraisers will then add or subtract from the average, distinctive features such as additional bedrooms, swimming pools, oversize lots, exceptional views, and anything else they believe adds or detracts from the value of the average home within that area. I refer to this as tweaking the value to make it more accurate.

Resales vs. new. There is also a value differential between new and resale homes. There does not seem to be a consistent price or value differential from region to region. In some places in the country, new homes carry a premium, but in others, comparing feature for feature and size for size, new homes sell for less money than more established homes. When you are evaluating your market, you need to research and factor in the new versus used value. Hopefully, in your area there will be a premium for the resale home.

What's new? A component of value that you should be aware of is the "bells and whistles" incorporated into new housing. Way back in the dark ages we remember when wet bars were introduced to the then standard ranch-style home. This was followed by the sunken living room, sunken tubs, walk-in closets, indirect lighting, wall-to-wall carpeting, and other features that are now standard in any new home. In recent years we have seen the addition of pot shelves, microwaves, double ovens, Corian® and granite countertops, and a wide variety of upgraded flooring materials. If and when you consider modernizing, upgrading, or expanding your current home prior to resale, you should look into and "value engineer" all of the new "gee whiz" desirable upgrades. It is very easy to overspend the value of this type of improvement. Don't forget to leave a little upgrading potential for your perspective buyer.

Housing Costs

I'd like to spend a little time here analyzing the components of cost related to homes when you are contemplating a purchase, as well as looking at the different types of leverage available for home purchases. The modern purchase of housing today includes components of cost that didn't exist ten years ago. Your local realtor would be able to fill in any gaps or add items that I have left unaddressed in the following list.

- Purchase price
- Closing costs
- Loan points
- Termite inspection
- Home inspection
- Roof warranties
- Appliance warranties
- Insurance costs including insured loss history on the home known as the CLUE report

Every individual item listed above has a very real dollar value attached to it. It's amazing how they add up. What is important is making sure that you include all of your costs associated with the purchase as part of your investment in the house. It is traditional that most lenders will include these costs in the total package when considering a mortgage loan application. A conventional loan today will allow you to borrow up to 80 percent of the total costs.

Leverage

There are many forms of leverage available to the prospective homebuyer, the most common of which is the mortgage. Mortgages today come in an infinite variety of choices. Let's look at some of the potential loan choices available to you when you buy a home. They are, but are not limited to, the following:

- Purchase money loan or seller-carry-back financing
- Contract for sale
- Wrap loan or an all-inclusive deed of trust
- Conventional 80 percent loan
- Adjustable-rate mortgage
- Interest-only loan
- Second mortgage
- Combination first and second loan
- Hard money loans

Sounds a little confusing doesn't it? We'll take a quick look at each of these loan types so that you understand what is available. I do not necessarily recommend any individual choice. It is, however, important to be aware of them in case an opportunity presents itself wherein any one of these might make good sense for your particular situation.

Purchase money loan. A purchase money loan is financing provided by the seller of the property. It is often found in raw land transactions. It becomes common in the housing market in times of tight money or high interest rates and is also quite common in a transaction where the buyer's credit is less than stellar. Terms for this type of loan are totally negotiable, but in general, interest rates and points are higher and more onerous than those found in more conventional bank financing.

Contract for sale. A contract for sale is almost exactly what the title implies. Buyer and seller enter into an agreement for the buyer to make payments to the sellers which accrue toward the purchase price. In most instances, the seller retains title to the home with a contract for sale recorded as

Definition

All *mortgage loan payments* have two components, principal (P) and interest (I). Some mortgages have two additional components required by the lender; tax impounds(T) and insurance impounds (I). So a mortgage loan that does not require impounds has a PI loan payment; one that does require impounds is referred to as a PITI payment.

a lien against the property; a portion of the payment will accrue to the purchase price; the balance of the payment is interest to the seller. When the contract is fully paid or paid down to an agreed upon amount, the deed is then recorded in the buyer's name, and the balance of the contract, if any, is then converted into a mortgage loan.

Wrap loan. A wrap loan is a loan granted by the seller which is made to the buyer leaving the seller's current financing in place. The incremental part of the loan (that amount over and above the seller's existing loan) is deemed to be "wrapped" around the existing loan. In most instances, the new total loan is at an interest rate higher than that of the existing loan. If you look at Table 5.2 you will see the effect of this type of loan on both buyer and seller. The virtue of this loan, from a buyer's point of view, is that this financing is available in times when financing is hard to get. From a seller's point of view, a wrap loan is a good deal as the override rate of interest on the old underlying loan only serves to increase the seller's rate of interest on his carried loan amount (the increment over the base loan).

Table 5.2—*Wrap Loan Analysis*

Item	Value
Existing mortgage value	$150,000
Existing interest rate	7% based on 30-year payout
Existing loan payment (7.2% APR)	$10,800/year or $900/month (PI)
New loan amount increment	$25,000
New wrap loan (total of the existing loan and increment)	$175,000
New loan interest rate	8.5% on 30-year payout
New loan payment (9.23 APR)	$16,152/year or $1,346/month (PI)
Yield to seller: new payment less existing payment	$5,352/year or $446/month
ROI to seller on $25,000 loan	21%/year

You can see why it's a good deal for the seller. While the buyer is paying a relatively conventional 8.5 percent interest rate on his home loan, the seller is receiving a whopping 21 percent interest on his incremental part of the loan. These types of loans proliferate during times of tight money and high interest rates.

Conventional loans. The most common loan in use within the United States has, since WW II, been a conventional 80 percent loan. This is typically a bank loan, and carries a preferred rate of interest due to the substantial down payment required by the terms of the loan. Other relatively widespread loans made by the banking industry are FHA and VA loans. The FHA loan can be obtained with down payments as low as 3 percent, and a VA loan requires 0 percent down. These loans generally carry a higher rate of interest and most of them require mortgage insurance. Mortgage insurance covers the difference between the 80 percent loan and the FHA 97 percent loan, or 100 percent VA loan. Almost all conventional mortgage loans today require tax and interest impounds.

Adjustable-rate mortgage. Increasingly popular today, and introduced over a decade ago, is the adjustable-rate mortgage. This loan came into being due to the increased value of the average home in today's housing market. To make homes more affordable, builders needed to lower the monthly payments so that their potential buyers could qualify for loans. The typical adjustable-rate mortgage starts out at a nominal low rate of interest for a period of years and increases or decreases based on a predetermined index such as the "cost of living," or "federal funds discount rate." In many of the loans, a clause allows the loan to "float" up or down and most lenders put a "floor" rate of interest below which the rate of interest cannot go. The middle-of-the-road compromise seems to be an adjustable-rate mortgage with both a "floor" and a "ceiling" rate of interest. As housing prices rise higher and higher, this loan becomes increasingly popular.

Interest-only loan. Taking matters a step further, today lenders are allowing interest-only loans as mortgages. Unheard of in the past, these are becoming very common, especially in areas where the appreciation rate of housing is equal to or greater than the rate of inflation. In the past, lenders used to rely on the 20 percent down payment in the case of the conventional loan, and mortgage insurance in the case of the VA and FHA loans. The lenders now look to home appreciation as protection against loss in case of foreclosure.

Second mortgages. Since our country's economy seems to be fueled by consumer debt, a new type of loan has become very popular. The universal use of credit cards has led many people into debt, and interest charged on credit card debt is 100 percent or more higher than interest rates charged on mortgage loans. Inflation and rapid appreciation in housing values has prompted lenders to loan against the equity in the home, over and above the first mortgage. This is known as the "home equity" loan or "second mortgage." It has become a popular way to pay off credit card debt, and it has the added cachet that the interest on this type of loan is tax deductible. Interest on personal loans, automobile loans, credit card loans, or any other form of loan except mortgage loans are, for the homeowner, not tax-deductible. Today it makes more sense to take a second on your home to buy a car than it does to buy a car with a conventional auto loan.

Combination first-and-second loan. Carrying this concept a step even further, there are companies such as ditech.com that advertise 100 to 125 percent financing. The concept here is that the appreciation will provide protection for the lender against a potential deficiency in the event of a foreclosure. These types of loans typically require better than average credit. There are even loans now offered by conventional bank financing, using a combination of first and second mortgages, offering a buyer 100 percent financing on a purchase. These loans, however, carry a premium interest rate commensurate with the risk.

Hard money loans. The lender of last resort is a group of private lenders known as the "Hard Money Lenders." These lenders charge 500 percent more in points and front-end costs, and as much as 5 to 8 percent more per year in interest. In addition, unlike the conventional financing offered by banks and other finance companies, these lenders require personal guarantees by the borrower for any recovery shortfall or "deficiency" in the event of foreclosure.

Lenders

Lenders are broken down into four major groups:
1. Banks, real estate investment trusts (REITs), and insurance companies
2. Mortgage companies
3. Other lenders; GMAC, ditech.com, e-loan.com, etc.
4. Portfolio lenders

Banks and insurance companies. By far the most common and prevailing lenders are banks and insurance companies. These two groups have been traditionally the largest and most consistent lenders in both the housing and commercial building industries. Periods of high inflation and tight money caused the rise of alternative lenders for real estate products. Commercial lending companies like GMAC, which was originally formed to loan money on automobile purchases, moved into equipment loans and real estate loans. Their first foray into real estate loans was usually the second loan or equity line of credit type loan, but today these companies and new companies like ditech.com are becoming more and more mainstream lenders.

Mortgage companies. Between the borrower and the lender, is a group of companies known as mortgage brokers or mortgage bankers. The difference between a broker and a banker is relatively simple. The mortgage banker represents a very limited and specific list of lenders, and the mortgage broker shops his or her potential loans to any lender in the market. In addition to making loans, the mortgage banker normally "services" the loans on behalf of the lenders represented by that company. Loan servicing generally means collecting the payments and distributing the funds to the lender as well as making payments from impound accounts. The mortgage bankers collect a fee, usually equal to or less than one-tenth of 1 percent of the funds collected. The mortgage banker's first allegiance (his or her "fiduciary duty") is to the lender, and mortgage bankers are referred to as the lender's "correspondent."

The mortgage broker, representing the prospective borrower, takes a loan application from the borrower, collects the borrower's credit history and other information, and shops the loan to any lender in the marketplace. Mortgage brokers do not service loans, but earn their living from "origination" fees. Origination fees are points charged as fees for making and/or arranging the loan. Not uncommon, the mortgage broker can be compensated by both borrower and lender. By law, these dual fees should be disclosed to both the borrower and lender.

Warehousing. An additional function of both mortgage bankers and mortgage brokers is what is known as "warehousing" loans. The warehousing of loans is the compiling of closed home loans in bundles of $1,000,000 or more. These bundled loans, generally in amounts of tens of millions of dollars, are then sold to investors in what is known as the secondary mortgage market, or secondary loan market. These bundles of loans are securities backed by a large numbers of mortgages on individual pieces of real estate, sometimes guaranteed by an agency of the federal government such as Fannie Mae, Freddie Mac, or Ginny Mae.

Fannie Mae, Freddie Mac, and Ginny Mae. The secondary market is populated by entities with funny names like those in the title of this section. Fannie Mae, otherwise known as the Federal National Mortgage Association, is a federal agency that guarantees repayment of home loans sold to investors. Ginny Mae and Freddie Mac are other agencies that fulfill basically the same function. Unless you are someone with a large amount of money to invest, you will probably never come into contact with any of these federal agencies.

Portfolio lenders. The last group of lenders, known as portfolio lenders, is, from the point of view of commercial loans, my all-time favorite. Up until the early 1980s, most life-insurance companies and commercial real estate lenders were portfolio lenders; that is to say they made the loans, serviced the loans, and kept them until they were paid in full. Starting in the 1980s, commercial lenders, mostly local banks, started making commercial loans and bundling them for sale in the secondary market. To make these loans easier to sell, the borrower was "locked" into the loan for a minimum period of time; that is to say that the borrower was precluded from prepaying the loan before the expiration of the term.

Prepayment penalties. In lieu of absolutely forbidding prepayment, commercial lenders instituted a fee roughly equivalent to the amount of interest that would be due and payable should the loan go to the full term. An alternative to this has been what is called a "yield maintenance" condition which edged its way into the loan market. It states that in the event of prepayment, the borrower must pay a fee equivalent to the difference between the projected interest yield on the loan and that which would be the prevailing rate in the market at the time the loan was repaid.

These two types of clauses enabled these bundled loans to be sold in the secondary market because the investor had the confidence that regardless of whether the loans were held to term or prepaid, the lender would make the promised yield on the loan dollars. From the borrower's standpoint, if the loan was committed at a time of high interest rates, it was very expensive for the borrower to prepay the loan as rates began to fall. Conversely, on a loan made during a period of low interest rates, the yield maintenance provision made it very easy for the borrower to prepay as the penalties became nonexistent.

Unfortunately, many lenders, including traditional banks and insurance companies, found that they could make good income from origination fees and commercial loans and an additional markup or "discount" on the bundled loans when sold in the secondary market. The result is that the prevailing loan in the commercial market today is the bundled loan with lock-ins varying from five to ten years. The lock-in or yield maintenance provision generally comes with a clause specifying that, in the last year of the loan, the borrower has a penalty-free window in which to refinance the property.

The portfolio lender generally allowed prepayment without penalty. This was of great benefit to the borrower, as he or she did not have to wait nine years to refinance the property. In addition, if the property involved multiple phases, it allowed the borrower and lender alike to roll the new phases into the old loan as they were constructed and put into service. From the lender's point of view, especially with a good loan, it keeps the relationship between borrower and lender close, allowing the lender an opportunity to make additional loans to a good borrower. All things considered, I like portfolio lenders very much, there are still some around, but they are so conservative that their loans make little or no sense to anyone but a REIT.

Which loan should you use? When you're buying a house or any other form of real estate, your rates of return on your investment are going to be better if you leverage the transaction. Having said that, I believe that there is no specific loan that fits every occasion. The best you can do is to familiarize yourself with what potential loans are out there, keep updating yourself annually, and make sure that you and your projects are as credit worthy as possible. In addition to your talent, your next best asset is your credit worthiness!

Financial Analysis

Table 5.1 takes a hypothetical look at the financial impact of the home you already own. In this section of the chapter, I would like to walk you through the analysis of other pieces of personal real estate that you might consider owning, specifically a second (vacation) home and a rental property. When delving into investment and development tools later on in the book, we will expand on these financial analysis charts in greater detail, but for now a quick look at the potential of different types of investment will get you thinking about what you might like to consider, at least in the residential arena.

The Vacation Home

If you look at Table 5.1, you'll think that Table 5.3 is relatively similar. Keep the assumptions the same as in the original table to make it consistent.

As you can see in Table 5.3, the only difference from table 5.1 is in the bottom of the chart where you have incurred a taxable gain. If you are an investor, you can argue that this house was a long-term investment, and, therefore, is eligible for capital gains treatment. I'm not at all sure that a profit on a vacation home would ordinarily be treated as a capital gain, and I'm not an accountant, so I would defer to your accountant's opinion on any subject regarding taxation.

Table 5.3—*The Vacation Home*

Item		Dollar Value
Purchase price		$160,000
Down payment (20%)	Conventional loan	32,000
Closing costs	Estimate	3,500
Mortgage amount	80%	128,000
Mortgage (PI) 8%/30 years (APR = 8.81)	(PI)= Principal + Interest	$11,276.80/year $939.73/month

Table 5.3—*The Vacation Home, continued*

Item		Dollar Value
Appreciation 10% x 5 years	Compounded—Year 1	$176,000
	Compounded—Year 2	193,600
	Compounded—Year 3	212,960
	Compounded—Year 4	234,256
	Compounded—Year 5	257,682
Initial investment	Down + Closing cost	$35,500
Gross appreciation/profit	End of Year 5	
New value less cost	$94,182	
ROI	On $35,500	265% or 53%/year
Annual tax benefit during ownership	Estimated tax write-off	$10,240/year
Taxable gain		$94,182
Tax rate	Capital gain	15%

The Rental Property

Looking at a rental property, using the same assumptions, the results will look like Table 5.4.

Table 5.4—*The Rental Property*

Item		Dollar Value
Purchase price		$160,000
Down payment (20%)	Conventional loan	32,000
Closing costs	Estimate	3,500
Mortgage amount	80%	128,000
Mortgage (PI) 8%/30 years (APR = 8.81)	(PI)= Principal + Interest	$11,276.80/year $939.73/month
Appreciation 10% x 5 years	Compounded—Year 1	$176,000
	Compounded—Year 2	193,600
	Compounded—Year 3	212,960
	Compounded—Year 4	234,256
	Compounded—Year 5	257,682
Initial investment	Down + closing cost	$35,500

Table 5.4—*The Rental Property, continued*

Item		Dollar Value
Gross appreciation/profit	End of Year 5	
New value less cost	$94,182	
Rental income $1,000/mo/5 yrs	$1000 x 12 x 5	$60,000
Less maintenance	$600/year	($3,600)
Net rental income	5 years	$55,400
Less interest	5 years	($51,200)
Net taxable profit	Ordinary income 5/years	$4,200
ROI	On $35,500	265% or 53%/year
Taxable gain		$94,182
Tax rate	Capital gain	15%

In Table 5.4, the bottom end looks completely different from the others. What you have accomplished with this rental property is that you have made a capital gain of $94,182, and rental income over a five-year period of $4,200, but the best part of it is that your tenant has paid the interest and principal payments over the five-year period. You lost your annual interest write-off of $10,000, but the trade-off is that you did not have to pay the $10,000 in interest every year; your tenant did that for you. The potential problems in achieving this are the selection of a decent tenant, maintaining the property in a competitive condition, and keeping it leased throughout the five-year period. In a hypothetical situation where you are in a 30 percent tax bracket, you lose the interest write-off, costing you $3,000 in after-tax gain, but you pick up $10,000 in rental income to offset it. That's a $7,000 tax-sheltered gain.

Multi-Family Rentals

A multi-family spreadsheet, while similar to Table 5.4, is necessarily more complex from the point of view of cost and income analysis. It will therefore be dealt with in greater detail in Chapter 9.

How to Shop for Your Next Home

The final section of this chapter outlines steps you need to take when looking for your next home. You need to perform a two-part analysis to satisfactorily locate a property that meets your needs for a "home" as well as a "house."

A House as a Home

What to look for in a home will not be very much different from what you have looked for during past purchases. You will have to consider at least the following items:

- Amenities required in the house itself, i.e., number of bedrooms, baths, and garage space.
- Transportation corridors (commuting), i.e., how close is it to your work, your spouse's work, and your children's schools?
- Does the area meet your needs for raising a family, your current station in life, your ego needs?
- Is the neighborhood consistent in value? Are housing values uniform in the immediate neighborhood, or all over the block? All over the block is not necessarily bad. It may provide opportunities for expansion and upgrading.
- Are all essential services, shopping, schools, medical, and recreation available nearby or close enough so as not to be inconvenient for day-to-day living?

Investment Considerations

Now that you are a savvy investor, additional considerations need to be contemplated:

- How much are you willing to pay for shelter, and how much are you willing to pay in addition for a good investment?
- Are you willing to pay anything extra for the investment potential of this property?
- What is the property's potential for upgrading, for expansion? Do you have the time to devote to anything other than normal maintenance? Will the neighborhood in the area support an upgrade or an expansion?

A financial projection. Before "pulling the trigger" on your decision on a new place to live, consider the following potential of the proposed property from an investment point of view:

- *Is it a quick turnaround possibility?* If so, do you want to go to the trouble and expense of moving in and out in a short period of time?
- *Two-year hold.* Is this an area that you can live in and move from within the two-year tax-free window or are you going to want to stay longer because of your family situation? If the answer is to stay longer, look very hard for an upgradeable property or expansion potential, as this will allow you to

maximize your capital gain during the increased period of time you're likely to hold the property.

- *If you are looking for a property that you need to spend more than two years living in, you should very seriously look at the potential of an upgradeable house and/or one that can be expanded.* To do this you must confine your search to areas containing custom homes with as large a spread in value as possible.

When you find such an area, you want to buy a house that is at the low end of the value spectrum, with adequate extra land and potential value so that you can, during your tenure at this house, expand it as you can afford the time and money.

The Silent Bonus—Added Value without Cost

After having ploughed through this book, you might decide that the entire process is beyond you or you don't want the hassles. Does this mean that you can't make money on your home? Absolutely not! Perhaps your existing home qualifies only for the lipstick approach, but there are moneymaking strategies when buying future homes. In fact, you can accumulate a surprising amount of money in a relatively short period of time. The most reliable way to do this is to make sure you live in an area where housing is appreciating consistently.

Strategies for Profit

How is this possible? The answer to this is you must live in an area with constantly rising demand. Today jobs are portable, and as long as you're going to work, you might as well live in an area that will also produce a profit for you in housing. Table 5.5 shows the areas of the country that are experiencing constant growth. If you live in one of these areas, this strategy will work for you.

I'm not suggesting that you immediately pull up stakes and move, only that you consider the consequences of doing so. Recently, a friend's daughter and her husband moved from the San Francisco area to Phoenix because they were starting a family and wanted to own a home. The cost of housing in San Francisco MSA was too high for two well paid middle management people to afford a decent size home. In Scottsdale, they could purchase a 2,400 square foot home with four bedrooms for just over $300,000. The same home in the San Francisco MSA, within a reasonable commute to their employment, would have cost them $850,000 to $1,000,000. Neither one had any trouble in locating comparable if not better employment. For those of you on the east coast, Florida has consistently led the nation in growth for decades. The mitigating factor about Florida growth is that most of the net in-migration is composed of retiring people. This has a dampening effect on both wages and house prices. That said, it is still a viable growth state.

Table 5.5—*Top Ten U.S. Cities with Populations of 100,000 or More*

RANKED BY PERCENT CHANGE IN POPULATION 1990 – 1999

Rank	City	1999 Population	1990 Population	Numerical Change	U.S. Rank 1999	U.S. Rank 1990	Percent Change
1	Henderson City, NV	166,399	65,109	101,290	123	223	155.6%
2	North Las Vegas City, NV	101,841	7,956	53,885	217	224	112.4%
3	Chandler City, AZ	169,053	90,703	78,350	117	210	86.4%
4	Pembroke Pines City, FL	121,279	65,454	55,825	174	222	85.3%
5	Plano City, TX	232,904	128,507	104,397	71	144	81.2%
6	Las Vegas City, NV	418,658	259,834	158,824	37	63	61.1%
7	Corona City, CA	119,594	76,181	43,413	175	221	57.0%
8	Scottsdale City, AZ	199,943	130,086	69,857	85	142	53.7%
9	Coral Springs City, FL	116,136	79,137	36,999	185	218	46.8%
10	Laredo City, TX	183,160	125,029	58,131	102	149	46.5%

Zero Cost Value

Why move to an MSA in a growth state? The answer is relatively simple. Housing in these areas appreciates reliably every year. For instance, Arizona has a net in migration in excess of 250,000 people every year. Every year, the *Arizona Republic* publishes a chart showing the Phoenix MSA historical housing appreciation; you can find a comparable chart for any area you are interested in. Usually the local newspaper is a reliable source for this type of infor-

> ### Heads Up
> You can count on it; wealthy people do not like driving to and from work with the sun in their eyes.

mation. Failing that, ask your local realtor. The National Association of Realtors routinely publishes data like this for its members. Many articles in our local paper routinely update us on the rising values of homes in our MSA. Assuming that you live in a reasonably prosperous MSA, and you look in your own paper for these types of articles, you will see that merely owning a home in your MSA, and keeping it in good repair, is a profitable enterprise. If you assume that you could conservatively expect an appreciation of 7 percent over the next ten years, you could easily expect to make some money. If you upgrade your home every two years, you can make more. Why upgrade? The answer is simple, 7 percent of $400,000 is more money than 7 percent of $200,000. What does this mean, and how can it affect you?

Table 5.6 is an example of a couple purchasing a home for $160,000 with 10 percent down and a loan at today's rate of 5.5 percent. What can they expect?

Table 5.6—*Appreciation Analysis*

Item	Cost
Home purchase	$160,000
Closing and loan costs	2,300
Total investment	162,300
Cash investment	16,230
Value after two years	183,184
Net gain in value	$20,884
ROI on cash invested	128%
Annual ROI	**64%**

This simple analysis in Table 5.6 indicates that just owning a home in an area of constantly growing demand can be a profitable venture. If the home is rotated

Heads Up

Do not exceed this price point. There are many statistics available in each area to guide you on your choice. Find the area in your MSA where price escalation is the most reliable and highest, and check the price point where this starts to peter out.

every two years, the cash profit, acquired tax free, can be reinvested in another home, keeping the debt constant or escalating the mortgage payments to keep pace with your job growth. This will result in ever-increasing profits that can in turn be reinvested. If you are able to work your way up to a home worth $400,000, you will be earning $28,000 per year tax free. I'll bet you can't make that much and save it on your day job.

Planning Ahead

All this sounds great doesn't it? Well, to take advantage of this, you need to plan ahead and be willing to move every two years. The single best ploy when doing this is to migrate from one economic level to another. You can start out in a starter home which with today's financing can be acquired for little or no down payment, and work your way up from that to an upper middle class home within a ten- to twelve-year period. To do this, you need to do at least the following:

- *Commit a fixed percentage of your net income to mortgage payments.* These payments will escalate every time you move.
- *Commit to selling every two years.* You might have to live in the first home three or more years to have the appreciation accumulate enough to offset the sales commission, but once you are over that hurdle, you can start moving every two years.
- *Select areas in your MSA where price escalation is the highest.*
- *When you roll into a new home, use all of the profit to make the down payment.* This, coupled with your fixed percentage of income dedicated to mortgage payments should guarantee you a significant upgrade in house price every time you move. Remember, the more expensive the home, the more gross dollars you're making each year.
- *Keep in good touch with the realtor community.* You want to confine your activity to home prices where sales velocity is the highest.

If, like everyone else, your funds are limited, you might have to start your march toward riches in a lesser neighborhood. Do not despair, you can move up as soon as you have accumulated enough of a down payment. Each MSA has different grades of housing, and most MSAs are predictable. The most exclusive homes will be found in the NE part of town, the middle value in the SE, the lower cost homes in the NW. The industrial area and low cost housing will be found in the SW part of town. This holds true throughout the country unless there is a geographical limitation like a mountain, lake, or other natural barrier to limit access to that part of town.

Maximizing Your Yield

How do you make this program really sing? In areas of constant growth, there are always new housing developments. These are tract homes, and the cost ranges from $110,000 to $850,000 in our area. I'm sure that will be the same in any area you choose.

When you start out, try to buy one of the first homes in the tract. Choose the one that is going to be the most popular, not the one you like the best. There is always one obvious choice, but if you cannot decide, get help choosing from an experienced realtor. By buying one of the first units, you will enjoy an extra boost, as the builder always raises the price on the most popular units as they start to sell out. This cost escalation will be an added bonus above and beyond the usual historical appreciation. Certain builders are more popular than others; pick a good one, and follow him or her around. Most builders today build in a variety of price ranges to protect themselves from market swings. Take the time to study the new communities; you should be able to spot those that will be hugely popular. Again, if you need help, ask your realtor; he or she is getting paid to know what's going on.

Heads Up

Most tract home sales pavilions are set up to sell without the benefit of you having a realtor, as they can save the commission. They will, however pay your realtor a commission if you show up with a realtor or register your realtor the first time you visit the new home sales pavilion. Your realtor will appreciate this and go the extra distance for you.

CHAPTER 6

Grow Your Equity

T his section looks at strategies in the short term in an attempt to cover all the bases that may pertain to your current situation. The short-term approach will deal with periods of six months; the medium term will cover periods of up to two years. Long-term strategies will deal with upgrade and renovation projects that can be implemented over periods of two to five years or more. There are many different strategies for improving your home, but all will be based on the market potential of your particular house. How to assess the market potential has already been covered, and once this has been completed, you should be prepared to create your battle plan. A realistic strategy to maximize the value of your home prior to resale should incorporate examining everything from the lipstick approach to a complete rebuild. Where your home fits within these two extremes will depend largely on your estimate of the market potential, your available resources, and the advice of your professional real estate broker.

It is essential during this process that you do not overreach yourself or over-estimate the potential sale price of your home. With your first attempt you should be conservative and rigorously realistic. While this may result in less potential profit than a more aggressive approach, it should ensure that you have a rewarding experience with your first attempt. After you have studied the buyer's approach in this book, you should be able to make a much better buy with your next home and there-fore set yourself up for a larger profit when you sell that home. Let's explore the range of potential improvements for your current home.

Heads Up

This is the crucial part of the entire process. I strongly recommend that you take as much time as you need to do your research and analysis of the market, your neighbor-hood, and your general area. The decision on what to do is the hard part, executing your plan is the easy part. Just remember the old adage that "you make your money when you buy." If you don't buy right, the potential for profit may be less than ideal.

The Lipstick Approach

The so called an "lipstick approach" is your basic fix-up, paint-up, and re-carpet job. Most of this work you can do yourself, and it is characteristic of this minimum cost and maximum result approach that yields such good results. You will employ this approach if you have limited resources, or if you live in a tract home where major vari-ation from the models is not a viable option. The basic part of any facelift is to make the existing house as pre-sentable as possible. This includes not only the house itself, but the front and back yards as well. Think of spruc-ing up your yard and landscaping as grooming the house to make it more presentable. The exterior of the house should look sharp: fresh paint and detailed trim is a must. Inside the home, each room should be either completely repainted or refreshed so that it looks demonstrably clean. Ask your realtor to take a long look at the home to suggest what clutter should be removed from the rooms to make them appear large and elegant. You should put this clut-ter in storage other than your garage until you move. All of your rooms should be simply decorated, free of clutter, and very presentable. It is strongly suggested that your garage be made as presentable as the rest of the home. While women tend to select a home for the family to buy, the man of the house will want to put his blessing on areas of the home that are important to him. Traditionally, the garage and potential workshop space are important items for the male buyer.

Timing and Leverage

As with most things in life, timing is one of the most important factors contributing to success or failure. Earlier we discussed the condition of the national and local economies and their relation to the current and potential value of your home. Unless you're forced to make a decision that does not seem compatible with what is going on in your area, I recommend that you time your decision and execution to coincide with a rising market or at the very least, a stable or growing market. Again, this is not rocket science; simply keeping an eye on what's happening on a day-to-day basis should give you ample understanding of this aspect of your project.

> **Heads Up**
>
> If you become comfortable with the idea of buying and selling every two years, you should pay close attention to the traditional three-year business cycle. By finessing your purchasess at the bottom of the cycle and planning your sales at or near the peak of the cycle, you should maximize your potential return on investment in a spectacular fashion.

Leverage will play a vital role in your percentage return on dollars invested. The difference between the all cash transaction and the transaction using borrowed money is known as leverage. Your use of leverage has made your money work harder for you, increasing your ROI from 20 percent gross to 100 percent gross, and your annual ROI from 10 percent to 50 percent. The same holds true when you go to fix up your house.

Keep the same example, but in this case if a few dollars are spent to fix up the house, it might sell for $130,000. The cost to improve the house for resale is determined to cost an additional $2,000. If you put the cash up yourself, and you are able to attain the increased sale price, your rate of return on this $2,000 will be 500 percent during the six month fix up and resale. This is an annualized rate of return of 1,000 percent. If, however, you borrow the money as a home improvement loan, your rate of return at the time of sale becomes infinite. This is the effect of leveraging the additional $2,000.

> **Definition**
>
> ROI is an acronym for return on investment, and ROR is an acronym for rate of return.

Given the above, does it ever make good business sense to have a paid-for home? From a strictly business point of view it does not. However, if you are retired or nearing retirement, having a paid-for home can be a great comfort. Therefore, once you are finished with buying and selling and are satisfied with the results, you should consider a paid-for home as a retirement gift to yourself.

How Far Can You Go?

How far can you push the value of your home? This is a very difficult question to answer and is what separates the amateur from the professional house remodeler. For your first attempt at maximizing your home value, as mentioned earlier, I would recommend you do not push the sales price too far. Once you have gained experience and pushed it a little bit further each time, you will be better prepared for taking the additional risk.

In a situation like this, what is the real risk? If you have lived in a home for a period of time and you do not live in an area where population and employment are stagnant or decreasing annually, your home will already have accumulated some appreciation. If your home is in decent condition, you do not need to do anything to pocket this appreciation when you sell other than to make your property as presentable as possible. Once you start spending money to increase the value of the house, you will incur two separate potential risks; one, that you might not recoup your investment after the fix up, thereby lowering your net profit due from the house's normal appreciation, and two, that you might do the wrong thing and lower the value or potential value of your home. If you have done your homework on your area as well as the potential market value, you should totally eliminate the potential of the second risk. The remaining risk is that you do not fully recover the cost of the fix up. This would be a pretty acceptable risk to most people unless their resources are so strained that they do not have the wherewithal to pay for the fix up in the first place. If you are in this category, just make your home as presentable as possible and put it on the market; save your fix up for your next opportunity.

Realtors are always making recommendations. Figure 6.1 is an excerpt from a Century 21 local realtor flier.

Knowing Where to Stop

Knowing how far to push the enhancement of your house is a delicate matter. The

Heads Up
Shooting from the hip is for gun slingers. Real estate investors must avoid hasty decisions and do the homework.

more research you do the more confidence you will have in your ability to make this decision. As a rule of thumb, in my business, I spend twice the amount of time researching and planning as I do in the execution of the plan itself. I've found that preparation and study is a major contributor to profit. It has been a long time since I have failed to recoup or make a return on my investments. I'm not blowing my own horn as a genius in this matter, merely testifying to the fact that I have proven to myself that the work of research and planning is the

Figure 6.1—*Century 21 Kern Realty Flyer about Remodeling*

REMODELING: *How Much is Too Much?*

Many homeowners choose to remodel existing rooms, or add on to their current plan, in an attempt to increase their home's value. But, what projects should you choose? And how much rehab is too much, in terms of recovering costs when you decide to sell?

First, always protect the character of your home. Nothing sticks out more than a new addition that is at odds with the architectural style. Recognize your home's character and stay within its framework.

The most financially rewarding areas to remodel are usually the kitchen and bath. Newly re-done cooking spaces, cabinetry and additional storage areas can attract more buyers and may command a higher price for the home than a comparable one on the market.

Enlarged bathrooms are very popular attraction for home buyers, according to the National Kitchen and Bath Association. Today, the most popular additions for younger buyers are sunken whirlpool baths and larger showers.

Replacing worn carpeting, tiles and wood floors can give your home an immediate advantage over similar properties.

Updating paint colors in all areas of your home can also prove beneficial. It's important that you use neutral colors, when adding new floor and wall coverings.

Replacing outdated drawer-pulls and door knobs and some light fixtures is another relatively easy project that can add a lot of appeal.

Try to stay simple when remodeling, and look at your home as though you were the buyer. If you find the upstairs bedroom could be brightened by a new coat of paint or a more modern light fixture, potential buyers will probably feel the same.

Concentrate on improving two or three areas in your home. More than likely, the time and money you spend adding quality to your home will be rewarded with greater profit when you sell.

Smart Home Tip:
Make a paste of lemon juice and salt to remove rust stains in the kitchen or bathroom areas, without scratching.

Figure 6.2—*Values as a Percent of Cost*

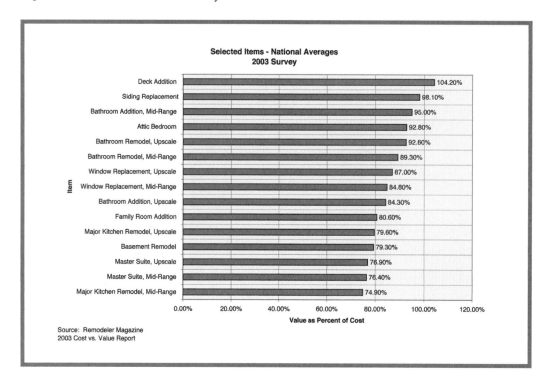

Selected Items - National Averages
2003 Survey

Item	Value as Percent of Cost
Deck Addition	104.20%
Siding Replacement	98.10%
Bathroom Addition, Mid-Range	95.00%
Attic Bedroom	92.80%
Bathroom Remodel, Upscale	92.60%
Bathroom Remodel, Mid-Range	89.30%
Window Replacement, Upscale	87.00%
Window Replacement, Mid-Range	84.80%
Bathroom Addition, Upscale	84.30%
Family Room Addition	80.60%
Major Kitchen Remodel, Upscale	79.60%
Basement Remodel	79.30%
Master Suite, Upscale	76.90%
Master Suite, Mid-Range	76.40%
Major Kitchen Remodel, Mid-Range	74.90%

Source: Remodeler Magazine
2003 Cost vs. Value Report

largest single contributor to the profits I have made. I believe that if you study the lives of successful business people, you'll find this approach to be a common thread behind most if not all of their success.

As a cautionary note, Figure 6.2 shows the relative cost/rewards for adding and/or upgrading various aspects of any house.

The Quick Turn Around and Taxes

In any given situation where profit is taken, there are tax implications.

> **Disclaimer.** What I say about taxes does not constitute tax advice, as I am not qualified to advise anyone on taxes. This is intended to provide you with some information to better understand and ask good questions of your tax professional.

My tax accountant has given me some guidelines to follow. For investments of less than one year, you can count on these profits being taxed as ordinary income. That is to say, these profits will be added to your normal gross income. Investments in excess of 12 months qualify for capital gain treatment. The current federal tax rate on capital gain is 15 percent. For housing used as a primary residence for a period *not less than* 24 months, profits are totally tax free.

Does this mean that if you have purchased a home only a few months ago you should not sell it for profit? Not at all, it simply means that if you do sell it in a period of less than one year, you will pay taxes at the same rate as the rest of your ordinary income. As a quick rule of thumb, look at your last year's tax rate and multiply it by your potential profit to see how much of that profit will be paid to Uncle Sam and taxes. To put this into dollars and cents, let's assume that you purchased the home for $100,000, and you can sell it for $120,000 without too much work. This will yield you a profit of $20,000. If you were in the 25 percent tax bracket last year, and assuming that this additional income does not boost you into a higher tax bracket, you would pay $20,000 times 25 percent or $5,000 in taxes on this profit. That would mean that your net profit would be $15,000 on an investment of $100,000 or 15 percent return on investment. With the ability to evaluate the tax impact of potential short term profit, you should then be able to make an intelligent decision about whether it is worth it to you to proceed at this time or wait for a better tax treatment.

If you find that you will be in a capital gain situation, you will have held the house for more than one year but less than two, you will be looking at paying a 15 percent federal tax on your profit. Using the same example above, your $20,000 profit will be reduced by 15 percent for $20,000 times 15 percent equals $3,000. Your net yield on this investment would then be $17,000 for a 17 percent rate of return. Again, you should evaluate the profit potential rather than its taxable impact. You'll find that if you incorporate the use of leverage in both situations, the tax impact should be very easy to reconcile.

Finally, look at the tax-free transaction to see what its potential impact would be, not only on your initial home, but if you continue to do this on a regular basis. Let's assume that you took advantage of the idea of leverage in the first place, and that you invested $20,000 to purchase your current home, and at the end of two years with a little fix up, your net profit was $17,000 after the cost to fix up. You now have in your hand a total of $37,000, none of which is taxable. If you take this $37,000 and purchase a $150,000 home, live in it for a

Heads Up

Over the years I have found that an opportunity to profit should never be overlooked. Having to pay taxes on a profit is better than not making any profit and all. When you are evaluating any potential project, focus on the positive aspects of the plan, plan for the potential negatives, and work hard to produce the best results.

period of two years, improving it as you live there, and sell it after the two-year period has expired for a net profit of $30,000, this means that in a period of time less than four years, you have increased your cash nest egg from $20,000 to $67,000.

All of this is after-tax income!!

If you are employed, you have to ask yourself how long it would take you to save $47,000 out of your current salary. If you're like most people in this country, it would take you a long time, and for every dollar saved, you have had to pay taxes on it. That means that if you're in the 25 percent tax bracket, you have to make a $1.25 for every dollar you save, and you can only save this $1 after you pay all of your bills. By using the capital invested in your home, rolling in every two years, you are able to accumulate a fairly large tax-free pile of cash in a relatively short period of time.

If you assume that you continue with the above scenario three more times with the same predictable results, that would mean that in a ten year period of time you would have parlayed your initial $20,000 into an after-tax cash income of $150,000. The price for this is moving every two years. Most people consider moving to be a dramatic event, however if you have made a game plan and stick to it, you should be more than compensated for the inconvenience. If you are looking to your day-to-day employment as a source for long-term retirement savings, you need to be in a situation where you can dramatically increase your income without substantially increasing the cost of living. If this is the case, then you will have several choices when planning to salt away money for your retirement. Most people, however, are not in the situation described above. Their income, even with steady raises and progression within the ranks, is relatively predictable and serves only to keep pace with their increased cost of living.

Capital Items vs. Eyewash

The primary purpose of this section is to address the investment opportunity represented by the potential of maximizing the value of the home you are currently living in. Under normal circumstances, whether you are dealing with this home or another home that you would be living in, you would be expected to maintain the home in a proper manner so that the value of the home would not deteriorate. The act of maintenance in and of itself is not profit producing; it does however, in an indirect way, produce some profit. Annually, through inflation and increasing scarcity of homes in your area, the price of housing rises. The value of a properly maintained home should rise with the rest of the homes in the area. While some of the increase in value can be attributed to inflation, there's also a component which is profit. In a normal situation, you would expect that your home should increase in value by the cost of routine maintenance plus inflation. In essence that recapture of the maintenance cost can be construed as a profit. You are essentially recapturing your cost of living in the home. Think of it, combined with your tax savings in interest paid, as free rent.

Maintenance vs. Capital Items

Maintenance is defined as keeping your home in good repair. In general, maintaining a home in good repair should at the very least include the following items of maintenance:

- Paint
- Wallpaper
- Floors
- Exterior paint and trim
- Landscaping
- Mechanical maintenance
    - Heating, ventilating, and air conditioning (HVAC)
    - Plumbing
    - Septic systems
    - Electrical
- Built-in appliances
- Common areas (in condo situations)

Taking care of these items are normal maintenance chores. Anything beyond this work, such as upgrading any of these items can be considered a "capital" item.

When you are attempting to elevate the value of your home, and you are contemplating something in excess of the lipstick approach, you will be dealing with capital expenditures. These costs must be added to the original cost of your home to determine your new basis for evaluating the potential profit you hope to gain at the time of sale. Table 6.1 is a tool for the purpose of analysis so that you can get a better handle on the process. To start with, let's put together a spread sheet to determine your actual cost to date. A typical spreadsheet would look something like Table 6.1.

Definition

A *capital item* is expenditure for the purpose of elevating the value of a home. Examples of this are better flooring, lighting, mechanical systems, or alterations of any kind.

As you can see, the home you thought you paid $100,000 for actually cost you $104,300. This is a relatively typical situation. In some cases like the situation

Table 6.1—*Basic Spreadsheet*

Item	Cost
Purchase price	$100,000
Closing costs	1,500
Loan costs	1,600
Title insurance	300
Termite inspections	300
Building inspection	300
Home appliance warranty	300
Total costs at closing	$104,300

involving FHA and VA home purchases, some of these costs were paid by the seller, and these should not be added to your cost basis. We will use this basic spreadsheet as a tool as we go along to illustrate how to analyze your actual investment and return on investment.

Cost and Leverage

A basic concept in dealing with any form of investment is leverage. Leverage is defined as using other people's money (OPM) to make your money work harder. The simple example of this is a home purchased for all cash for $100,000 and sold for $120,000 will yield a profit of $20,000. This is a 20 percent profit over the time of ownership. If the same home were purchased with a conventional 80 percent loan, then your actual investment would have been $20,000. This alters the profit picture at the time of sale, and the same $20,000 profit becomes a 100 percent profit or ROI, based on your actual investment of $20,000.

Definition

ROI is synonymous with rate of return, cash on cash return, or percentage profit. It should always be annualized to reflect your ROI per year on your investment.

If, in the example above, you lived in the home for two years before selling, then your leveraged ROI would be a gross return of 100 percent for two years or an annualized return of 50 percent. If you have had any experience with investments of any kind, a return like this should impress you.

To take this a step further, we should expand our initial spreadsheet by adding the information just covered. It will look something like Table 6.2.

Table 6.2—_Cost Basis_

Item	Cost	Cash Invested
Purchase price	$100,000	
Closing costs	1,500	
Loan costs	1,600	
Title insurance	300	
Termite inspections	300	
Building inspection	300	
Home appliance warranty	300	
Total costs at closing	104,300	
Loan dollars	−81,000	
Equity		**$23,300**

At this point, we have documented your house purchase and shown that you have in fact made a cash investment in it of $23,300. As we follow the transaction through, you will be able to track your investment accurately, and if you are the true bean counter type, you can add in your annual principal repayment to your cash investment. For the sake of this book, I'm going to assume that your annual tax savings will more than offset your annual principal payments, and this refinement will not be alluded to in the rest of this book.

Spreadsheets and Planning

Now that we have some basic tools, how do you use them to analyze your project? It's quite simple: Add to it as you formulate your plan. Assume the following as part of your battle plan:

- The neighborhood is sold out—that is to say that the original builder has no more new homes for sale.
- The homes in the neighborhood are at least five years old.
- Your home is a three-bedroom, two-bath home with a two-car garage on a one quarter acre lot (i.e., an average suburban home).

Heads Up

Returns on investment in real estate can be quite spectacular when they are planned properly. You might even come to the conclusion that you can make a career out of this type of transaction. At the very least, real estate investing can provide you with a low-risk, high-yield, tax-free nest egg.

- You have made no capital improvements to your home as yet.
- Prices for your model home are now at $115,000 to $120,000 depending on condition.
- Some of the homes in the neighborhood have been improved with capital additions and are worth more than the average.

What's your battle plan to be? If you've done your homework, you have found out that several homes have upgraded appliances, some have upgraded carpet and flooring, and some have added space, bedrooms, family rooms, playrooms, and workrooms. What should you do?

Your research should reflect how much these modifications have affected the selling price of these particular homes, but if none of them has yet sold, there may be no reliable way to guess what they might sell for. For some guidance in this area, you can consult your local Realtor® and your local residential appraiser. If there is no definitive answer, you might be better off not taking a chance on the additions; just play it safe on this move, and make a more versatile purchase next time. If this is the case, then you will want to contact the realtors that handled the sales of your model and determine what made some worth $5,000 more than the others. Armed with this information, you can make your plan to maximize this home without taking any heavy capital risks.

If, on the other hand, you find out that the homes that have made some capital improvements have sold for significantly more money, then you can consider not only a good lipstick approach, but perhaps an addition prior to sale. If the upgraded homes have been selling the extra square footage at the same price as the basis home, say $80 per square foot, then you know that if you can add some space at a cost less than $80 per square foot, you can make a profit. If construction costs in your area are around $50 per square foot for additions, and they sell for $80 per square foot, your profit potential is $30 per square foot.

For the sake of this example, determine that you have found out that the best sales included a modest kitchen upgrade, and an added family room of 250 square feet, and you can make a profit at this. Look at the potential deal and put it into perspective using the following assumptions.

- A complete lipstick job on your place will cost $1,000.
- The kitchen upgrade will cost $1,500.
- The 250-square-foot family room addition will cost $50 per square foot or a total of $12,500.
- The basic house will be worth at least $120,000 and with the addition no less than $140,000, ($80 per square foot for the additional 250 square feet family room).

- Brokerage commissions are 6 percent in you area.
- Fully improved, you house should sell at worst case for $140,000 less the 6 percent commission or a net of $131,600 to you. How does this stack up? Take a look at Table 6.3.

Table 6.3—*Gross Profit with Addition*

Item	Cost	Cash Invested
Purchase price	$100,000	
Closing costs	1,500	
Loan costs	1,600	
Title insurance	300	
Termite inspection	300	
Building inspection	300	
Home appliance warranty	300	
Total costs at closing	104,300	
Loan dollars	−81,000	
Equity		**$23,300**
Lipstick job	$1,000	1,000
Kitchen addition	1,500	1,500
Family room addition	12,500	12,500
Total investment		**$38,300**
Sales price	$140,000	
Less commission	−8,400	
Net yield/cash after loan paid off	**$131,600**	**$50,600**

If you could sell the home for $120,000 without the additional expenditure of $12,500, you would have yielded as shown in Table 6.4.

Table 6.4 illustrates that the addition costing $12,500 will yield you an additional $18,800 in gross cash yield, or an additional net profit of $6,300. The addition alone will yield a 50 percent profit over the short time you will have the additional money invested. Annualized, this component of your project produces a 100 percent per annum yield.

Table 6.4—*Gross Profit without Addition*

Item	Cost	Cash Invested
Purchase price	$100,000	
Closing costs	1,500	
Loan costs	1,600	
Title insurance	300	
Termite inspection	300	
Building inspection	300	
Home appliance warranty	300	
Total costs at closing	104,300	
Loan dollars	−81,000	
Equity		**$23,300**
Lipstick job	$1,000	1,000
Kitchen addition	1,500	1,500
Total investment		**$25,800**
Sales price	$120,000	
Less commission	−7,200	
Net yield / cash after loan paid off	**$112,800**	**$31,800**

Potential Profit and ROI

Now that your plan looks pretty good, how should you proceed? In case you have not noticed, we have assumed that the costs of preparing your home for sale will be paid for in cash. Do you have that amount of cash to invest? If you do, do you really want to invest it in this project? What are the alternatives? You can take out a home improvement loan; for the sake of this example, assume that the interest rate will be at 8 percent. It will take four months to do the work, and an additional three months to sell the house for a total project duration of seven months. How does this affect the deal? Go back to the spreadsheet to find out. By referring to Table 6.4, with the family room addition included, you can see that you will yield $50,600; subtracting your total investment of $38,300 and the net profit is $12,300 or a 32 percent ROI. Remember, the addition yielded a 50 percent ROI, so your total yield went up substantially by doing the addition. If you look at the home improvement loan, realistically I believe you could expect that you could borrow 100 percent of the cost. Putting these numbers into the spreadsheet would look something like Table 6.5.

Table 6.5—_Leverage Analysis_

Item	Cost	Cash Invested
Purchase price	$100,000	
Closing costs	1,500	
Loan costs	1,600	
Title insurance	300	
Termite inspection	300	
Building inspection	300	
Home appliance warranty	300	
Total costs at closing	104,300	
Loan dollars	−81,000	
Equity		**$23,300**
Lipstick job	$1,000	
Kitchen addition	1,500	
Family room addition	12,500	
Loan dollars	15,000	
Loan cost Interest	700	700
Total investment		**$24,000**
Sales price	$140,000	
Less commission	−8,400	
Net yield/cash after loan paid off	**$131,600**	**$36,400**

You can see that by leveraging the costs, your cost went up by the interest cost of $700, but the bottom line went up by $3,800. This is the effect of leverage. Your gross yield on dollars invested is now calculated by taking your net profit of $36,400, deducting your investment of $24,000 for a total dollar yield of $11,400, or an ROI of 47 percent.

Almost without exception, you can leverage your plan by doing the research and backing it up with proper cost analysis. Your lender understands the process, and that is how they earn their money. Let their money work for you.

Heads Up
Leverage has increased your yield from 32 percent to 49 percent in just seven months.

CHAPTER 7

The Details— Inside

Everything I know about housing and how to modify it is a monster of a subject, so I have broken it into two parts: inside and outside. The following chapter deals with outside detail. There are many authoritative sources for home renovation, and I suggest you seek out more sources than these two chapters. They will, however, get you launched. I can find no documented proof that specific remodeling of your home will add value specific to your home, and while it is necessary to keep your home well maintained and groomed, modifying your home beyond that point may not necessarily line your pockets with additional profits. The key to profitable renovation of your home is to do enough to keep the home current within the context of the home's design and the general neighborhood. This will guarantee that you will get the maximum possible yield from your particular house, and ensure a prompt sale when the time comes to sell. Major renovations and additions are covered in Chapters 11 through 16.

Interiors

American homes have evolved in recent years and have added features and rooms which are today considered essential. Thirty years ago the American dream home was a three-bedroom, two-bath ranch house, on a quarter acre lot with a two-car garage. Today the most popular home is a four-bedroom, two-and-a-half bath house with a three-car garage. The lot size varies all over the country from a quarter acre down to 7,000 square feet.

The internal configuration of the housing has also changed. Older homes have smaller rooms with fewer amenities. The art of remodeling or redecoration now includes modernization and adding to older homes to make them more competitive in the marketplace. They must compete with new homes under construction. In this chapter we will cover and describe briefly the ideal configuration of the modern home. Within each type of room, innovation and design have created features that are now considered essential to modern living.

These features are not really essential. They are, however, very desirable to buyers looking for new homes. Our society has become one of instant gratification, and because of the money available for mortgage loans, the ability to satisfy people's desire for instant gratification has been extended to the home buyer.

In some areas it is now possible to borrow 100 percent or more of the cost of a new home. The rule of thumb for most mortgage underwriters is that they will allow the borrower to allocate one-third of his or her income for mortgage payments. The net effect of this is that people are able to buy more expensive homes at a younger age. With this kind of buying power the American public can exercise complete discretion when buying a home. This has forced the sellers of older homes to modernize, and in some cases, add to the size of their homes before placing them on the market.

This is not all bad, as a renovated home can compete effectively with new housing. By modernizing and renovating your home, you can show a decent profit. There are some people who do this for a living. The big trick is to know what to do and how to do it at the least possible cost.

Rooms

One of the fundamental differences between the older home and the new home is room size. One hundred years ago, people in this country were considerably smaller than they are today. In addition, incomes were more uniform than they are today. This resulted in smaller homes with smaller windows, and considerably fewer amenities. Typical room sizes today are shown in Table 7.1.

Table 7.1—*Typical Room Sizes*

	Minimum	Optimum
Public Areas		
Entries	Placement to provide joining public spaces more important than square feet. Dimension and separation varies with floor plan configuration. Should be large enough to allow entry without fouling with front door. Review sight lines from entry for views of unsuitable areas (bathrooms, kitchen, and other private spaces).	
Living room	12' x 12'	14' x 16'
Family room	12' x 12'	14' x 16'
Great/living/dining rooms	12' x 20'	14' x 24'
Dining room	12' x 12'	12' or 14' x 14'
Kitchen	8' x 8' (galley) 8' x 9' ("U" shape)	12' x 12' (island)—work triangle 16' to 20'
Breakfast area	6' x 6' (nook) 8' x 8' (table—no circulation) 10' x 10'	12' x 12'
Pantries	18"w x 24" d (cabinet)	6' x 8' (walk-in)
Washroom/laundry room	6' x 6' (room) 3' x 6' (laundry closet)	7' x 12' (mud room)
Guest closet	Provide 3 LF rod & shelf	4 LF R&S
Powder bath	3' x 5' or 4' x 4'	3' x 6' or 5' x 5'

	Minimum	Optimum
Privacy Areas		
Master bedroom	12' x 15'	16' x 18'
Master bath	6' x 6' vanity, 3'—1 sink/ 6' x 8'—vanity 5'—2 sinks	9' x 12', 6' vanity, 2-sinks/ 10' x 12', 8' vanity, 2-sinks + sit-down, incl. sep tub and shower
Master closet	Linear—8'/walk-in 4'6" x 8' (L-shape)	walk-in 6' x 8' (18 LF)/closet

Table 7.1—*Typical Room Sizes, continued*

Privacy Areas		
Secondary bedrooms	10' x 10'	12' x 12'
Den	10' x 10'	12' x 12'
Office	10' x 10'	12' x 12'
Guest bath	5' x 5'—single sink	5' x 10'—dual sink, compartmentalized
Stairways	4' tread	6' tread

Exterior Spaces		
Covered patios	10' x 10'	12'–14' x 16'–24'
Garages	12' x 20' (one-car) 20' x 20' (two-car)	24' x 30' (three-car)

Room dimensions represent net usable space and assume allowance for traffic areas within separate rooms. To the extent that spaces are combined, traffic zones can be overlapped. The dimensions are guidelines for modest and mid-priced contemporary production homes. Dimensions may vary considerably from market to market. Room sizes that are significantly smaller or larger than in homes in competitive areas may affect value.

The perceived value of the arrangement and emphasis of the rooms will vary based on the stage of life of the potential buyer. For example, young families emphasize the public areas and their separation from the private areas, while couples without children are less concerned with the separation of public areas from the private areas.

You need to take the above list and roughly compare this to the room sizes in your current home before you embark on any significant renovation project. Once you go beyond the standard lipstick approach, you start entering the realm of the legitimate renovation project. What you need to determine when you get into this type of project is what your goals are and how you plan to compete with other homes for sale in this economic bracket. I'm not suggesting that before entering this type of project you turn your existing home into a carbon copy of some of the newer homes. What I am suggesting is that you should determine what you're competing against, so that you have a better ability to come up with a strategy to compete effectively. Sometimes it is not necessary to rebuild your rooms, but merely to add to them the amenities that have become expected in the new housing constructed today. Some of the items that you will encounter in these new rooms are as follows:

- Plant shelves
- Generous dual-pane windows
- Maintenance-free flooring
- Enhanced lighting
- Ceiling fans
- Electrical outlets every 8 feet.
- Minimum ceiling height of 8 to 10 feet.
- Vaulted ceilings
- Varied wall textures
- Light-colored walls
- Enhanced communication options such as cable TV, computer wiring, and high-speed telephone lines

The above items are relatively easy to incorporate into an older home. They just require some planning and some expenditure.

We will look at individual rooms and discuss what would be an ideal situation to create in advance of the sale of your home. Do not look upon this as necessarily a goal when you're trying to sell your home, merely look upon these ideas as guidelines if you plan to make more than fundamental changes in your home. What is discussed here is not only the ideal for each room, but also items that can be incorporated into your existing rooms without any dramatic changes to the rooms themselves. When you approach your project, you want to do it in the most economical manner rather than attempting to match the ideal. The entire thrust of this exercise is to make a profit, not just spend to your money.

Heads Up

I strongly recommend that before you put your home on the market you go to see the homes that are already on the market. Try to look at homes that are in the economic bracket you wish to target based on the research you have already done. Every time you see something that appeals to you, make a note of it. You may use that list when putting together your battle plan for your property. At the very least, you will have a list of things that you deem desirable.

Entries

Unless you are dealing with homes in an upper economic bracket, a separate entry is not a large item. Most middle-of-the-road housing incorporates the entry into the living/dining room area. In homes that sell above the average price, entries tend to be larger and more elegant. If you do not have an entry on your home, it is relatively easy to create an entry by adding onto the front of the house. This is only possible if you're setback requirements will permit it.

Living Rooms

Unlike other rooms in the modern home, the living room has become a smaller room than in the past. The American way of living has become less formal, and, therefore, the family room has replaced the living room as a place to gather and entertain. On a daily basis, Americans use the family room to gather around a television set. A living room needs to accommodate, comfortably, at least a three-person couch and two easy chairs. Beyond that, you get into the realm of the above average home.

Family Rooms

Today's family room has become a rather elaborate affair; it is not only larger, but also can incorporate things such as a wet bar, a media room, an office, and an eating area. It is most often adjacent to, or part of, an extended kitchen separated only by a counter. This room has become the focal point of family living, and is usually the largest room in the downstairs portion of the home. If you have an older home that has a standard living room, family room, or in the case of a really old home, a parlor and a living room, restructure the dividing wall to make the room closest to the kitchen more like today's family room.

Great Rooms

Very popular in current housing construction is the great room. This room is a combination of both living room and family room. It is usually built in conjunction with an expanded kitchen and dining area. The use of the great room allows the space generally allocated to the formal living room to be reallocated to additional bedrooms, storage, and other amenities.

Dining Rooms

Most small- and mid-size modern homes do not have a formal dining room. The current custom is to incorporate a dining area in the formal living room. Other than for entertaining, the dining room gets little use by the modern American family. More popular today is the eat-in kitchen between the kitchen and the family room. If your home can be reconfigured to accommodate this you'll find that this will become an attractive feature at the time of resale.

Kitchens

The up-to-date kitchen tends to be fairly spacious, with a central island for food preparation and eating. Areas usually found in today's new kitchens include a generous pantry, and sometimes a laundry room. Expanded amenities include, but are not limited to, the following items: dishwasher, double oven, microwave oven, four-burner cook top, garbage compactor, refrigerator/freezer, telephone, TV, computer outlets, and pantry.

Master Bedroom Suites

The master bedroom and bath have become a major focal point of current housing design. Marketing people have determined that the kitchen and the master suite are two rooms that are essential to get right to entice today's discriminating buyer. Items commonly included in the minimum master bath are his and her sinks, separate tub and shower, and generous walk-in closets. The bedroom absolutely must be able to contain a king size bed and several large chests of drawers. If your home does not incorporate these items, as a minimum, this would be an ideal place to consider an expansion of your home. You may not have to build additional space; you might be able to demolish and reconfigure. To attract the attention required to sell your home, you will have to have a very attractive kitchen and master suite.

Master closet. The master closet is essential to the modern home. Today's women look for a minimum 8-by-12 walk-in, with men being accommodated in separate and smaller walk-ins or traditional straight closets.

The Guest Bath

The guest bath comes in an infinite variety of styles and sizes, from the standard combination tub and shower, toilet, and sink, to the more elaborate separate tub, shower, and toilet room. Other variations include the Jack and Jill bathroom which is shared between two bedrooms, but not the rest of the house, and the combination guest bathroom and powder room.

Other Bedrooms

Other bedrooms are not as vital as the master bedroom, but it is essential that when selling new homes you have at least three additional bedrooms. You might not be able to compete in this area, but do not despair because you will be in the majority at the moment, as most homes are this way. The reason for the fourth bedroom is that people today deem a home office to be an essential part of any new home.

Guest closet. The guest closet has been completely overlooked as an area of emphasis in modern housing. A standard five or six foot long closet will suffice. The modern touch today would be to have bifold doors rather than sliding doors, but that is generally overlooked by buyers when they are looking for a home.

The Den

The den is another popular room, and if you do not have four bedrooms, but you have an area that you can create or designate as a den or office, you will have created a space that will serve as an office. Some older homes have a library and this is ideal for today's office requirements. The only thing you want to make sure of is that the requisite electrical and communication wiring is in place.

The Office/Media Room

As mentioned above, the home office has become a desirable feature of the new American home. Few houses built today lack this amenity, and it is either provided for as a fourth bedroom, or a separate den/office, or media room.

Utility Room

Today's utility room is typically placed between the garage and the kitchen, and the modern variety is as spacious as possible. At the very least this room must be able to contain a separate washer and dryer and sorting table. If you have an old-fashioned home with a generous garage, you might be able to incorporate a portion of the garage to accommodate this function.

Stairways

If you have a two-story home, the stairway may be a fairly important feature. The modern stairway has at least one landing, and sometimes two. Older homes usually have a fairly steep, narrow, and rather utilitarian stairway. If this is the case, and you do not have the room to renovate this feature in your home, you have to make it as attractive as you can. If possible you should try to incorporate at least one landing with as much width and depth of stair tread as possible.

Pantries

Pantries are very desirable areas, and you should make the effort to have one incorporated into your kitchen or at least accessible to the kitchen. Several areas to investigate when attempting to accommodate this amenity are the washroom, and the coat closet or linen closet. A pantry would be a more desirable feature than a large utility room or coat closet. When tackling this, the larger the better is the general rule of thumb.

Patios

While patios are probably more properly dealt with as part of the backyard, it is essential to the modern house that you have a covered area for outside seating that runs off either the family room or the living room, preferably both.

Garages

In a large part of the country the garage has become a vital area of the house. In the east and midwest most homes have basements, but in the west a large garage is essential. In the past, the size of garages has varied considerably east to west and state to state, however, the minimum size today for a two-car garage is 24-by-24 feet. Some older garages were built 20-by-20 feet, and this can cause a problem. Whether a home has a two- or three-car garage is less important than the dimension of the garage in front of the parking space. The additional 4 feet not only allows people to move around the garage, but provides an area for storage essential to a home without a basement. It was the lack of a basement that was the impetus for the third-car garage added to the modern home. Most people in the west use the third-car garage for storage.

Basements

If you live in the part of the country where basements are the norm, having a basement is obviously essential. The modern basement has more headroom than older ones; this provides room to utilize the basement as additional living space. If you have an older home that has a basement with very restrictive head room, there isn't much you can do about it. In this condition you need to simply make your basement as presentable as possible so that it can be used for storage. It is also an ideal area for a utility room or a play room for the children. To be counted as part of the living space of a home, any area must be heated and/or air conditioned. This rule of thumb includes any spaces and add-ons that were converted in any other areas of the house. If you convert an old porch into a dining room or expanded living area, you must extend the heating and cooling into this room to have it included as part of the living space of the home.

Kitchens and Baths

What is an older home? I think the answer depends on where you live. In New England, homes can be over 100 years old and still be desirable places to live. In fact, restoring these old homes has proven to be a profitable enterprise. Out west, a 25-year-old home is considered old and in need of modernization. What's the case where you live? The easy way to find out what is old in your neck of the woods is to talk to an appraiser or a realtor. While you will not get a guaranteed answer, you should get a pretty good idea where your home stands. In my mind, a house that qualifies as old has definite possibilities. Old homes tend to have advantages that new ones do not have.

Old Houses

What sets the older home apart from new housing? The old home usually has the following advantages:

- It sits on a bigger lot.
- It is larger than the newer homes.
- It has more rooms.
- It has washrooms and pantries.
- It was better built than the new homes.

While this might not be true of all older homes, it most likely is the case. What are the disadvantages of older homes? They likely have the following problems: inadequate wiring, antiquated plumbing, basements with low headroom, smaller rooms, detached garages, and antiquated kitchens. While some of these problems are potentially expensive, all have a solution, and when rectified could very well put your older home in a better place within your housing market. In many areas of the country, for the last 20 years, people have been buying up older homes, Victorians, brownstones, and cottages and renovating and expanding them at a profit.

Size. One big advantage of the older home is that the kitchens were always large, and sometimes had walk-in pantries and wash rooms. Size has again become fashionable in new homes as people invest more time and money in their residences. Renovating a kitchen can be expensive, and taking an old kitchen all the way to the latest and greatest will most likely not pay back all of your investment. If you have an older home, I suggest you modernize it enough so that it meets the minimum requirements for the modern kitchen. It must have the following appliances:

- Garbage disposal
- Double sink
- Microwave oven
- Family-size refrigerator (23 cubic feet minimum)
- Four-burner cook-top and oven

The counters should be in good condition, and, at the least, covered with a good grade of Formica. The kitchen cabinets should be freshly painted or stained, and the floor should be tiled or covered with a good vinyl. To go beyond this could take a great deal of money, and you won't necessarily get it back in the short term. If the layout works well, and all the basics are there, the buyers can upgrade whatever they deem necessary. If they are going to be there for a while, they can recoup the upgrade better that you can in the short term.

Expense. When dealing with an older home, the focus should be to make sure that the basic systems, electric, plumbing, and HVAC, are brought up to code, and are functioning properly. Unless you are going for a total remodel, demolition, and addition, you should concentrate on these items and not get into glitz and glamour. If you look at the potential of any older home, you should view it as a project to be broken down into stages, wherein each stage has a risk/reward ratio. Depending on the level of upgrade you are contemplating, your project can be limited in scope at the last stage. Your project, broken down into phases, would look something like this.

1. Conduct market research
2. Determine how far you want to go
3. Make a plan and do the numbers
4. Draw the plans, line up the money, and get the permits
5. Demolish and upgrade the power, plumbing, and HVAC
6. Build it out, installing the basic amenities
7. Finish the interior based upon the market potential (basic, if it's skinny, and all the way if you can push it to the top).

Cosmetic vs. functional. Step seven above contemplates the difference between general upgrades and true renovation and refinishing. Beyond upgrading the infrastructure, power, plumbing, and HVAC, the refinishing can take on a very broad range of upgrading. New Formica counters are about 10 percent of the cost of stone counters. The fact is that Formica will do the job, but stone is needed when you are shooting for the top of the market. Chances are that, if your home is average, you should go for the functional and let the buyers provide more if they feel they

> **Heads Up**
> The infrastructure is functional, and everything else is cosmetic. Functional renovation is necessary, and cosmetic renovation must be discretional. Do not overdo the cosmetic as you might not get your money back.

need it. If you overdo your remodel, you will most likely not recapture your investment. Figure 6.2 in Chapter 6 contains a chart that shows the cost recovery of different renovations in different markets. You should be guided by its warning.

Appliances. Appliances are an extension of the kitchen. They must cover the basics and be functional. Unless you are going for the gold, they need not be top of the line. Items like built-in refrigerators, double ovens, and other refinements should be saved for the top-of-the-line market. The only real way to recover these items is to live with them long enough for the market to catch up. If you live in a dilapidated mansion in the Hamptons, Palm Beach, or Beverly Hills, you can take the remodel all the way all at once. If you are upgrading an older home in a neighborhood that has started to improve but still contains un-renovated properties, you would be wise to limit your remodel to adding space and basic amenities. Let the serious upgrade wait until all homes catch up with modernization requirements. Gentrification can wait until the second round when the neighborhood has caught up with the fashionable set.

Bathrooms. Bathrooms are a bit like kitchens; they need to be modernized, but not necessarily state-of-the-art. These days, in new housing, the master bath has become a component of the master suite which includes bedroom, sitting room, baths, and closets. The ultimate setup contains his and hers sinks, and closets, a separate toilet room, perhaps a bidet, separate shower and Jacuzzi tub. The floor should be tiled with granite or marble counters around the sinks, with top of the line, very fashionable fixtures.

Do you need to go all the way with the master bath? Certainly not, unless you are shooting for the top of the market. You do, however, need to incorporate as many of these basics as possible in the master bathroom:

- At least one sizeable walk-in closet
- Separate toilet room
- Separate tub and shower
- Two sinks and generous counter space

In older homes, where the master bedroom and bath were traditionally pretty basic, you might need to cannibalize an adjacent bedroom to incorporate the additional space needed. In my home, we added a room off the bath to contain the walk-in closet and expand the bathroom space. Some of the tricks to adding class can be found in decorating books. One of my favorites is to make one sink a pedestal with a medicine cabinet over it. This is the man's sink. The other should have abundant counter space, and, perhaps, a place to sit. The pedestal sink gives the bath a classier look, and men can handle the lack of counter space. Tub enclosures should be sliding glass instead of curtained, or better yet, if you can have a separate shower and tub, make the tub a Jacuzzi and use the glass door on the shower. Jacuzzi tubs come in all sizes and are not that expensive. People like the idea of the Jacuzzi tub but seldom use it. It does, however, make a good selling point. Finally, if you have the space, the addition of a bidet gives the setup the ultimate in cachet.

Traditionally, the second bath opens to the hallway, to be used by the occupants of bedrooms two, three, and four. It should have two sinks, a separate toilet room, and a combination bath and shower. If you create anything fancier than this you might not get your money back. I recommend a tiled floor, but carpeting is acceptable. They can also be made to open only into two bedrooms, and thereby become a so-called "Jack and Jill" bath, used exclusively by the occupants of the bedrooms. Another variation is a bath that opens to the hall for guests, as well as to the guest room as an attached bath for the guest "suite." The extra door to the hall can be closed and locked when company is in residence.

The powder room. The extra bath, known as a half bath because of the lack of tub and/or shower, is traditionally known as the powder room or guest bath. If you have the space for it, it can add real value to the home, but if not, the setup allowing guests to use the second bath will suffice. It should be modern and well lighted and have a decent mirror, so people can use it to put on cosmetics, etc.

Fixtures. The bathroom fixtures should be modern. By modern, I mean the toilets should be the new low-flow flush models, with elongated bowls and comfortable seats. Sinks should have combination hot and cold faucets, and tub and shower should have combination mixing fixtures as well. Chrome or polished brass accessories are the most popular and easy to get. All fixtures should have matching accessories (handles) and be clearly from the same pattern. This will appeal to the buyer, and not be very costly. If you cannot upgrade the fixtures, at least upgrade the accessories and trim.

CHAPTER 8

The Details—
Outside

Housing exteriors deal with everything from architecture to configuration. As we discussed briefly earlier in the book, architecture varies from area to area and within each area. The difference between a Cape Cod and a Victorian should be understood by anybody who's looking to improve an existing home. Exterior modifications must be planned and executed within the context of the architectural style of your house. In some instances, with a little help from an architect, you might even be able to transform one architectural style into another.

Most likely you will easily recognize those architectual styles that are in use within your community and geographical area.

The National Association of Realtors® (NAR) has an online graphic of a sampling of architectural styles. Some of the styles they discuss I have never heard of, but you might have. You may access them by logging on to their site (www.realtor.org) and go to Architecture Guide where you can view the specific details.

- *Art Deco.* Homes built in this style feature geometric elements and a vertically oriented design.
- *California Bungalow.* A forerunner of the craftsman style, California Bungalows offer rustic exteriors, sheltered-feeling interiors, and spacious front porches.
- *Cape Cod.* A true classic, Cape Cod homes—square or rectangular one-story to one-and-a-half story structures with gabled roofs and unornamented fronts—were among America's first houses.
- *Contemporary.* Unmistakably modern in feel, Contemporary style homes are identifiable by their odd-sized windows, lack of ornamentation, and unusual mix of wall materials.
- *French Provincial.* Balance and symmetry define the French Provincial style, which includes a steep hip roof, balcony and porch balustrades, and rectangular doors set in arched openings.
- *Georgian.* Two- to three-story brick structures crowned with multiple chimneys, roof balustrades, and pedimented
- *Pueblo.* Flat roofs, parapet walls with round edges, straight-edge window frames, earth-colored stucco or adobe-brick walls, and projecting roof beams typify Pueblos.
- *Ranch.* Similar to the Spanish Colonial, Prairie, and Craftsman styles, Ranch homes are set apart by pitched-roof construction, built-in garages, wood or brick exterior walls, sliding and picture windows.
- *Saltbox.* This New England Colonial style gained the Saltbox nickname because its sharply sloping gable roof resembled boxes used for storing salt.
- *Split Level.* A modern style, split level design sequesters certain living activities, such as sleeping or socializing.
- *Tudor.* Half-timbering on bay windows and upper floors, and facades that are dominated by one or more steeply pitched cross gables typify Tudor homes.
- *Victorian.* A popular housing style, Victorian architecture, which dates from the second half of the 19th century, has two main styles: Second Empire and Queen Anne.

Configuration

Architecture is primarily concerned with vertical design and trim. Configuration deals with things like layout of the home on the lot, number of stories, and the design of rooms within the home. Configuration may also be extended to deal with lot layout and additional buildings. If extensive renovation is contemplated, configuration must be taken into account along with architecture, to ensure that the final result will be harmonious within the context of the overall architectural design. The primary thrust of configuration is to provide a harmonious group of living spaces that flow one into the other. The size and shape of individual rooms is as important as their relationship to each other. You would not want to have a pantry and washroom immediately adjacent to formal living, and you wouldn't want a children's playroom next to a formal dining room. The sizes and shapes of these rooms, as well as their inter-relationship, is what constitute a livable home layout. These types of considerations will be raised only in the event of a substantial renovation or remodel. They are of no concern at all to a standard lipstick job.

Paint and trim. Whether dealing with a quick and dirty lipstick job or a complete renovation, exterior paint and trim is essential to create a pleasing first impression. Routine home maintenance requires periodic painting of the exterior, and obviously if you're going to get your home ready to sell it is absolutely essential that the exterior of the home have a clean and fresh appearance. Having your home presentable is a requirement to maintaining its value. A new paint job, in and of itself, does not guarantee any increase in value of the house; rather, it is essential to maintaining the basic value of the house. All things being equal, a freshly painted home will sell more quickly, and most likely, for more money.

Basic. A basic paint job is generally two-tone. Typically, the bulk of the house is painted one color and the door jams, roof trim, and window frames are painted with a contrasting and complementing color. The reason for the differing color on the trims is to "frame" the basic paint job of the house.

Revitalized. Depending upon the architectual style, variations on the above could include several different paint colors, and several different trim colors. Other decorative items such as millwork, awnings, and decorative trim can be added and painted in contrasting colors.

Landscaping

Landscaping is a very important item for most housing. Depending upon where you live, the prevailing tastes in landscaping range from broad expanses of lawn and stately trees to rock and cactus. The basic purpose of landscaping is to decorate the home and the site around the home, and/or to provide shade and privacy for the occupants of the home. Most homes are landscaped in a fairly haphazard manner or in a basic way by the original builder. To really maximize the impact of landscaping, I suggest the use of a landscape architect to help you with the design and plant selection. In the short term, if you're preparing a home for sale, cleaning up and adding some color here and there is probably all you can manage for a quick sale. If, however, you are taking a longer view, you might employ the services of the landscape designer to come up with a long-range plan for your home. With this in hand you can, over a period of time, expand your landscaping with this ultimate design as a goal.

Trees . Trees are major features of landscaping, and they bear some consideration before planting. You can purchase trees for planting in sizes starting at one to five gallons up to 48-inch box size and larger. You can even pay to have mature specimen trees transplanted to your home for an instant result.

Definition

A *one-* or *five-gallon tree* is so called because it is planted and raised in that size (one or five gallon) container. A 48" box tree is a tree whose roots are confined to a 48" x 48" x 48" box. The general rule is the larger the container, the larger the tree, and the higher the price for that tree.

Trees are either deciduous or evergreen. Deciduous shed their leaves in the fall, and evergreens are fully leafed year round. There are also other considerations, as some trees are more densely leafed than others. The densely leafed trees will screen the home from view, and others, such as the willow or Palo Verde, will allow the home to be seen while providing some shade. The type of tree you pick will alter the effect of the curb view to the public. In the end, it is a matter of individual choice and personal maintenance considerations.

Shrubs and ground cover. Shrubs and ground cover are used to cover up the dirt and to keep the dust down. Most communities require that residential property be landscaped and all of the bare dirt covered with either grass, ground cover, or some form of decorative rock. While the practical effect of this is to control dust and erosion, the economic results of good landscaping are that the home with upgraded landscaping will sell for more money, and more quickly, than a haphazardly landscaped property.

Ornamental features. Other features that can be found within the definition of landscaping are both ornamental and practical. Items such as a fish pond or aviary can be wonderful additions to a landscape plan. Common items found as ornamental additions to landscaping are columns, arches, sundials, gazebos, greenhouses, fish ponds, swimming pools, spas, and arbors.

The first impression. If you remember the old adage that "you never get a second chance to make a first impression," then you will understand the importance of curb appeal. What lies between the house and the street is an opportunity to dress up your home. It can be used to show off the house, hide its bad features, and ensure privacy for the occupants. Landscaping is an important amenity on any property, as it provides the dressing for the building as well as privacy, wind breaks, curb appeal, and a sense of shelter.

Lot Size and Amenities

Once a subdivision is built, all the houses have been placed within envelopes established by the original subdivision design. Outside these envelopes, but inside your property lines, are no-build zones known as setbacks and easements. You might wonder what use these areas are to your home, and why you should have to purchase and maintain them. These easements provide for the utility companies to serve not only to your home, but all the homes in your area. The setbacks are part of the zoning regulations designed to enhance the area in general and provide a uniform quality-oriented approach to the development process. These "dead" areas cannot be built on, but you may landscape them. The only dead area that I recommend you not spend a lot of money on is the right of way portion in your front yard. It is there so that the city can widen the road in the future, and when that happens, you will not be compensated for your loss of investment in landscaping. What you can accomplish with a building lot depends largely on the size of the lot. Multi-family lots are so small, you are lucky to have a private patio and a bush out front, but your average residential lot of ¼ acre will provide ample opportunity for buildings, as well as recreational amenities and extensive landscaping. When you take on a remodel, it is important to realize that a little well-placed landscaping can really make an impression. In general, planting is less expensive than building modification. Hiding less-than-desirable features on any building with plantings is very cost effective.

Small lots. When you have very little to work with, it is necessary to use the space carefully. In small lots, usually the front yard is regulated and maintained by the condominium association, but the back plot is all yours. If you are working with a small patio or a balcony space, the use of potted plants on the floor and hanging plants can give the impression of a pleasantly cool and shaded space.

The normal ¼ acre lot. The average lot is about ten thousand square feet, or approximately one hundred feet wide and one hundred feet long. Most subdivisions will have the street frontage dimension a bit smaller, and the depth a little larger. For the sake of illustration, use a lot with the dimensions of 80 feet wide by 125 feet deep. With 10-foot side yard setbacks, a 20-foot front setback, and a 20-foot wide driveway, you have left a patch of land 40 feet wide for large landscaping in the front. The depth will be a minimum of 20 feet and possibly more if the house is pushed back on the lot. Most home builders push the house as close to the street as possible to maximize the back yard, but for aesthetic appeal, the customary dimension is 40 feet; this leaves a good planting area, but remember, the utility easement must be able to be accessed, so you had better not plant any trees in it. The side yard setbacks are fine for planting large trees. Shrubs and lawn can go anywhere. I'll have more on the backyard later.

Large lots. These generous lots can be a little more difficult, as it takes more of everything to fill them up, and once planted, the landscaping must be maintained. A good ploy is to cluster the plantings around areas of lawn or decorative rock. The clustering will give the impression of masses of green and set off the defined open spaces, maximizing the effect. You can use rock and other features to good effect as well. Homes in the eastern part of the country enjoy more rainfall than in the west, so landscaping must ensure that there is space to enjoy each plant or tree, avoiding overgrowth. In the west, to achieve an overgrown look, you must have copious amounts of irrigation.

Basic planting. When a developer builds a home, the landscaping will be minimal. A front yard starter package looks something like this:
- (2) 24-inch box trees
- (3) 15 gallon trees
- (8) 5 gallon shrubs

Most nurseries have weekly specials on this type of planting package. Our local one is offering one this week, at $699 planted and guaranteed. If you are doing a rebuild, you can take advantage of these weekly specials to spruce up your project with a small expenditure. Most nurseries will allow you to substitute and mix and match. New homes seldom have any planting in the backyard, and it is not uncommon to encounter a newer renovation prospect that has a backyard where there has never been any planting done. When a newer home becomes a renovation candidate, it is because the owners did not have the money to maintain the mortgage, far less the house and yards. It then falls to you to provide a suitable backyard for the resale.

Enhance or hide the building for increased street appeal. The most eloquent argument for landscaping in a fixer upper project is curb appeal. You want people to notice your project and stop to see it. You can't sell it if they haven't seen it. Good landscaping in the front yard will have them pulling over to write down the number on the sign. An astute landscaping package can dress up an ordinary house very nicely. It is much more effective than architectural decoration of the building, and much more cost effective. If you have a feature on the house that you want to hide, plant something in front of it. If you want to emphasize some feature, frame it with landscaping.

Creating an oasis. With the current trend of cocooning, you may want to consider a more elaborate approach to landscaping on your more ambitious projects. Families today are spending more and more time at home, and their dwellings are starting to reflect this. Additions of media rooms, swimming pools and other amenities allow people to recreate right in their own homes. In the old days, formal gardens and mazes were very popular, and today a private and secluded atmosphere is very desirable. I'm not suggesting that you install a pool, as it is not cost effective, but if you can transform the backyard into a private oasis, you will have scored a home run with the average buyer.

Heads Up
What is needed is lush landscaping, privacy, and low maintenance; remember the irrigation system.

The need for privacy. Privacy is a big factor in modern living. In the western part of the country, fences and walls are accepted as part of a normal subdivision, so most of the houses have a private backyard. In the eastern part of the country, fences are not as common, and privacy must be achieved with planting hedges, etc. With the plentiful rainfall in the east, rows of trees and shrubs grow quickly and achieve the same effect as fences and walls.

Front yards are another matter. Many subdivisions preclude heavy planting in front so that homes are visible from the street. This is a safety issue. You can achieve privacy by planting trees and shrubs in front of windows to screen views into the home from the street. They can also block views from the house. Most view lots situate the house so that the views are visible from the back of the house rather than the front, so that is not generally an issue. Judicious planting can achieve a great deal of privacy, and provide a good selling point, as shown in Figure 8.1.

Planting—deciduous vs. evergreen. Remember when planting, and depending on your location, you should choose plants and trees that hold their leaves year round. Obviously, for color and seasonal variety, you can sprinkle in a few items

Figure 8.1—*Landscape Plan Emphasizing Privacy*

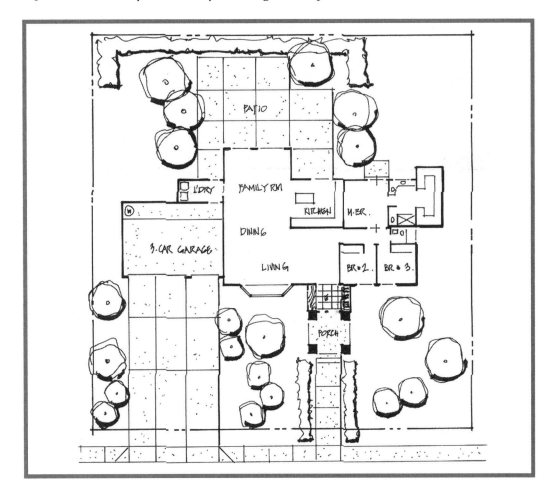

that are deciduous, but at all costs avoid too many, or your house will look naked during the winter season. This will dramatically affect its curb appeal. Be sure to plant your trees and shrubs as far ahead of your anticipated sale date as possible. The more mature your landscaping is, the better it will be for you.

Maintenance and salability. For your own sake, while you own the home, and for the long term, choose plants, trees, and irrigation materials that will hold up well. In four-season climates, be sure that your irrigation system can be drained and made freeze proof. Winterizing irrigation will ensure a long service life. Quality materials and planting techniques are the least inexpensive in the long run. If you have a limited budget, install a quality piping system, along with wiring for future automation, and run your system manually for a few years. Then add electronic controls and better dispersion heads.

Exterior Remodeling

Tackling the modification of the exterior of a home can either be simple, such as adding or modifying trim details or major, such as adding additional rooms, porches, and overhangs. These latter types of renovations are considered to be major modifications due to their structural requirements, rather than because of their cost or function. Most, if not all, of this type of modification requires both architectual design and a building permit. Unlike interior modification work which can be done with little or no permitting process, exterior and structural renovations always require plans, building permits, and inspections.

Awnings and patio covers. Some items that can be used to dress up a home are awnings and patio covers. These are relatively light structures and will require little or no modification to the house itself prior to addition. Awnings are built and installed by specialists, and I strongly recommend that if you're considering this type of an addition you start out by talking to the specialists. As far as patio covers are concerned, these can be designed and constructed by anybody who's handy with a hammer and saw. They need not even be attached to the house itself. In fact, if you're doing it yourself, I recommend that you consider building them freestanding. The most important consideration when adding something like this to your house is to make sure that it fits in with the overall architectual style of the house itself.

Siding. If you live in an area where homes are sided with wood or other similar materials, it is a relatively easy proposition to change the siding on your home. In most cases this will require modification and/or changing the design of the trim that frames the siding. This is a fairly costly step, and you must be convinced that this will add significant value to the house before you consider this type of change. Again, I strongly suggest that you consult with a house designer or architect to see if the change you are contemplating fits with the architecture of the home. Another easy change is to replace your wood siding with stucco. This can be done easily, but should only be done in areas where stucco is a recognized exterior housing finish material.

Additions. The granddaddy of all home renovations is the addition of space to the home itself by demolition and replacement of major components of the existing home. It is not uncommon to see someone add a second floor to a home or a new room or a series of rooms. Another common major modification is the demolition of existing interior walls and the reconfiguring of the living space within the existing home. Both of these types of renovations are considered major and potentially structural and will require the services of a home designer, structural engineer, or architect.

Other structures. Other major renovations that would be classed as exterior would be the addition of freestanding structures to the lot on which the house sits. These could be garages, guest quarters, or decorative structures such as gazebos. These will require design engineering and permits separate and apart from any work being done on the home. This type of renovation or remodel would be tackled only if the home is considered to be eligible to take it up a class or two. In areas of estate housing there may be situations where a smaller home on a large lot could be elevated to the class of the surrounding estate home neighborhood. This smaller home would be a prime candidate for this type of renovation.

All about Roofs and Roofing Materials

One of the most effective modifications to the exterior of the home is to change the roof design. You probably have noticed that there are many different types of roofs and roofing materials. Certain types of roofs go with certain styles of architecture. In Chapter 12, I include some pictures of different architectural styles, and in this chapter, I'd like to walk you through the variety of roof styles and discuss the alternative materials that you can use to alter the look of the home to complement the shape of your roof. In certain instances, you can change the roof style completely, giving the home a totally different character and potential value. The most common remodel is to transform a flat roof design to a sloped roof design. This is considered to be a major structural and architectual alteration and will always require approved plans and inspections during construction. It is one of the few things that you can do that will make a significant change in the design of the house. It can potentially transform the design from, let's say, a simple ranch style home to a southwestern design. By adding or modifying a specific style of roof, you can transform a mediocre home into a fairly spectacular looking one. On homes where the roof is already sloped, you can also change the design by adding things like dormers, cupolas, and

Heads Up

An architect uses the roof in the same manner that a woman uses her hair. It is a major style statement. In the case of the roof, it is the most prominent feature of the architectural style.

overhangs. Most of the roof modifications you will see will require some form of structural modification of the house. Therefore, I recommend strongly that when you're considering this option you deal with a house planner or architect in deciding that this type of remodel might be a viable option for your renovation. Some modifications, such as dormers and cupolas, may be added to your home without serious structural modification so long as they are cosmetic in nature rather than being integrated into the roof itself.

Roof Design

All roofs are sloped, even the so-called "flat roofs." The reason for this is simple: weather. In most places around the country, we have rain, and in some places snow. These conditions drive the roof design. Both snow and rain can cause damage from intrusion and weight. In some areas where snow is prevalent, the freeze/thaw cycle compounds the potential damage.

Most roof design calls for the roof to overhang the exterior walls, thus protecting them from water and other intrusions. (See Figure 8.7.) Flat roof designs are treated in a different manner, and the use of the so-called flat roof is generally confined to geographical areas with less than average rainfall and less than severe freeze/thaw cycles. In addition to the potential of water incursion into the home, water and snow are heavy. Water weighs over eight pounds per gallon. Snow, while less dense, is also heavy, as eight inches of snow are equivalent to one inch of water.

Snow, rain, and roof loads. All buildings are designed to carry certain loads, and these design criteria are applied to floors and roofs. The load design criteria differ in various parts of the country and are set up to address the local weather conditions. In addition to accommodating the weight of the roofing material, roofs are designed to carry live loads (people working on the roof), dead loads (the weight of snow, ice, and water), and wind loads. The most common roof design and the simplest structure is

Heads Up

The roof is the driving force in design. Its shape and treatment will be the primary determinant in which architectural style your home belongs. You can take one style, which is less popular, and turn it into another, thereby enhancing the value of your investment.

the shed roof, or a one-slope roof. It is high on one side of the structure and slopes to the other side. More common is the two-slope roof which slopes from a center ridge to the two eaves. These are the simplest form of pitched roofs. Pitched roofs come in a variety of shapes and materials. The basic component of any pitched roof is the roof slope or the amount of "pitch" required to meet the design criteria. The most common slope is the 3-in-12 (3/12) roof. The designation of 3 in 12

Figure 8.2—*The Shed Roof and Two-Slope Roof*

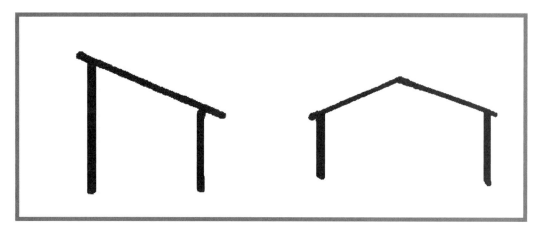

means that the roof has three feet of fall from the ridge for every 12 feet of width of the slope from the ridge to the eave.

Different slopes. As architects exercise their design skills, roofs take on many different and complicated shapes. In general, the more complicated the roof, the more expensive to build, and with more shapes, the more opportunities are created for leaks. Where two different roof slopes come together, valleys are formed to transition from one slope to another (see Figure 8.3). These valleys are places where leaks can occur, and the changing temperatures in all climates affect these transition areas more than any other part of the roof.

These areas are compound slopes, and require specialized construction techniques to create a waterproof area. These junction areas also slow down the roof's

Figure 8.3—*Simple Slope Roof and Compound Roof Slopes*

ability to shed water and snow. Snow and ice can jam in these valleys and cause a damming effect on the roof. When this happens, more water (weight) is retained on the roof, requiring the entire structure to carry more weight. In winter climates this is compounded by the daily freeze thaw cycles. This water, snow, ice combination expands as it freezes, tearing at the roofing material itself. Improper designs fail, and roof leaks can occur.

Roof construction. How a roof is constructed is as important as the materials it is constructed with. To perform properly, the roof must be a structural element independent from the rest of the house. Above the ceiling, the roof structure is insulated for two reasons; one, to protect the interior of the home from the outside temperature, and, two, to make sure that the roof structure is maintained at the same temperature throughout. If there is a temperature difference, the snow and ice on the roof will freeze and thaw at different times, causing more damage than if they had a consistent cycle. Even without the snow and ice, daily changes in temperature cause the roofing materials to expand and contract at different rates. This causes wear and tear on the materials themselves, causing roofs to fail over a period of time. Most roof designs are rated as to their expected useful lives. In the industry we refer to roofs as being 10-, 20-, or 30-year roofs. This designation means that the manufacturer of the roofing materials and the builder putting the roof together guarantee the performance of the roof for the designated period of time. To avail yourself of a manufacturer's warranty, you simply pay for it. The manufacturer of the roofing then inspects the job during construction and issues you the warranty.

Heads Up

The roof warranty is widespread in the commercial building industry, but is available to all. Just ask your builder.

Curves. Less common than the pitched roof is the curved roof. It is seen fairly often in commercial work, but can be seen occasionally in residential construction. Even though the roof surfaces are not flat, they follow the same design criteria for load and wearing. See Figure 8.4.

Flat roofs. Very common in commercial construction is the "flat roof." This is a misnomer, as there is never a truly flat roof. These roofs seem flat, because the exterior walls of the building seem all the same height. In fact, the flat roof is constructed inside these perimeter walls, with several slopes to channel the rain and snow to various points of discharge. This avoids damming water on the roof which might cause the structure to fail when the design loads are exceeded. See Figure 8.5.

Figure 8.4—*A Rare Roof—Curved, Poured Concrete with a Widow's Walk*

Figure 8.5—*A Flat-Roofed Home*

When you hear of a roof collapse, it is most likely a flat-roof design where the drains have become clogged, and water has ponded on the roof, exceeding the structure's load capacity. These interior slopes of the so-called flat roofs are called crickets and can be any shape and slope required to rid the roof of water as reliably as possible. The water is drained over the side of the roof by scuppers and down-spouts, or internally within the building by piping it down through and out of the building. Proper insulation is even more critical for this type of roof, because the aim is to keep the water load consistent throughout the roof structure. If water or snow builds up in a non uniform way, the structure suffers from eccentric (uneven) loading and can fail.

Roofing Materials

Basic roof structures are composed of insulation, membrane, and wear surfaces. All roofs are framed, and then covered with wood or metal to support the roofing itself. The three components of the roof are insulation, either on the roof or under the roof, the impervious membrane, and the wearing surface. This construction holds true whether the roof is pitched or flat. There are many types of materials in use today, and the industry is changing rapidly. In your existing home, you will most likely have a pitched roof composed of felts covered with some kind of shingle or tile. Older flat roofs were composed of felts and sand and gravel wearing surfaces.

The membrane. This material used to be felts sold in a variety of weights. Today this membrane can be very high tech, lighter, and better than the old felt rolls used in the past. Manufacturers are also able to guarantee the roof for longer periods for less money. The wearing surface for sloped roofs will remain fairly constant, and provide ample choices to decorate the house. You can choose from, but are not limited to, the following:

- Asphalt shingle
- Wood shake
- Clay tile
- Concrete tile
- Metal
- Concrete

Each of these materials has fans and detractors. They have been used success-fully all over the country. Perhaps the most common and widespread and least expensive is the asphalt shingle. It comes in a variety of weights, colors, and tex-tures, and provides a good 10- to 20-year roof, depending on the climate it is used in and the shingle installed. The wood shake is popular in California, and has a great look. It weathers well, but is affected by severe heat. Untreated, it can have a limited useful life. It is also more costly than the asphalt shingle, and can attract critters to live in the roof material. A better choice is the clay tile roof. It lends itself particularly to western architecture and has a long useful life. The disadvantage of the clay tile is its fragility. It breaks easily when walked on, and requires much skill to be used properly. Rapidly replacing the clay tile and the wood shake roofs is the concrete tile roof. These tiles can be had in a variety of colors, weights, and textures, and are available all around the country. Their disadvantage is their weight. They weigh at least ten pounds per square foot, and the roof structure must be designed to accommodate this extra weight.

Metal roofs are used almost exclusively in commercial buildings and on homes in areas where a lot of snow is the norm. It is very expensive, but one of the best roofs you can buy. It is very long lived, and comes in a variety of colors and materials.

Poured-in-place concrete roofs are rare, except in high-rise urban buildings. More common are poured concrete porches over living areas. These can be a maintenance problem and expensive to build, and are generally avoided except in very expensive homes. See Figure 8.4 for a rare look at one.

Flat roofs or built-up. Flat roofs come in two varieties, the built-up roof and the spray-on roof. Both need to be properly sloped. The built-up roof is the traditional felt and sand and gravel roof, and the spray-on roof is composed of a spray-on sponge-like material, coated with a waterproof membrane. The new spray-on roof seems to be gaining in popularity despite its greater cost. If you are contemplating a flat-roof project, I suggest you consult the architect and the manufacturer to determine what guarantees are available, as well as the expected lifespan of the material you want to use.

Potential changes. When looking at a renovation or upgrade project, wherein you might like to dramatically alter the appearance of your home, the roof is an obvious choice of an area where you can have some very real impact. The roof literally crowns the house, and changing it will alter the architecture of the home forever.

Flat to pitched. The most dramatic change would be taking a flat-roofed home and putting on a pitched roof. By adding the appropriate trim and exterior finish, you can literally achieve almost any architectural style. The converse is also true. You can take off a pitched roof and install a flat roof for all or a part of the home. The most effective and modern approach is to have a combination of pitched and flat roofs with a collection of different masses with a variety of different elevations. This sounds complicated, but it just takes time and money.

From single to multiple slopes. Perhaps the easiest way to dress up a home with a simple two-slope pitched roof is to add some other roof structure at right angles to the existing roof. This alters the roof to a multiple slope and provides a lot of curb appeal. You could use the roof to add a new entrance to the home, or cover a new porch or an added garage. This type of renovation is not too costly, and relatively easy to do.

Combining pitched and flat. Sometimes people use the existing garage for new rooms for the home. This renovation is relatively simple, as the structure is already in place, you need only add plumbing, walls and electrical work without disturbing the exterior. You might need to add a window or two to make the new rooms more habitable and appealing. Now that you have used the old garage, and assuming that you have the space on your lot, you can add a new garage with a roof profile that contrasts and complements the older part of the home. It is quite common to see a home with a pitched roof attached to a garage with a flat roof. They tie together nicely, forming a new harmonious whole with architecture that is more interesting than the old house. See Figure 8.6.

Roof gardens. Some variations for urban dwellers is the addition of roof gardens to their homes. Urban homes very often have flat roofs, or roofs of poured concrete. If this is the case, you can modify the roof to include an area for seating and a garden. It would require the construction of a covered stairway and exit to the roof, but can provide you with an exceptional new outdoor area. If you are fortunate to have a view, it can be a very valuable addition to the amenities of the home.

Figure 8.6—*Combination Roof Style*

Widow's walks. Very popular in New England waterfront towns is the widow's walk. This is an area built into the roof, and accessible from within the home, that allows you to sit or stand on the roof with a railing. It was popularized by sea captains' wives in seafaring villages; so called because the wives could go out on the walk to see the ships as they entered the harbor. See Figure 8.4 for a look at one.

Change and impact. A minor change that can have a tremendous impact on your home is the substitution of roofing materials only. Asphalt shingles can be traded for shake, concrete tile, or metal roofing. The results can be dramatic. When contemplating concrete tile, you will need a structural engineer to look at your roof framing to determine whether you can add the weight. This does not cost much and can be done quickly. Most structures are over engineered so that these changes can be made without any problems. I would be concerned only in buildings that are more than 20 years old.

The modern touch. To achieve the modern look despite the architectural style, you need to add certain touches to your home. As these relate to roofing, you need to update the wearing surface to what is now fashionable in your area, and you can find out what is selling by simply touring some of the new subdivisions. Another must is to finish the building eaves. Typically, older homes had unfinished overhangs. These should be boxed and refinished, with the appropriate touches added, such as gutters and/or venting. You should look at the roof slope to see if the addition of some simple new shapes can accent the home in a more dramatic manner. See Figure 8.7.

Building masses are interesting when the roof line is varied. Look at your home to see if a simple change in the roof line over one area of the home could

Figure 8.7—*Old Overhang and Finished Overhang*

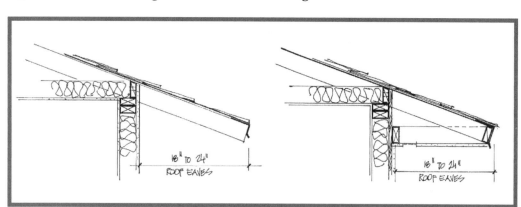

make a more dramatic statement. These types of changes are not mandatory; they only provide additional choices for you when you contemplate an upgrade for your home. By doing the research and consulting with realtors and architects, you can develop a better feel for the potential value of this type of alteration. Tearing the roof off of a home is not cheap, but it might move your home up several categories in value. If the neighborhood and the area can support the new value, you just might hit a home run.

Gutters. If you live in an area that experiences a great deal of rain or snow, you will find that gutters are a mixed blessing. They control the water cascading off the roof, but they are a maintenance nightmare, especially if you have many trees around the home. In addition, the freeze/thaw cycle tends to dam up the water at the eave and gutter line, forcing water back up the roof, and under the roofing material, causing roof leaks. The only solution is to keep the gutters free of debris, and install a heating system to melt the ice and snow from your roof. Do not get discouraged with the details of the exterior. Think of it as dressing the home, and the interior will provide the substance. Both are valuable and contribute to genuine value when you are renovating or expanding a home.

Once you understand the nuts and bolts of it all, you will be better able to evaluate a potentially profitable house when you see one.

Renovations and Additions

Selecting a Specific Property

I n this chapter we examine the acquisition of a new personal home, plan for its investment potential, and examine the purchase of an additional house for investment only. Working with housing is a bit of a specialty, so you need to pay attention to those things peculiar to housing that give value to the houses themselves.

Market Research

As with any investment, your project should start with market research. I know I've mentioned this before, and I will mention it again. Researching your target market is a critical aspect of any investment whether it's in real estate or any other type of investment.

You may choose to do your own market research, work with your realtor, or a market research company.

What to Look For

What you are looking for in your market research is trends in values and absorption (velocity) rates. For any segment of the market that you're interested in, factor in the historical trend, what's going on today, and what your realtor thinks will happen tomorrow. Calculate the per-year value rise, and average it over a 5–10–15 year period. Find out how many homes sold in a given year, and in what price categories. You're looking for the hot seller, the most popular segment of the target market. Check at least the following characteristics:

- Size
- Number of bedrooms and baths
- Garage size
- Land size
- Living room and family room versus great room
- Formal dining room
- Kitchen size and type
- Age and design (Victorian, Cape Cod, Contemporary, etc.)
- Condition

These facts should give you a fairly good basis for projecting your thoughts onto tomorrow's market. Research, as it relates to housing, is a relatively accurate proposition today. The modern computerized MLS systems in use around the country make the compiling of statistical trends a relatively easy chore. Just remember, the key component of market research is you; you must make decisions based on the facts you have been able to gather.

Market research is largely a matter of gathering data and then putting your interpretation on the data gathered. My experience over the last 25 years has been that data can be manufactured as well as researched. Fortunately, in the housing industry, accurate data is universally available to all who are in the industry. You'll find that this is not the case when dealing with commercial properties; I would strongly suggest that when you're dealing with commercial property, you spot check your data periodically to verify its accuracy.

Residential Targets of Opportunity

Where to look for a new home is always a dilemma. In addition to your personal considerations for housing, you have now added an extra layer of analysis because you are, from here on out, also going to look at your own personal housing as an investment. This approach will quickly change your thinking as investment considerations may come into direct conflict with your personal housing preferences. You might find, for instance, that you really enjoy the homes in a certain area, but upon doing the research, you find that homes in this particular area have only appreciated 2 percent per year while the overall market in your immediate region is enjoying an average appreciation of 8 to 12 percent per year. While this might prove to be a wonderful place to live, it might also be a lousy investment. You need to pass on this one, and come back to the neighborhood after you have made your pile. This is a very common phenomenon, and it exists in every major city in the United States. A lot of this property is still viable from a business point of view but from a residential point of view, it lacks the cachet and appeal of newer and more stylized developments.

Your Home and the Market

If you run across this situation, what do you do? The choice is simple, you can buy the house anyway and look elsewhere for an investment, or you can bypass this house and keep looking. This is a time when you and your spouse need to be in total agreement on your investment plan. There is no such thing as the one and only perfect house for you and your family. Like most things in life, sound decisions are based on compromise, and housing is no different. When you are looking for a home, what are some good areas to look in? Some of my pet areas are listed below:

- Custom home developments in the path of growth.
- Established areas where older homes (30 years old or more) are being acquired and renovated by young families.
- Rural locations and housing which may have excess land.
- Urban areas in locations where the trend to downtown living has once again become a factor in the marketplace.
- Light industrial areas between the suburbs and downtown (these areas are becoming increasingly popular for loft living and may present a development opportunity).

This is only a partial list of potentially profitable locations where you can look for a place to live. I'm sure, knowing your area, that you can come up with a list of other potentially profitable locations. One of my favorite areas can be found in regions fortunate enough to have a lake, an ocean, or a mountain. These types of areas have the added cachet of having potential recreational and vacation draws. In Chapter 12, one of the case studies will take a look at a long-term renovation project of a property with a lifestyle, vacation, or second home location. Another aspect of your search will deal with your investment strategy.

Again, consider how long you intend to occupy the home you're about to buy. I think it's unlikely that anybody is going to consider purchasing a home to live in for a quick turnaround. Moving is expensive, and you need to make enough money not only to pay for the move, but to also provide a profit on your investment. Most people who are looking at a home for investment consider a home that will be an investment for the medium- or long-term. This limits your choice to two categories of houses: ones that can be upgraded, or ones that can be totally renovated and/or expanded.

The upgradeable home would be a home that has medium-term potential; this is an ideal choice if you are looking to rotate your home every couple of years. Upgrading a home can be a relatively simple and not too disruptive process that will allow you a harmonious occupancy while you are doing the upgrades. However, a home that can be renovated and/or expanded is a major undertaking, and you should know what you are in for before you embark on the project; in some instances, during a major home rebuild, the house may become temporarily uninhabitable.

Within this same mixed area, and away from a major arterial, you'll get into neighborhoods of older housing. As a general rule, the farther you get from the major arterial the better the quality of the older houses, and the greater the potential for upgrading and/or renovation and expansion. Many of these older homes have incredibly appealing features that are no longer included in the new homes built today. They are generally larger, with more generous rooms, and represent good upgrade and renovation possibilities.

Heads Up

The two houses pictured in Figures 9.1 and 9.2 sit side by side on the same street. The home on the top has not been upgraded or modernized and the other has—in fact it sold for about $325,000. Older homes like the one on the top, in this neighborhood, sell for about $185,000. This is definitely a potential project, clearly visible from the street.

Neglect. Another fertile field for potential upgrades involves homes that have been neglected from a maintenance point of view. It is not uncommon in these relatively volatile and economic times that homeowners may fall into a situation of financial disadvantage. Unfortunately, someone's misfortune is potentially someone else's opportunity. As the old wive's tale says, "it's an ill wind blows no good." This type of opportunity can exist anywhere in any neighborhood in any economic bracket, and the only sure way to find something like this is to have your realtor be on the lookout for properties that fit this profile or, be constantly on the alert, looking for these types of properties as you drive

Figure 9.1—*Potential Project*

Figure 9.2—*Completed Project*

around involved in your day-to-day activities. These are the types of homes that lend themselves to the quick turnaround or lipstick approach. If you're going to deal with this type of property, you will do well to have your own real estate sales license. In addition to that, having some fundamental skills with a paint brush, wallpaper, and carpeting will serve you, too. The quick turnaround opportunity does not lend itself to hiring others to do the work. You'll find that this remains true unless the home you're dealing with is a very large and potentially very expensive property.

You can look at this mixed-use area and pick an area that, due to the volume of traffic on the arterial, is an obvious choice for assembly of land for the development of new commercial property.

Physical obsolescence. Other potential project opportunities involve buildings, whether residential or commercial, that have achieved some measure of physical obsolescence. Physical obsolescence comes in many forms; residential obsolescence can be achieved by low ceiling heights, single bathrooms, small living areas, and carports. Other problems can involve lack of insulation, noncompliance with building codes, old plumbing, wiring, and general dilapidation. This is relatively common in vacation properties or in areas that evidenced extreme home construction expansion after World War II.

Neighborhoods in Transition

If you have plowed through the above, it must be apparent to you that a neighborhood in transition may represent a very profitable opportunity. How do you find these types of neighborhoods, and how do you know that they're going to represent an opportunity for you? The answer to this will rely primarily on your common sense, but there are other sources of information about this type of phenomenon. If you're going to get into this business with any degree of seriousness, you need to make some reliable friends in the business. You'll need a good realtor, a good appraiser, and an honest contractor. There are a lot of other people you'll need, but the realtor will help you find the opportunities, the appraiser will help you verify that the opportunity is real, and the contractor will help you bring your plan to fruition. Few people contemplating this type of business come into it with all of these skills. If you have one or more of these skills you are way ahead of the curve, but even if you lack the skills, they can be had for affordable price.

In your daily travels, you most likely pass through areas of potential opportunity. In the eastern United States and the midwest, you'll find a host of old well-established communities. Each and every one of these communities will have neighborhoods in transition. Take the initiative, drive around, and see if you can spot some potential areas yourself. If you see areas completely run down and neg-lected, these are areas that are going to soon become pockets of opportunity. If you run across rundown neighborhoods with one or two newly refurbished homes and/or businesses, you can bet that these are areas that have been discovered and are in the process of rejuvenation. I would suggest that for your first venture, you seek out the latter neighborhood.

Urban, Suburban, or Rural

Where should you choose your first renovation project? Your choices are in the city, the suburbs, or a rural setting. Most likely you'll probably want to kick it off in the area that is most familiar to you. You should, however, give some thought to other potential areas that may be readily accessible to you. Urban areas have some advantages and disadvantages that you should be aware of. First there is a plethora of old buildings, and, therefore, no end of buildings with renovation potential. The drawbacks are, but are not limited to, some of the following:

- City bureaucracies are large and slow-moving.
- City building codes are more complex than rural codes, and infrastructure can be very complicated.
- Construction projects require a lot of space for material storage and con-struction staging; this is in short supply in the average city. Because of this one of the most important people on inner-city construction jobs is the expe-diter; it is his or her job to make sure that the materials are scheduled to be put in place as they are delivered.
- Urban real estate tends to cost more than suburban real estate due to the density, or potential density, of city properties.

Does this mean that you should forget dealing in the city? Not really, but for your first effort, unless you live in the city and are familiar with this bureaucracy, I would suggest you take a more low-key approach either in the suburbs or in a rural setting.

In suburban venues, the most common areas in which to explore the possibil-ities for renovation work are close-to-the-city locations (the fringes). Older prop-erties are ideal to examine for commercial renovations. The immediate residential transition area, adjacent to these fringe commercial properties, should be fertile field for residential property renovation. Both of these areas should feed off each other and complement each other, as these will always be transition areas between suburbs and city allowing for convenience commercial and closer-in residential.

The final place to look for potential renovations is in the country area sur-rounding your target market. Rural areas have limited commercial and industrial possibilities, but unlimited potential residential possibilities. Residential properties in rural areas typically start at one unit to the half-acre and are as large as the typical family farm. As mentioned before, this excess land has a development potential of its own, and most truly rural housing is of a more mature vintage than those found in the average suburban location. The older homes have great upgrading and redevelopment potential.

Renovation Potential

To recap this chapter briefly, take a look at what you can do with various types of renovatable property. What you can do is truly limited only by your imagination and the market potential for the area in which you are choosing to work.

Housing

Relative to housing, the choices are, but are not limited to, the following:
- Subdivide the property and sell off or develop the excess land.
- Refurbish the house and resell it.
- Remodel and modernize the house, working with the existing structure, without adding on.
- Remodel and modernize, and expand the house to its potential without significant demolition.
- Tear down and rebuild, utilizing at least a significant portion of the old structure.

There are endless permutations and combinations of the above, but this is basically what housing renovation boils down to. Chapters 10 through 12 will tackle the nuts and bolts of this process.

Rural settings. When you are dealing with rural housing, some of the best potential lies with the land. At the very least, a large lot may be split into two lots if the configuration allows it. Earlier in the discussion regarding land, we covered lot splits, so the procedure should be familiar to you.

If you are fortunate enough to find a home on a large parcel of land, in excess of 40 acres, you may consider what we call a lifestyle subdivision. A lifestyle subdivision is one that is built around a common theme. Around the country, you will find subdivisions built around an airport where you can taxi your airplane down the street into your own hangar. Other subdivisions are built around waterways where you can park your boat in your own water garage. A recent arrival in the lifestyle subdivision business is built around the wine business. Very common around the country are properties built around a central equestrian facility, complete with riding trails, indoor arenas, stables, and veterinary facilities. Whatever the theme, the process is quite simple. In Figure 9.3 you see a typical family farm layout, and in Figure 9.4, you see it transformed into a lifestyle subdivision.

Obviously, layout and lot sizes will vary with the type of subdivision, but the principle remains the same for all forms of subdivision; the layout becomes a designer's or engineer's work.

Tract home limitations. When dealing with potentially renovatable property, you must pay particular attention if you're looking at tract homes. The tract home and its potential for profitable rehabilitation/remodeling is directly related to the minimum and maximum values within the tract itself. You cannot, for instance, go into a tract containing only single-story houses and add a second-floor to one of the homes. This will create an over-improved situation where the value, or perceived value, cannot be substantiated by comparable housing. The best move when dealing with tract homes is upgrading and minor additions. Some other things you can do with impunity is to add a room, a bathroom, an extra garage, convert carports into garages, and add amenities such as a swimming pool or extra landscaping. Do the research carefully within your target tract and see what,

Figure 9.3—*Typical Family Farm*

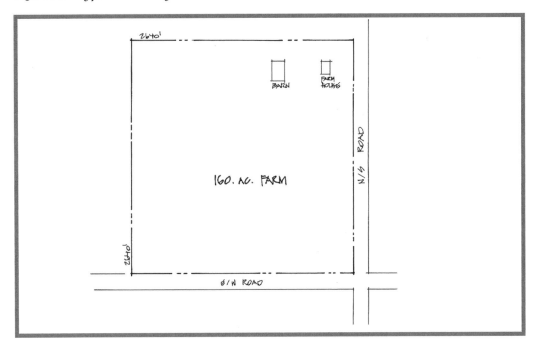

Figure 9.4—*Lifestyle Subdivision*

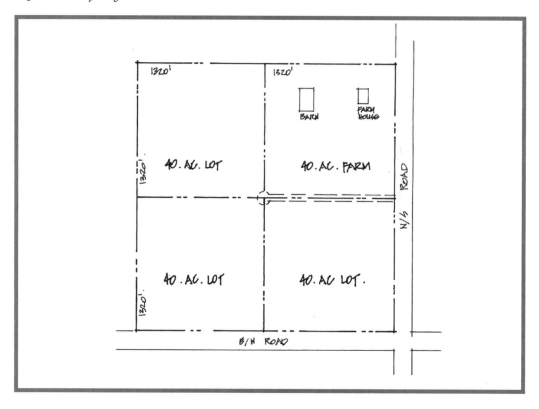

if anything, has been done before in the way of upgrading and/or expansion. I would recommend confining your activity to tracts that have already experienced some degree of modification.

Apartments and condos. Other types of housing products that have built-in limitations are multi-family units, apartments, and condominiums. These types of dwellings are even more uniform than the tract home. Therefore, you must exercise extreme caution when considering upgrades for these types of units. I have seen situations where someone has purchased two condominiums side-by-side, broken through the common wall, and created one very large unit. This ultra size unit always proves to be very difficult to sell. Having said that, it is not uncommon in urban areas for people to purchase two floors in a co-op building, and create a two-story living unit with a gracious stairway connecting the two floors. Due to the scope, size, and cost of this type of living unit, it seems to have a decent resale potential among the wealthy home buyers. I do not recommend this type of approach for your first project.

Converting apartments into the condominiums is always a potentially profitable project. For such a project to be successful, the apartment project must have certain design characteristics in place before you start. The units must have a moderate or high degree of privacy built into the design. It is handy if the units' utilities, such as gas and electric, have been designed to be individually metered. This is not necessarily crucial, as retrofitting is possible; it's just expensive. Another thing to look for is the potential of converting carports into individual garages. Private, secure parking is a big asset when dealing with potential condominium conversion. Most people in this type of business tend to be experienced and well-capitalized, so I think this would not be an ideal choice for your first project.

Quick Results vs. Long-Term Strategies

When you're approaching a project involving a house, you must look at the entire spectrum from the quick-and-easy lipstick process, to the upgrade, and to the demolish-and-renovate approach. All three of these approaches have occupancy, financial, and living implications, not the least of which is a return on the cash invested. When looking at any form of investment, you need to consider the cash-on-cash rate of return and the timeframe in which the return can be realized. This is similar to a cost-benefit analysis; I recommend "running the numbers" on any project you undertake before you launch. As you saw in Chapter 8, it is a relatively simple process to take a quick look at the potential for any project's appreciation only. To make it relevant for improving the home, you need only add the cost of improvements to the analysis. If we stick with the home we were looking at in Chapter 8, using the same initial assumptions, then our new cost-benefit analysis would look something like you see in Table 9.1.

Table 9.1—*Cost-Benefit Analysis*

Item		Dollar Value
Purchase price		$160,000
Down payment (20%)	Conventional loan	32,000
Closing costs	Estimate	3,500
Mortgage amount	80%	128,000
Mortgage (PI) 8%/30 years (APR = 8.81)	(PI)= Principal + Interest on $128K	$11,276.80/year $939.73/month
Appreciation 10% x 5 years	Compounded—Year 1	$176,000
	Compounded—Year 2	193,600

Table 9.1—*Cost-Benefit Analysis,* continued

Item		Dollar Value
Convert garage to office		15,000
Expand kitchen		18,000
Paint, carpet, and landscape		20,000
Initial investment	Down + closing cost	35,500
Upgrade costs		53,000
New home value		305,000
Sales commission (6%)	(18,300)	286,700
Profit on sale	(Sale price) – (cost) – (renovation cost)	70,200
ROI	$35,500 + renovation costs ($53,000) ($88,500) total investment	79% or 39%/year
Annual tax benefit during ownership	Estimated tax write-off	$10,240/year
Capital gain taxes		$0

As you can see by going through the project outlined in Table 9.1, in addition to the home's appreciation during the time you owned it, your upgrade of the home resulted in additional profits. In as much as you lived in the home for 24 months or more, your capital gain profits were tax free. This is the type of project that you can do again and again, reinvesting your profits as you go. By reinvesting your profits, you can either purchase increasingly larger homes or take some of the cash generated from this process and invest in a project that is separate and apart from the home you live in.

Short-term cash generation. The project outlined above can be classified as a short- or medium-term type project. A large-scale demolition and renovation project would be, if you occupied the home during the process, a long-term project. Once you have several generations of the above project under your belt, you will have generated enough cash to consider a separate house as an additional investment. There are several different ways that you can go about adding the second project to your investment plan. You can:

- Tackle a project that is a quick lipstick project, turning over two or more per year.
- Purchase a rental property, lease it out, and sell it later for a capital gain.
- Purchase a rental property and upgrade it with the cooperation of the tenant.

- Purchase a renovation property and go for the big one.

The first option will generate ordinary income unless the property is held in excess of 12 months. Typically, the lipstick approach is a quick turnaround, one to four months, and is a relatively small but quick profit on your investment. The only drawback with this quick turnaround project is the fact that the real estate commission at the time of resale represents a large percentage of your potential profit. I, therefore, recommend that if you are going to look at these types of projects, you become a licensed real estate salesperson. This will save you at least half of the real estate commission. The remainder of the list falls into a capital gain tax mode, and as long as you hold them for a year and a day, you can claim long-term capital gain.

Combine home and house. An ideal plan of attack when dealing with residential properties is a combination of two homes at all times. Live in and upgrade one, renovate, and expand the other. Every two years, you'll have a nontaxable profit on your own home, and, if your renovation project takes twelve months or more, you will have a capital gain on the second house. If you look into financial analysis of this type of approach over a ten-year period, you'll see that your net worth should have a dramatic increase.

Planning and Financial Analysis

The prospects for profit when purchasing a home are relatively certain if you do the research. All that remains prior to purchase is coming up with a plan. Any plan involving a house purchase should be responsive to two considerations: time and investment. Time relates to how long you plan to live there, and investment relates to how much cash you intend to put into the transaction, both at the beginning, and during the execution of your plan.

Chapter 9 looked at the financial impact of simply buying and holding a piece of property, and, in the scenario just outlined, you can see the impact of upgrading a home while you live there. Assume that:

- You started with the original investment of $35,500.
- You borrowed the $53,000 for the upgrades.
- At the time of sale, you now have $105,700.

This represents three times the working capital you started with a little over two years before. In addition, the $70,000 increase is tax free. Part of your forward planning will be to decide whether to take most of this money and buy a new home, or split it up and buy two houses. Assume that you wish to be a little aggressive with your financial planning: you would most likely split the investment and purchase either a rental property or an upgradeable property with part of the money. Using some of the assumptions from Chapter 8 about a rental property, and the same assumption used in Table 9.1 for your personal home, then at the end of two years, you should have accomplished the following:

1. By living in and upgrading your home you should have produced an additional $70,000 of profit.
2. By purchasing, leasing, and reselling a comparable rental property, you should have accomplished what you see in Table 9.2.

Table 9.2—*Rental Property Investment Analysis*

Item		Dollar Value
Purchase price		$160,000
Down payment (20%)	Conventional loan	32,000
Closing costs	Estimate	3,500
Mortgage amount	80%	128,000
Mortgage (PI) 8%/30 years (APR = 8.81)	(PI)= Principal + Interest	$11,276.80/year $939.73/month
Appreciation 10% x 2 years	Compounded—Year 1	176,000
	Compounded—Year 2	193,600
Initial investment	Down + closing cost	35,500
Gross appreciation/profit	End of Year 2	
New value less cost	$30,100	
Rental income $1,000/mo/5yrs	$1,000 x 12 x 2	24,000
Less maintenance	$600/year	(1,200)
Net rental income	2 years	22,800
Less interest	2 years	(22,552)
Net taxable profit	Ordinary income 5/years	248
ROI	On $35,500	84% or 42%/year
Taxable gain		30,100
Tax rate	Capital gain	15%
After tax gain		**$25,585**

By extrapolating the results, and adding the $25,585 to the $70,000 you made on your own home in Table 9.2, you realize that in this second round of investment, you've taken your original $35,000 in capital and increased it by an additional $95,585 over and above the $70,000 you made on your first home rotation. You now have $201,285 of available, after tax, capital.

Another thing you need to consider is that this rental property yielded only $25,000 in gain on $35,000 invested because you only held the property for 24 months. Since this investment property is not going to be a tax-free investment property, there is no reason for you to sell out after 24 months. Referring to Table 9.3, you can see the results of having held this property for five years. You should, therefore, consider modifying your plan to do the following:

1. Rotating your own home ownership every 24 months.
2. Splitting the cash yield generated by rotating your home each time, for purchasing a rental property every two years.
3. Hold all the rental properties until you decide to consolidate your investment portfolio.

Continuing to use these assumptions for income property profit generation, we can see that, after the ten-year period, assuming no compounding of price escalation, your financial situation should look something like that shown in Table 9.3.

Table 9.3—*Ten-Year Investment Property Schedule*

Item	Year	Cost	Invested	Appreciation
Rental 1	1–11	$160,000	$35,500	$176,000
Rental 2	3–11	160,000	35,500	128,000
Rental 3	5–11	160,000	35,500	96,000
Rental 4	7–11	160,000	35,500	64,000
Rental 5	9–11	160,000	35,500	32,000
Total appreciation	Yr 11		$177,500	$496,000
ROI		Average	279% or 28%/year	

If we assume that prices escalate 10 percent per year, and we compound the yields as shown in Table 9.3, then the escalation per unit would be greater than the straight percentage of the purchase price in Table 9.3. Annual value escalation would be more like that shown in Table 9.4.

The effect of compounding yields the returns shown in Table 9.5.

In addition to profiting on your five rental properties, you will have turned your home over five times for a total tax-free profit on your home of $350,000. Adding these two investment returns together, you will now have $948,133 of capital to

Table 9.4—*Rental House Ten Year Projection*

Item		Dollar Value
Purchase price		$160,000
Down payment (20%)	Conventional loan	32,000
Closing costs	Estimate	3,500
Mortgage amount	80%	128,000
Mortgage (PI) 8%/30years (APR = 8.81)	(PI) = Principal + Interest	$11,276.80/year $939.73/month
Appreciation 10% x 5 years	Compounded—Year 1	176,000
	Compounded—Year 2	193,600
	Compounded—Year 3	212,960
	Compounded—Year 4	234,256
	Compounded—Year 5	257,682
	Compounded—Year 6	283,450
	Compounded—Year 7	311,795
	Compounded—Year 8	342,974
	Compounded—Year 9	399,282
	Compounded—Year 10	415,000
	Compounded—Year 11	$456,500

Table 9.5—*Ten-Year Profit Recap—Rental Unit Investment*

Item	Year	Cost	Invested	Appreciation
Rental 1	1–11	$160,000	$35,500	$293,000
Rental 2	3–11	160,000	35,500	148,295
Rental 3	5–11	160,000	35,500	119,950
Rental 4	7–11	160,000	35,500	70,576
Rental 5	9–11	160,000	35,500	30,100
Total appreciation	Year 11		$177,500	$661,921
Taxes	15% capital gain			(99,288)
Net cash gain after taxes				$562,633
ROI	Average	Pre-tax gain 372% or 37%/year		
		After-tax gain 316% or 31.6%/year		

work with after liquidation of all your properties. This total is comprised of your profits plus your original $35,500 investment.

Obviously, there are many variables that will occur during a ten-year investment period, but you get the general idea. Before you say to me that compounding distorts the potential appreciation of a home, let me cite you examples from my own experience.

1. In 1974, I purchased a duplex (half of a two-family house) for $38,000; in 2003 it sold for $620,000.00.
2. In 1977, I purchased a single-family home on 1.5 acres for 180,000 and added about $60,000 in renovations; it is currently appraised at $4.2 million.
3. In 1979, I purchased a single-family home on 2.5 acres for $280,000 and added $200,000 in renovations; it is now appraised at $2.8 million.
4. The exception that proves the rule is that in 1984 I built a home at a cost of $285,000, and sold it four years later for $290,000. The market for that home was totally flat, as it was at the top end of the market. I had overbuilt the market.
5. My current home was purchased for $115,000 in 1992 and since then, I have added $225,000 in renovations and additions. The current market value is over $700,000, with more renovations to come.

Heads Up

Unfortunately, I did not have the money or the wisdom to retain ownership of homes 1, 2, and 3. If you can hold on to your real estate, it will make you rich.

The only thing that may differ from my experience with the above properties and your potential investment experience is the location of the homes. All three of the above homes were purchased in California and Arizona where we have a built-in growth factor due to migration and normal population growth. The fourth house was built in a small town with a very dollar-conscious buying public. By researching the historical appreciation in your market, you should get a pretty good idea what to expect from your potential investments.

Multiple Property Investment

In the investment scenario above, you will find that you would probably be quite busy buying and upgrading your own homes as well as purchasing and managing your five rental properties. In general, you'll find that after ten years of this, you will probably want to consolidate your investments into something more manageable. Once you have made a good start on long-term capital accumulation, you will probably back off from rotating your personal home every two years, and, instead, buy bigger homes, expand them, and periodically rotate them for additional tax-free capital gains.

Many people grow tired of dealing with multiple residential rentals, as they are a 24/7 proposition. Once you go beyond the realm of multiple properties, you will have to look into multi-family investment properties. Any property with more than one dwelling could be classified as a multi-family property, but in the investment game, multi-family rental properties usually start with eight-unit properties and above. It is quite common to see duplexes, triplexes, and four-plexes. These units are usually purchased and lived in by retired investors who want not only a place to live, but some handily managed investment property for income purposes. It seems that the efficiency of management of apartment rental units demands a size of approximately 150 units or larger. This is due to the fact that most properties of this type are professionally managed, and you need a certain minimum-sized complex to amortize the cost of professional management. Besides the day-to-day operation of the complex, the leasing of units, and collecting of rent, there is always a sizable maintenance responsibility that demands day-to-day, full time professionals. In addition to the efficiencies of operation, there is a different financial analysis that pertains to this size of investment property. Properties of this type are sold and priced based on capitalization rates typical for that industry and that part of the world. In Table 9.6 you'll find an income and expense analysis for a typical multi-family property of approximately 150 units.

Table 9.6—*Income and Expense Analysis, 150-Unit Apartment Complex*

Items Income	Notes	Subtotals Annual	Totals
50 studio	$550/month	$330,000	
40 one bedroom	700/month	336,000	
60 two bedroom	900/month	648,000	
Gross potential Income (GPI)			$1,314,000
Less vacancy allowance of 5%	(65,700)		
Effective gross income (RGI)			$1,248,300
Expenses			
Operations	Average 25–40%	(312,075)	
Management	4% of EGI	($49,932)	
Total operating expenses	($362,007)		
Net operating Income or NIBDS			886,293
Capitalized value	@ 8.5 Cap rate		10,426,986
Loan value	Generally 75% of capitalized value		$7,820,232

Average expense percentages were given to me by my friends at S-101 Management in Sunnyvale, California. They own and operate apartment rental projects for a living. As you can see, the property is a little more complex, and its value is calculated, not by comparable sales, but by capitalizing the NIBDS. We will have more on capitalization rates (Cap rates) later in the book. The calculation is simple, merely take the NIBDS ($886,293) and divide it by the cap rate, in this instance 8.5 percent or 0.085. The result is $10,426,986, the market value of the complex. Typically, you can borrow up to 75 to 80 percent of this value when purchasing this type of investment.

When you have tapped out your patience with managing six separate properties, you might want to consider cashing out your equities and investing them in one larger property such as an apartment complex or a commercial property. Life will be a little easier, and, depending on the market trend, more or less profitable. One thing for sure, your time will be freed up to look around at some new possibilities.

CHAPTER 10

Creating Your Team

I n this chapter, I'd like to take you through the components of a building—any building, whether residential or commercial. In addition, we'll review the potential players and look at source material for your ideas. It is vital to any renovation effort that you understand the nuts and bolts. Once you go beyond the lipstick/new décor approach, you will need to understand what you are physically dealing with. For people who do not work with buildings for a living, the physical interrelationship between the components of a building may be somewhat mysterious. Once you have been through the nuts and bolts, then we'll deal with the people who can help you with demolishing, rearranging, and/or rebuilding these components, and where to find information on what to do and where to buy your materials.

Putting the Pieces Together

In general, I like to take people through the component parts of a building in the order that it would be constructed so that it makes sense in a logical way. When creating a building, the architect/designer has to go through the same steps, in the same order, to "build" the building on paper. The only difference between doing it on paper or on the ground is that the architect first designs it from an external and floor plan point of view so that he or she knows what to construct on paper, starting with the structural design and foundations. On the ground, the contractor starts with site preparation, utilities, then foundations.

Information Gathering

Before starting on any building, a designer needs information about the ground on which the building is to be built. This is accomplished by a survey, topographic map, and soil test. The survey contains data showing the size and shape of the land parcel, the utilities that are available to the site, and their location. The topographic map shows the contours of the land. In addition, a soils engineer has tested the ground and designed the soil compaction requirements for the foundations. From that as a starting point, the project can be designed and built.

Site Preparation and Utilities

Any building must sit on a site that is prepared for it. This is accomplished by preparing the ground to receive it and bringing the necessary utilities to the building pad.

This process is known as rough grading. Once the building is completed, the site will be fine graded prior to receiving curbs, gutters, landscaping, and paving.

Definition

A *pad* is a piece of land, prepared and ready to build on. The soil has been graded level and compacted for the foundation, and the utilities have been brought to the building perimeter, ready for distribution within the building.

Foundations

Foundations are comprised of compacted soil, footings, and foundation walls. This is a rather simplistic explanation, as footings and foundations come in a variety of shapes and configurations depending on the soil-bearing capacity and the requirements of the building itself. It is enough that you know the basics as the experts will determine what you need to hold the building up.

Slabs. Another component of the foundation is the "on-grade" slab. On-grade implies that the slab is resting on prepared ground rather than suspended over a basement. It serves two purposes: pulling the footings and structural components together, and serving as the underlying floor for the ground floor of the building.

Structure

Attached to the footings and other foundation elements is the building's structure. A structure can be many different types; in housing, there are two basic types of structure, perimeter load-bearing walls and post-and-beam. Commercial structures are generally a combination of the two due to their size, or, in the case of mid- and high-rise structures, they can be a steel skeleton on which the rest of the building is hung.

Post-and-beam. Post-and-beam construction is a system that uses walls and columns tied together to form the structure of a building. The side-to-side bracing that protects a building from wind or seismic events is provided by the material that connects the structural components. This element provides the "shear" component of the structure.

Load-bearing outer walls. Perimeter load-bearing walls provide the ultimate flexibility for the building's interior. With this structural system, you can demolish all the interior walls with impunity as they do not contribute to the structural integrity of the building. In post-and-beam structures, you need to consult the architect or engineer before removing any walls. Most homes today are constructed with exterior load-bearing outer walls. They are said to be "clear-span" buildings. The roof and upper floors are held up by prefabricated trusses that span from one outer load bearing wall to another.

Roof Design and Construction

Roofs may take many shapes, from flat to peaked and everything in between. They can be angular, rounded, or, in fact, almost any shape that can be imagined. The support component is generally trusses, but may be as exotic as cables. It all depends on the designer and the shape. The roof is composed of the underlying structure of trusses and either wood or steel panels to support the roofing material. The roof itself is then constructed of traditional shingles or built-up roofing, composed of felts, tar, and a wearing surface. Modern "flat" roofs are now also offered in sprayed-on foam with a watertight membrane over the foam. Shingles vary from the traditional asphalt to wood, concrete, clay, and slate. Another alternate for peaked roofs is a metal roof, as simple as the old corrugated roofing to modern prefinished standing-seam metal roofs.

Interiors

Interiors are generally divided by non-load-bearing walls. In post-and-beam structures, some of the walls are permanent load-bearing; the rest can be moved around at your pleasure. All walls are constructed from two components: studs (uprights, either wood or steel), and sheetrock or other wallboards. Insulation within the wall is optional. The finish is then applied to the surface of the wallboard.

Acoustic walls. In areas within a home, there is sometimes a need for acoustical privacy. Most simple interior walls stop at the ceiling. The acoustical wall can extend above the ceiling, is fully insulated, and has a sound blanket draped over the top of the wall, extending at least four feet on either side of the wall. The resulting sound-dampening is generally enough for the owners' need for privacy. These walls are usually found separating bathrooms, media rooms, or offices from the living area.

Mechanical Systems

A building's services are provided by its mechanical systems, comprised of the utilities, power, water, sewer, gas, telephone, cable TV, data distribution, and HVAC.

Definition

HVAC stands for heating, ventilation, and air conditioning.

Electrical power. A home's electrical distribution is accomplished by several means; first of all, there is a main power distribution panel, perhaps some sub panels, and then the power is fed to different locations by individual circuits designed to handle the anticipated loads. In a home, there is usually a 100-amp panel unless the house is a large one, and then the panel may be sized at 200 amps. Before attempting an extensive add-on project with a home, check with your electrical contractor or electrical engineer to determine whether the existing electrical service can accommodate the additional circuits needed for the addition. Commercial buildings generally have a large main panel, and sub panels for each tenant. Most of today's new buildings provide for individual metering of power for each tenant in order to control the operating costs of the building.

Plumbing. Plumbing is very straightforward; water in and sewer out. Modern structures are using new materials for the waste lines, but most incoming water lines are still built with copper pipe. In the older buildings, hot water was provided by a central boiler or water heater, but now builders can choose point-of-use water heaters, greatly simplifying the water distribution process. The utility distribution within a building is installed before the walls are finished so that these mechanical services are concealed from sight. In renovation projects, you will need to demolish the wall surface to accomplish moving any of these service lines.

HVAC. Today's modern home is climate controlled. The building codes establish criteria for this, defined in number of air changes per hour to ranges of acceptable temperature differential between the inside and the outside of the structure. These mechanical systems can be separated with one system providing heat, another cooling, and some combine both. They all use electricity, plus gas or heating oil, or a combination of all three. In some climates, primarily those with winter weather, boilers are still in use, but in parts of the country where the temperatures are more moderate, a combination unit known as a "heat exchanger" or "heat pump," is used. The air is heated and/or cooled in an air handling unit and distributed throughout the building by ducts within the walls, floors, and ceilings.

Windows, doors, and hardware. Once the interior and exterior walls are completed, and the utilities covered up, the holes in the walls are filled with windows and doors operated by hardware. There is an infinite variety of choices for these units, limited only by your imagination and wallet.

Finishes. The last touch is applying the finishes—paint, wallpaper, etc.—inside and out, and the structure is complete.

Landscaping and site work. The real finishing touch to any building is the site landscaping. There are many different elements to the site, such as driveways, parking, walks, and landscaping. These can be designed and executed by you, your landscaper, or a landscape architect. Essentially, you must think of landscaping as dressing up the building. Obviously, high-rise buildings are only peripherally impacted by landscaping once you leave the street level, but a combination of softscape (plantings) and hardscape (physical improvements) can sell any building.

Consultants and Contractors

The people that put it all together start with the consultants who collect information and create a design, and move on to the tradespeople who actually do the work. Each is a specialized occupation, and has a specific function in any project. You will get to know them if you are going to be in the remodeling business.

Consultants

The consultants who gather information and design the buildings are comprised of surveyors, engineers, architects, planners, or designers.

Engineers. The engineering professionals are broken down into the following categories: civil, structural, mechanical, and electrical.

- *Civil engineers* are concerned with land development and utilities. Part of that function involves gathering information, and a subspecialty is surveying. Another subspecialty of the civil and structural engineer is the soils analysis and compaction design. The soil is tested, and the recommendation for compaction and engineering is passed on to the structural engineer. Once the data is gathered, the civil engineer prepares a grading plan, parking plan, foundation preparation plan, and utility plan based on the desired location and proposed elevation of the new building. This plan is then forwarded to the structural engineer.
- The *structural engineer* takes the architect/designer's design including floor plan, size, shape, and location, combines it with the civil engineer's grading plan and soils report, and produces the foundation plan and the structural design.
- *Mechanical engineers* handle plumbing, waste lines, elevators and people movers, and HVAC design. They take the architectural drawings and the civil drawings and distribute the required services throughout the house. Often, they advise the architect, structural, and civil engineers of special requirements, such as floor loads and stress counteraction requirements necessary for these building components. It is common that, in home design, the licensed subcontractors get involved in this process, as their day-to-day familiarity with the installation and operation of these components make them a logical choice for a design-build option.
- The *electrical engineer* provides power and distribution to all other building systems as well as the tenants. He or she must gather all the other professions' requirements to make sure that the power supply is both adequate and efficient.

Architects and designers. The people who actually design the building are the architects. In the case of houses, there is a profession called house designers whose practitioners are allowed to design homes. All other buildings are designed by architects and engineers. In the case of the house designer, he or she must have the structure designed by an engineer licensed in that state. The architect prepares the detailed building plans, and sends them to the mechanical engineers to add the required utility drawings.

Planners. A cross between the architect and the civil engineer, called a land planner, has evolved into a specialty for large projects. Rather than taking the strictly numerical approach of the civil engineer, the land planner strives to design the site so that it maximizes not only the building but also the aesthetics and sales appeal. Personally, even on small projects, I like to start with a land planner and then move on to the architect and engineer; I find that I get better projects by doing it this way.

Builders

The building profession is loosely divided into residential and commercial companies. In general, the residential builders are non-union, and the commercial contractors are union companies. This is somewhat confusing in right-to-work states like Arizona where there are no laws requiring union labor. In these states, the breakdown is housing, nonunion; small commercial, generally nonunion; and high-rise and municipal projects, union labor. Within each category, there are two types of contractors: general contractors and subcontractors. Whether residential or commercial, union or nonunion, all contractors are required to be licensed.

General Contractors Licensing

The general contractor is licensed to oversee the construction of the projects and may or may not provide his or her own labor for one or more of the sub trades. Typically, the general contractor provides a construction superintendent or foreman and hires the specific work to be done by specialty subcontractors. The licensing procedure is the same for union and nonunion companies. Each company must have a "qualifying party" to have a license for the company's use. That party must take a test and meet the practical experience requirements to become licensed.

Subcontractors

These companies represent many specialties such as earth moving, underground, gas, steam fitting, plumbing, electrical, drywall, structural steel, framing, roofers, glazers, and equipment operators. All companies must have a qualifying party for the company to be licensed.

Licensed vs. Unlicensed, Laws, and Liens

The licensed contractor must post a bond to be placed into a recovery fund for the customers so that shoddy work or substandard materials can be replaced. There is a limit to what the recovery fund can pay on a single claim, so it is vital that you choose contractors, general and sub alike, that are financially solvent, experienced, and clearly qualified to do the work. A licensed contractor with a signed contract can enforce payment for completed work through the lien process. If the contractor has not been paid in a timely fashion, he or she is allowed to record a "mechanics and materialman's" lien on the property. This class of lien provides for people working on the property as well as people who supply materials to the project. To perfect a lien, several things must happen.

First the contractor must have a contract directly with the owner of the project or the contractor or supplier must send a pre-lien notice to the owner prior to starting the work stating that he or she is providing labor or materials to the project under a subcontract with the general contractor. Then, if the contractor or supplier is not paid on time, he or she may file the lien, and with the two notices, the lien is deemed "perfected." Just because the lien has been filed and perfected does not mean that payment is automatically owed or will be paid. The owner may dispute the lien in court, and if successful, the lien may be voided. This lien must be paid before the property can be sold with a clean title.

Resources

In addition to the people outlined above, you will be able to draw on additional people to guide you in the remodeling process. There are many professions involved, and you are free to use or not to use any or all of the potential sources of talent, skill, and advice.

Front Line and Back Office

We have talked about most of these people before, and by now you should be familiar with most of them. They are, but are not limited to, the following: Marketing consultants, real estate brokers, title companies and lawyers, advertisers, interior decorators, handymen, mortgage brokers and bankers, lenders, accountants, bookkeepers, and property managers.

Information

The other resource you need is information not provided by anyone with a potential profit motive. There is an almost infinite amount of material available to you for this type of project. There are remodeling industry publications, building design information, product design and installation manuals, and web sites galore. Specific sources include, but are not limited to:

- How-to books such as the *Time-Life Series* on home remodeling and construction and the following publications:
  - *Family Handyman*
  - *Home*
  - *Old House Journal*
  - *This Old House*
  - *Workbench*
- Trade publications such as *American Homebuilder*
- Manufacturer's brochures
- Online information

All manufacturers publish specifications and installation manuals on their home building products that are readily available wherever these items are sold. All retailers are broken down into four basic types: local neighborhood hardware stores like Paul's True Value Hardware and Ace Hardware, local lumber yards, large discount hardware stores like Lowe's and Home Depot, and specialty stores such as Color Tile, Standard Brands Paint, Pella Windows, etc. All of the lumber stores will cut your lumber to fit and sell it as a package right from your plans, and the larger stores will entice you with a full package.

Online information. By far the most up-to-date information is available from the internet, but it can be overwhelming. Recently, I typed "home remodeling" into my search engine, and received over 35,000 hits. I suggest that you try to narrow your searches and select things like how-to reference books, financing, building plans, and contractors. This will give you a better selection of sites and potential contractors in your area. If you are taking a modest step into renovation, a little more aggressive than paint and wallpaper, you can attend free seminars given monthly by Home Depot and Lowe's. They have seasoned professionals teach the basics of skills like sheetrocking, plumbing, working with ceramic tile, etc. These will allow you to tackle the modest projects without the necessity of dealing with contractors. Homeowners are legally allowed to do their own work as long as it is inspected at the proper progress points. It's a great way to get started.

CHAPTER 11

What You're Allowed to Do

Zoning regulations were discussed briefly in Chapter 2; this chapter will provide you with more detail so that you know what regulations govern any prospective project or acquisition you are contemplating. Once again, if you are only tackling a redecoration project, you can skip this chapter and come back to it when you have decided to undertake something more complicated.

Zoning and Building Codes

If you are into remodeling, purchasing investment property, or development, this chapter is vital to your understanding of the environment in which you seek to invest your hard-earned cash. Fortunately, although we live in a free society, it's a highly regulated free society. By and large, the regulations are there for everyone's benefit, and while they are restrictive, they tend to create cohesive master plans, uniformity of value, and proper methods of construction. That is their function. In isolated cases, such as in California, land use regulations can be, and are, used to control growth, and in some cases, halt it completely. No matter what type of project you are contemplating, you will need permits for anything beyond a change of décor. Can you do the work without a permit? The answer is yes; many people add on to their homes without permits. But if you decide to do so, you may run the risk of getting into trouble. Even a home addition can cause problems. First of all, when you sell the home, you are legally required to disclose any work done on the home and whether the work was done legally with a permit. If you fail to disclose that information, and it comes to light at a later date, you might be liable to the municipality and to the buyer, long after the closing of the sale. You will most certainly be liable for any latent defects. What is permitted in any area is governed, first by the general plan, and then, specifically, by the zoning for the particular parcel of land.

The General Plan

In our computerized world, most of these regulations are available on the internet and are readily accessible. If you call your local planning department, they will give you the web address for the web site. For example, I have just completed work on a project in Mesa, Arizona, and their website is accessed at www.city ofmesa.org/planning/.

A municipality's masterplan can be accessed on most city web sites, as most municipalities have put these services and information on the internet to save money. Having staff available to meet with people to answer basic questions costs a great deal of money, and budgets are stretched thin. Most, if not all, of the forms for making applications are also available online, together with checklists of requirements and a schedule of fees for each process. The online Mesa General Plan is over 180 pages long, and provides more information than you will ever need. Always start with your planning department when you are doing research for property acquisition and improvements.

Zoning classifications. In Table 11.1 you will find a chart showing a typical municipal or county zoning classification breakdown. This will vary state to state and county to municipality. Rest assured, however, that your area will be represented unless you live in Houston where there is no zoning, and you can build what you want where you want.

Table 11.1—*Zoning Classifications*

Agricultural District	
AG	Agricultural activities, minimum ten acre lot
Single Residence Districts	
R1–go	Rural low-density housing, minimum 90,000 sq. ft. lot
R1–43	Rural low-density housing, minimum 43,560 sq. ft. lot
R1–35	Suburban low-density housing, minimum 35,000 sq. ft. lot
R1–15	Suburban low-density housing, minimum 15,000 sq. ft. lot
R1–9	Urban density housing, minimum 9,000 sq. ft. lot
R1–7	Urban density housing, minimum 7,000 sq. ft. lot
R1–6	Urban density housing, minimum 6,000 sq. ft. lot
Multiple Residence Districts	
R–2	Transition from Single Residence Districts, maximum 12 du/ac
R–3	Medium Density, maximum 17 du/ac
R–4	High Density, maximum 25 du/ac
Commercial Districts	
0–S	Office-Service: nonretail, small-scale offices, residential services on minimum 6,000 sq. ft. lot
C–10–2	Neighborhood Commercial: large-scale offices, small-scale retail Limited Commercial: indoor retail, shopping centers, group commercial developments
0–3	General Commercial: variety of outdoor and indoor commercial activities
Industrial, Manufacturing, and Employment Districts	
PEPM–1M–2	Planned Employment Park: regional
Town Center Districts	
TCR–1	Low density residential within Town Center Boundary, minimum 6,000 sq. ft. lot
TCR–2	Medium density residential within Town Center Boundary, maximum 12 du/ac
TCR–3	High density residential within Town Center Boundary, maximum 40 du/ac
TCB–1	Business district within Town Center Boundary, medium density residential, professional offices
TCB–2	Business district within Town Center Boundary, intensive commercial, light manufacturing, access to arterial and rail
TCC	Town Center Core: highest intensity land use with development incentives
Public Facilities District	
PF	Public Facilities: large-scale governmental, public utility, recreational, and educational facilities on minimum ten acre lot

The breakdown in Table 11.1 is not overly significant as it will change from jurisdiction to jurisdiction. What is important is that you realize that every piece of land or existing building you work with will be governed by regulations like these. We'll pick a category in this breakdown and follow it to the logical end so that you can see exactly what these regulations encompass. That way, you'll know how to analyze a project, whether it's a house you want to rebuild, a project you might want to acquire, or a new development you might want to undertake. Since most people will want to start their investment career with a house, let's follow along with the typical single family home designation, R1-9. This effectively produces three to four homes to the acre, and coast-to-coast is the most prevalent existing single family home.

Residential Zoning

To start with, look at the governing parameters for this zoning classification. The city's rationale behind these low density districts is stated as follows: "This zoning category identifies locations where detached, moderate-sized lot, single–family residential housing is desirable. The target density for these areas is three dwelling units per acre (du/ac).

Appropriate locations offer collector road access, connections to potable water and sanitary sewer, and proximity to public safety services. The provision of park and open space (15 percent of net area excluding street system) is encouraged to provide opportunities for recreation and non-vehicular pedestrian connections like pathways, trails, etc. Other uses permitted in this category may include office and neighborhood commercial building of less than ten acres where deemed appropriate by the city." With this as a given, then, how do they regulate what you can do within this district? This specific regulation is contained in the guidelines for the R1-9 zoning category in the building department's regulations. Table 11.2 provides the general guidelines.

In Table 11.2, you can see that for the R1-9 zoning district the following restrictions apply:

- The minimum lot size must be 9,000 square feet per home.
- The lot frontage must be al least 80 feet.
- The minimum lot depth must be 100 feet.
- The maximum units per acre cannot exceed 3.3 for conventional design, and 4.84 with a PAD overlay.
- The buildings cannot exceed 30 feet in height and two stories.
- Minimum building setbacks are:
  - Front: 25 feet
  - Side: 7 feet and no less than 17 feet for both side yards

Table 11.2—*Typical Zoning Table*

Zone Dist R1–	Max Lot Size			Max Du/Ac			Max Height/ Story	Minimum Yard Setbacks						Max Roof Area
	Area	Width	Depth	Conv.	PAD			Front	Side		Street Side	Rear	
									Min	Total			
90	90,000 sq. ft.	150'	—	0.5	0.48	30'/2	30'	20'	40'	20'	30'	20%
43	45,560 sq. ft.	130'	—	1.0	1.0	30'/2	30'	10'	30'	30'	30'	20%
35	35,000 sq. ft.	130'	150'	1.0	1.24	30'/2	30'	10'	30'	10'	30'	30%
15	15,000 sq. ft.	115'	120'	2.1	2.9	30'/2	30'	7'	20'	10'	30'	35%
9	9,000 sq. ft.	80'	100'	3.3	4.84	30'/2	25'	7'	17'	10'	25'	40%
7	7,000 sq. ft.	70'	94'	4.0	6.22	30'/2	20'	5'	15'	10'	20'	40%
6	6,000 sq. ft.	60'	94'	4.7	7.26	30'/2	20'	5'	15'	10'	20'	40%

  - Street: 10 feet
  - Rear yard: 25 feet
- The total roof area cannot exceed 40 percent of the lot size. For example, if the lot is 9,000 square feet, then the maximum allowable roof is 3,600 square feet including all structures.

Definition

A *PAD* zoning overlay is a "Planned Area Development." This allows for specific project designs approved by the city council or county board of commissioners. It allows the developer to exceed certain minimums in exchange for other concessions or amenities.

You're probably asking what does all this have to do with me? Unless you are the original developer, you are only interested in the restrictions on what you might add to the home. For instance, if you wish to add a room or another garage, the maximum roof coverage or the mandatory setbacks might affect your ability to do so. You might be forced to go up rather than out with your addition. The roof restriction allows a single story home and garage combination of 3,600 square feet, but you can have 7,200 square feet in a two story configuration, and 10,800 square feet with two stories and a full basement configuration. These restrictions, together with market restrictions, completely govern what you can build or rebuild.

There are also other zoning and building regulations that you must consider and abide by. They cover, but are not restricted to, such things as:

- On- and off-street parking
- Types of vehicles that may park outside the garage or on the street
- Whether you can work on your car or truck in the driveway
- Restrictions on recreational vehicle storage in the driveway, such as RVs, motorcycles, wave runners, boats, and snowmobiles
- Number and type of animals permitted
- Number of occupants, if unrelated
- Paint colors
- Roof shapes, etc.

You get the idea. All these restrictions and regulations are spelled out in the zoning and building codes. You should check them all before you start planning any significant renovation project.

Overlay districts. Not too common, but out there nonetheless, is the zoning overlay district. This is formed and put into effect for a specific purpose, such as preserving a historic neighborhood, ensuring consistency of architectural design, allowing the city's overall height limit to be exceeded for a downtown high-rise district, or permitting gambling within a specific city area. In short, a jurisdiction can impose any legal additional zoning requirements and/or restrictions to further the jurisdiction's goals for that purpose. This imposes yet another layer of compliance on projects within these districts.

Building Codes

An adjunct to zoning regulations is the local building code. These additional regulations tell exactly how you are to construct any type of building or manmade structure. The master code is the national Uniform Building Code, or UBC for short. This code sets minimum standards for design and construction and is overseen by the Occupational Safety and Health Administration (OSHA), which regulates how job sites are to be managed to ensure minimum safety standards for the workplace. Specific additional regulations cover both mobile and modular home construction. There are additional regulations and standards that cover the following items:

- Soils and bearing capacity
- Design loading of roofs and floors
- Special zones
- Hurricane, seismic activity, and snow loads

There are also local standards applied to the UBC to accommodate special areas of the country affected by potential natural disasters such as floods, earthquakes, and excessive snow. These are supplemental codes applied to the UBC for local areas.

Working with the Regulations

What you need to know as a homeowner/renovator/developer is how to work with these laws and regulations. They will come into play when you want to:

- Split a parcel of land into two or more lots and sell the land to the public
- Renovate or add on to your home
- Build a house or a commercial building
- Change the use for a parcel of land
- Put an existing or proposed property to a non-permitted use
- Create a residential or commercial subdivision

If you are changing the décor of your own home or of an investment property, chances are that you will not require any permits unless you are contemplating some major changes to the building exterior. The town will not care whether you

Heads Up

Now you know why you need all the consultants and specialists covered in Chapter 10 when you start designing and building anything. It's not as tough as it sounds. All these people know their specific areas of responsibility, and coordinating the design and building effort to meet all the requirements is "all in a day's work" to them.

add trim or change the outside color unless there is an ordinance regarding exterior paint colors, but your local committee of architecture or homeowners association may have something to say about it. See the section "Other Constraints" later in this chapter.

Some of the major items that you may be called on to handle in connection with a renovation/remodel/development project are the following:

- Changing the general plan
- Changing zoning
- Variances
- Special use permits
- Building permits

Changing the General Plan

This is a major undertaking, but from the municipality's or county's perspective, a rather routine one, as a general plan is considered to be a work in progress. Most states require that jurisdictions routinely revisit and revise their general plans, and also provide for citizen- or developer-initiated changes between the mandated revision periods. The process is simple and routine but takes planning and research, and in all cases, the change in the general plan is also accompanied by a rezoning request. Depending on your local jurisdiction, your requirements may include, but not be limited to, the following:

- A signed application (by the current owner of the land and the applicant if they are not one and the same)
- Payment of fees
- A narrative outlining the proposed request and your justification for the request as well as the anticipated impacts of the change in plan and zoning
- Site plans and proposed architectural drawings and renderings
- Traffic studies
- Environmental Impact Report (EIR) or Environmental Impact Statement (EIS in California)

Once the application is submitted, it will be reviewed by the jurisdiction's planning staff that will request dialogue with you and suggest some changes that would make the application more palatable to the planning staff, as well as the planning commission, city council, or county board of supervisors. In some cases, you may need to get approval for the proposed changes from the state highway department, the Army Corps of Engineers, or some other governing body. In California there are some doozies: The California Coastal Commission, and in San Francisco, The Bay Area Development Commission. In all, it is generally an exhaustive, lengthy, and expensive process. Timing from the date of the completed submittal varies from a brisk nine months to two or three years, depending on your area. As a general rule, if you are successful and your zoning change is approved, the value of the land should be substantially enhanced, and you can make some good returns on your investment.

Changing zoning. Changing the zoning for a specific parcel of land is much the same process. If the use is permitted by the general plan, you may proceed without having to modify the general plan. You can refer to the previous list for the requirements, as they will all apply to a rezoning as well as the general plan amendment.

Variances. Variances, mentioned earlier, are requests to waive specific zoning or building code requirements such as setbacks to accommodate one-of-a-kind existing conditions or special requirements. These follow the same approval process from staff to planning commission, and on to the city council or county board of supervisors. Once granted, these variances are a permanent part of the entitlements for that specific parcel of land in rare jurisdictions, there are time limits for a developer to act, and if not met, the variances can expire. The rule of thumb for this type of submittal is, but not limited to, the following:

- A signed application by landowner and applicant
- Fees
- Site plans and architectural layout
- Written consent or rejection of the request from the neighbors
- A narrative of what you want and why you need it, as well as an assessment of the impact on your land and on your adjacent neighbors' land

Special use permits. These applications are for the right to use the property for use that is not premitted in the zoning code. For instance, while restaurants are permitted in most C–1 zones, you need a special use permit for the restaurant to serve liquor by the drink. The alternative is a rezoning to C–2 which permits that type of restaurant. Another example would be seeking a permit to operate a bed-and-breakfast or a halfway house in a residential area. These petitions and permits, if granted, expire when the use is terminated. This permit does not run with the land. The application process is similar to that of the variance. The time it takes to obtain a variance and use permit is usually only a matter of months.

Building permits. To construct anything within a municipal jurisdiction, you need a building permit. Some rural counties do not require a building permit, and this may cause you some trouble when you are dealing in a rural area. I once built myself a home in the country, and the only permits I needed were a permit to drill a well, and a septic system permit. These were also the only items inspected during the entire construction process. This is wonderful when you are building, but may give you pause when you are buying the product of someone else's energy and entrepreneurship. Most people build to code whether required to or not, but some people just dig a hole and start banging boards together. The results can be spectacularly bad, even dangerous. If you are going to buy something in the county, hire a good inspector, and make sure you know what you are getting into.

Other Constraints

There are other regulations that are what I call civil restraints, imposed voluntarily by landowners to help the parcels of land within a specific development. They are, but are not limited to, the following:

- Covenants, Condition, and Restrictions (CC&R)
- Neighborhood Architectural Committees
- Homeowners' Associations

Here's a quick look at these requirements in a little more depth.

CC&R. These documents, known as "Covenants, Conditions, and Restrictions" set out guidelines for construction and operation of a specific development or subdivision, and are recorded against all the parcels within a defined development. In doing so, they become a deed restriction, or a voluntary restriction by deed. Buyers of these parcels have these restrictions fully disclosed to them in the preliminary title report or abstract of title. They buy the land knowing full well the restrictions that apply to their land or home. CC&Rs are designed to preserve uniformity of design, quality of construction, and ease of administration for the project. In the beginning, the management of the CC&Rs is done by the developer, and when the occupancy of the project reaches a certain percentage, generally 50 to 75 percent of the total houses, the neighborhood homeowners association takes over. In a tract home subdivision, all design and construction is controlled by the developer; in a custom home subdivision, it can be controlled by the developer and a separate and independent architectural committee, ensuring that the developer's initial design guidelines spelled out in the CC&Rs are followed. This committee is responsible initially to the developer, but once occupancy has reached a certain percentage, the committee then reports to the homeowners' organization.

Neighborhood Architectural Commitees. In addition to the government, the neighbors can have a say in what you do and any exterior changes to your house. The

Neighborhood Property Owners' Association (NPOA) generally has to approve any exterior changes to your home. They do this by having their appointed Architectural Committee look over your plans and issue you a permit from the association. They will inspect the property during construction and issue their own certificate of occupancy.

Homeowners' Associations. In general, homeowners' associations deal with quality issues such as keeping undesirable vehicles off the street or front yards, making sure landscaping is installed and maintained, and ensuring that new additions are compatible with the original architecture. Their intent is solely to maintain quality and enforce the CC&Rs.

Once the homeowners' association takes over, problems start occurring. The administration becomes political and is subject to the usual large frog in a small pond syndrome. If you can get rid of people on the board that are on a power trip, then things can go smoothly. The intent is to preserve value for all homeowners by preventing abuses of parking, maintenance, and building modification. Due to abuses by homeowner boards, homeowner associations are increasingly coming under fire and are ending up in court as irate homeowners feel that they have been singled out for unfair enforcement. Most people feel that these associations unfairly and arbitrarily infringe on their property rights. Properly run, homeowner associations are an asset to a community, but when they go bad, they can lower property values and make homes within the jurisdiction hard to sell.

Heads Up

In recent times, abuses by homeowners' associations have prompted the courts to intervene to prevent abuse and hardship imposed on individual homeowners' by capricious boards of directors. As a result, it is increasingly common for homeowners associations to be run, by contract, by professional property management companies. This is an effort to forestall abuse and provide prompt and uniform service to the homeowners.

CHAPTER 12

Tear Out and Rebuild—Case Studies

I n relation to housing, single family housing in particular, the most profitable investment will be found in expanding a home to its maximum value within the marketplace. There is and will always be a differential between the cost of construction and the completed value of housing and commercial buildings. That's what keeps developers and contractors gainfully employed. You too can capitalize on that fact. In this chapter, will look at three typical examples of this type of project.

The first deals with a ranch-style home that can be found anywhere in the country. This home is expressly, however, not found in a tract, because tracts, unless they are quite old, impose limitations on value that make profiting from an expansion project difficult.

The second project is a complete rebuild of a seasonal home in a vacation neighborhood. It is intended to capitalize on the expounding upper middle market catering to the baby boomers who do not mind a good commute.

The final look is at the conversion of an old single family home found on Main Street, anywhere in the country, to a commercial use, in this case, a restaurant. As people move to larger homes in the suburbs, more and more towns are being revitalized by small business expansion into the older homes along the main drag.

To create this series of examples, I sat down with my architect of 30 years, Bozidar Rajkovski, AIA, and created these projects from scratch. Although I commissioned the drawings, Bo outdid himself taking much more time and putting in much more thought and detail than he was being paid for. The result is a very realistic and plausible step-by-step transformation of three very ordinary buildings into creations much more valuable and immensely more appealing in the marketplace. I would wager that your realtor could find you existing buildings exactly like the ones we started with.

The Ubiquitous Three-Bedroom Ranch

In the series of drawings that follow in Figures 12.1 through 12.4, you will see a typical three-bedroom, two-bath, two-car garage, single-family home transformed

Figure 12.1—*Typical Ranch Plan View*

Figure 12.2—_Typical Ranch Elevation_

step by step into a larger, and more upscale version of itself. It is done in stages so that you can see how it can be done while you are living in the home. Of course, you can always move into a rental, and do it all at once.

In Figures 12.1 and 12.2 you have the raw material. It's a house you can find anywhere, usually on a quarter acre lot. It has three bedrooms, two baths, and a two-car garage. For years this was the average home in America, built, with minor variations, coast to coast. Figure 12.3 is its first transformation.

In Figure 12.3 you can see the start of the transformation. An entry area has been added along with a porch. This accomplishes two purposes. It adds to the

Figure 12.3—_The First Step, Plan View_

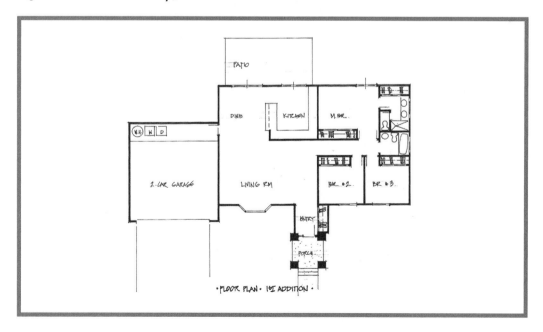

Figure 12.4—*The Second Step, Plan View*

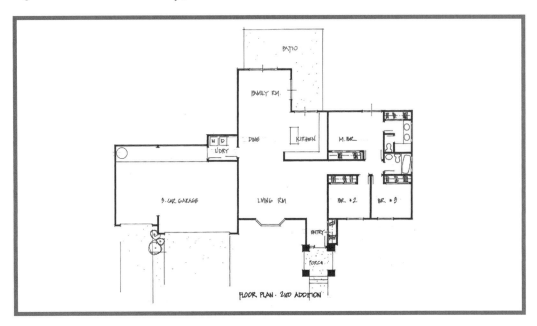

architectural character of the home by breaking up the roofline along the front of the house, and takes the foyer out of the living room, leaving more living space while providing an entry that can also double as a mud room in inclement weather. You will note that the new foyer has a closet for coats and boots as well.

In Figure 12.4, you can see the beginning of the expansion; the garage has been expanded to a three-car garage, and a laundry room has been shoehorned into the back of the original garage; the kitchen area has been expanded to the rear of the home, modifying the kitchen layout, and creating a dining area off the kitchen and a family room. The home, in its present configuration, is definitely a more desirable family home. You could, in fact, just stop there. We, however, did not. Read on.

In Figure 12.5 you can see that the living room has been expanded by pulling the living room's front wall toward the street and adding a bay window. At the same time, a center counter in the kitchen has been added to make it more workable and "modern." You might have noticed that we have, as yet, not touched the sleeping areas or the baths. Guess what's next.

In step four (Figure 12.6), the master bath has been expanded to incorporate a more spacious bathroom and a dedicated walk-in closet. It's not truly elegant as the tub and shower is still combined, but there is room for his-and-hers sinks. This step could be more dramatic if there is more room in the side yard for a larger

Figure 12.5—*Step Three, Plan View*

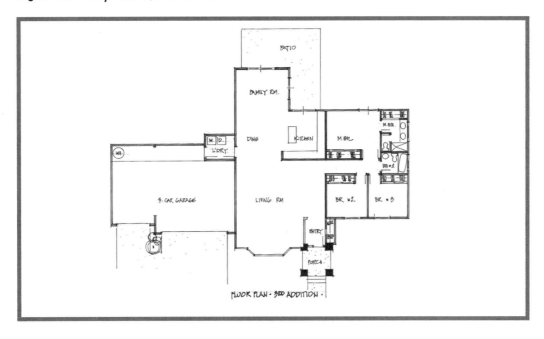

Figure 12.6—*Step Four, Plan View*

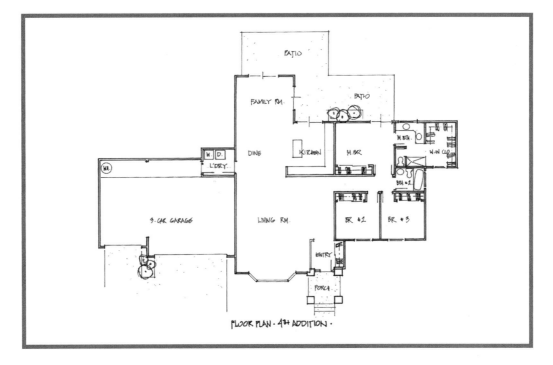

expansion. The only limit is the space and your pocketbook. In addition, we could consider expanding the other bedrooms and adding more.

As you can see from Figure 12.7, this can go on and on, including a slight variation in the closet addition shown below. Figures 12.8 and 12.9 show a completed project, both plan view and elevation.

It is hard to stop playing with this house because it is so common and constructed everywhere. It is worth spending some extra time on. This is not a very complicated project, and the demolition and structural modifications are relatively straightforward.

Figure 12.7—*Potential Future Addition Plan View*

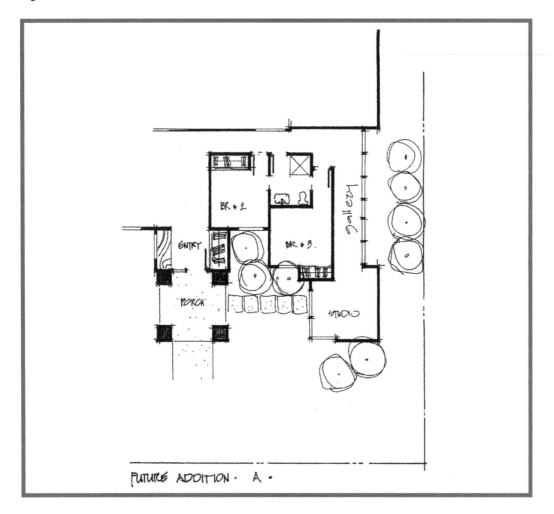

Figure 12.8—*New Ranch Elevation*

Figure 12.9—*New Ranch Plan View with Variations*

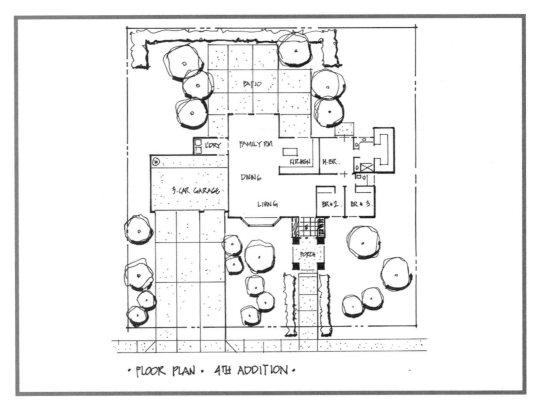

In Figure 12.10 the dotted lines show where the walls were removed; the rear kitchen wall, the left garage wall, the living room wall, and part of the original master bath. While you cannot simply tear these down without bracing and structural modification, all these modifications are relatively routine in nature.

Figure 12.10—*Demolition Plan*

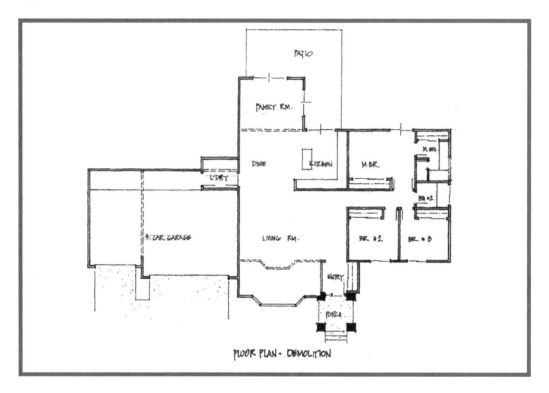

FLOOR PLAN · DEMOLITION

Seasonal Home to Primary Residence

Throughout the country, on lakes, seashores, rivers, and mountains, there are vacation cottages. These structures were generally built for summer occupancy, uninsulated, and completely without frills. As the country grew after the post-World War II era, cities and towns expanded, gradually encroaching into heretofore outlying areas. These buildings are now within modern commute times of employment centers. Those that are not are most likely now integrated into locations that have been transformed into lifestyle communities or retirement communities.

This project is another step-by-step approach so that you can envision the process over time and perhaps tackle it while living in the home. It also can accommodate newlyweds and tract the expansion of their family, transforming the home as the family expands.

Figure 12.11 is a typical cottage, very basic and uninsulated. The project will start by insulating the roof and all the outside walls. As we progress from area to area, we will replace all the windows with modern double-pane windows for

Figure 12.11—_The Vacation Cottage_

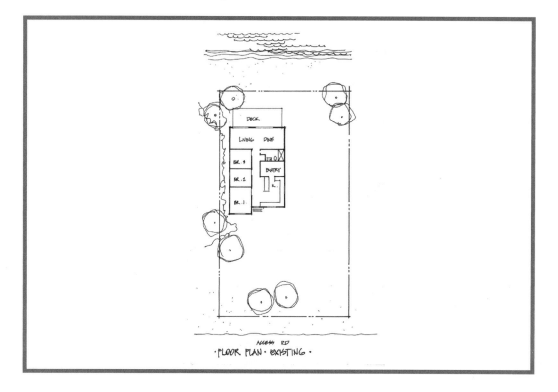

·FLOOR PLAN · EXISTING ·

increased insulation. You will note that the home sits to one side of the property; that is typical of many vacation home layouts so that the lot can accommodate the required parking and outdoor recreation necessary for a vacation property. The changes to this building are designed to accommodate that layout, but you can adapt to any site configuration as long as there is room to expand.

In the adaptation shown in Figure 12.12, we complete the insulation, demolish the middle bedroom, and create a Jack-and-Jill bathroom between the two remaining bedrooms. In addition, we have added an enclosed entry off the kitchen to free up room in the kitchen area for our next step. This provides a permanent all-weather entry to the home. We also start the window replacement for the rooms that will remain as permanent parts of the finished home.

Figure 12.13, Phase Two shows a major overhaul of the kitchen to accommodate a growing family and to set the stage for the first major changes in the home's configuration.

In Figure 12.14, Phase Three you can see where we are headed with this project. The right side of the home is expanded, the rear entry eliminated, a garage added,

Figure 12.12—*The First Step*

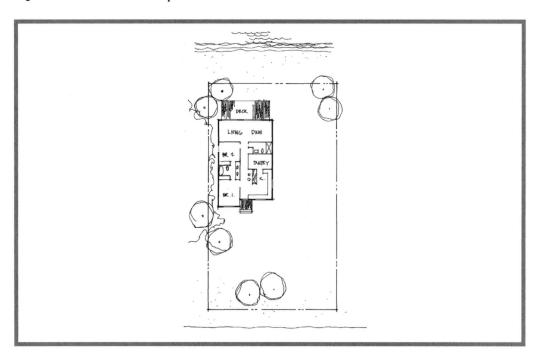

Figure 12.13—*Phase Two*

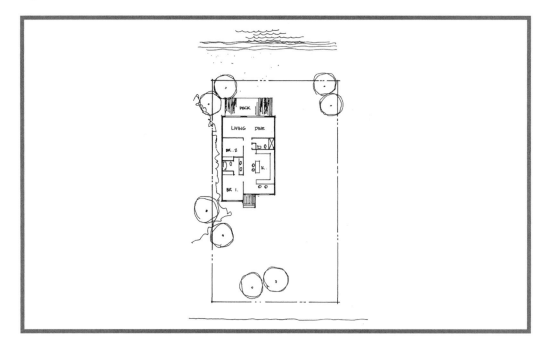

Figure 12.14—*Phase Three*

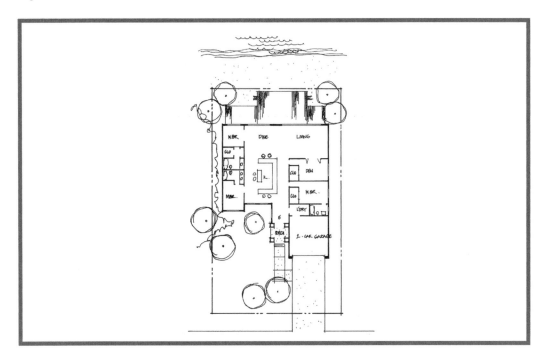

Figure 12.15—*Phase Four, Plan View*

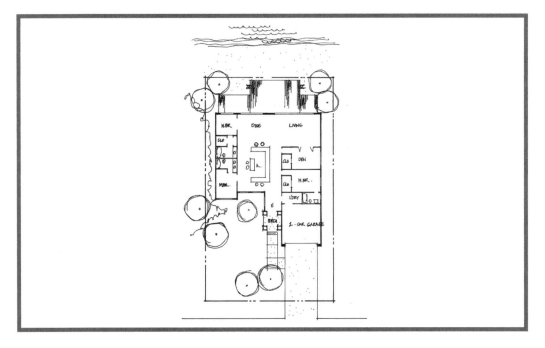

Figure 12.16—*Roof Plan*

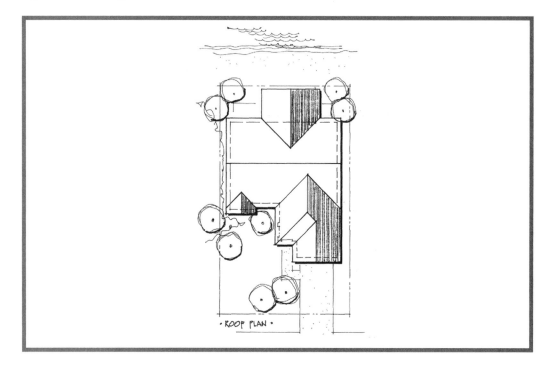

· ROOF PLAN ·

the old living and dining room reconfigured to accommodate a den, a new dining area, and a living area. The new space is created as two more bedrooms and a second bath. We now have a fairly livable single family home. There's more on the way!

In Figures 12.15 and 12.16 you can see the final touch. The porch has been expanded and fully enclosed to provide more all-weather living space. The new porch roof has been added to pull the entire project together. We have, over a period of time, transformed a small, basic vacation home into a spacious, year-round, single-family house.

The Commercial Conversion

This series of sketches will show you a step-by-step transformation of a typical Main Street dwelling that has been converted to a small business. These can be found coast to coast, inland and at the seashore, in the mountains and in the heartland. It is a great use for a home that has suffered the encroachment of commerce. Start with the original dwelling.

Figures 12.17 and 12.18 depict a rather plain contemporary two-story home on a lot with an old-fashioned detached garage. I would bet that you could track

Figure 12.17—*The Original House Elevation*

Figure 12.18—*Site Plan and Plan View*

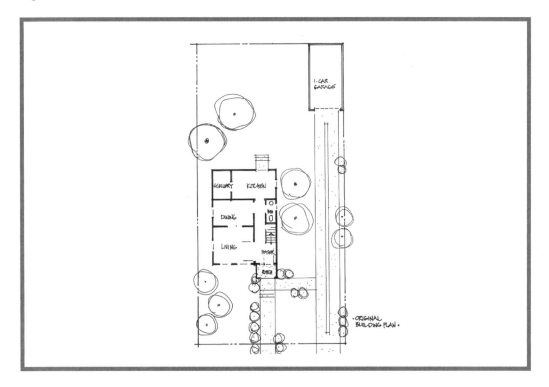

down quite a few of these in your own stomping grounds. This particular transformation is going to be modeled after an actual renovation project in my old town of Danville, California. This renovation is not what actually happened to that particular building, only what might have happened. The site layout is surprisingly similar, and the results are designed to emulate the actual building in use today.

Since no one is living in the home and since it is to be transformed into a new use, we will do it all at once, albeit step-by-step. We need to use the site to stage materials and workmen to do the work. First we will demolish in the main building and finish the exterior, then, move on to the rest of the site. The dotted lines on the plan view (Figure 12.19) indicate where walls are being removed prior to rebuilding the building.

With the demolition complete, the original building is closed in, the new space added and finished. You can see in Figure 12.20 a new dining room in front, with the kitchen, stairs and restroom in the rear. A walkway from the street has been created, and a reception area inside the front door. There is also a path connecting the main building to the old garage.

In Figure 12.21 you can see in some detail the finished product. What is not shown is more dining areas and restrooms on the second floor. The old garage

Figure 12.19—*The Demolition Plan*

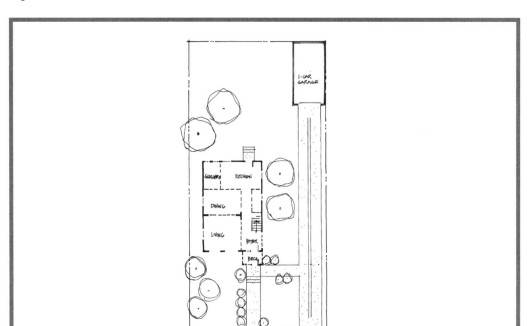

Figure 12.20—*Phase Two*

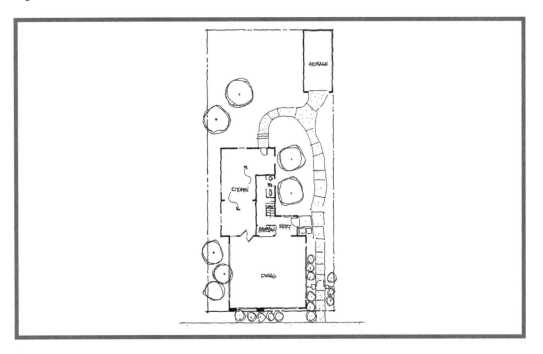

Figure 12.21—*The Finished Site Plan*

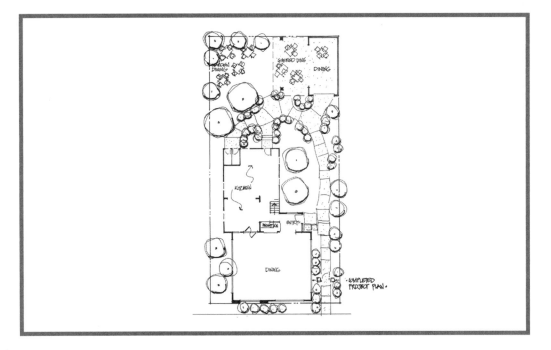

Figure 12.22—*The Finished Elevation*

· NEW ELEVATION ·

is now additional dining area, connected to an open air patio. The landscaping adds the final dressing, and you now have a charming turn of the century restaurant. In figure 12.22, you can see the finished elevation.

The three examples in this chapter illustrate what is possible starting with relatively modest dwellings. I must reiterate that the physical transformations shown here are not the single most crucial part of making money on renovation; although you will have to be canny and cost conscious, it is the marketplace that can absorb this type of project that is the crucial ingredient for success. You need to look for opportunities in an organized fashion, weeding out the marginal and going for your projects in areas that can clearly stand the upgrade. Fertile areas to look at are along the old tree-studded main streets in small towns where people are moving to get out of the cities, and in areas where good architecture abounds. Converting old Victorians or brownstones is great fun and generally very profitable. Older housing areas with the three bedroom ranch homes of the 1950s and 1960s just cry out for a good rebuild. Have at it!

Basic Business Considerations

CHAPTER 13

Money and Paperwork

Sometimes you may not have the necessary ready cash; this has been the case for the duration of my career. I started in the commercial development business with $6,000 in the bank, and my first two deals cost over three million dollars each. Since then, I have raised money for every transaction I have undertaken. I'm not suggesting that you take the approach that I did, merely that you become aware of the resources that are potentially at your command. The day will come when you will need to reach out to these resources, and then you'll know where to find them. Equity money, i.e., that portion of the project's cost over and above that which can be borrowed by conventional means, can be acquired by borrowing or through some form of partnership

Heads Up

Think of interest, points, and participations as rental rates for the use of the money you need.

arrangement. Most of this chapter will not apply to your first venture, or maybe not even to your tenth, but if you get serious and quit your day job, you might really want to pay attention to the possibilities offered here.

Obviously, your cash is the first primary source for any deal, but often ready cash is not enough to accomplish what you want to do at any given moment.

Where to Look for Cash

Where you look will depend on what you are up to. Since this book starts with your home and moves on from there, let's first look at funding sources for home-oriented deals.

Housing

Housing, especially your primary residence, is the easiest asset to raise money on because lenders and investors correctly believe that this is the sole asset that you would not be likely to walk away from in a disaster. On the average, this has proven to be so true that today you can actually borrow more than the home is worth, using the home as collateral. The first place to look at for ready cash is the equity built up in the home.

Since there is always an inflation factor in this country, however modest it might be, there will always be a time when your home is increasing in value due to the country's overall inflation. In addition, if you live in an area where the homeowners keep their homes in good repair and style, your home's value will rise with the neighborhood. That means that no matter what you borrowed on the home when you bought it, your home is worth more than you paid for it. This is your equity and you have the right to use it for investment purposes. To tap into this equity source is a simple matter of borrowing. You can borrow against your home's equity up to, and in excess of, 100 percent of value. There are several ways to do this:

- You can refinance the home with a new first mortgage.
- You can take a second mortgage, known as a home equity loan, or second mortgage.
- You can take a personal loan using your combined assets as security.
- You can take on a partner.

Partners in housing are nothing new in real estate; they have, however, in recent years, become more popular as people have started to realize the potential profit in real estate deals. Probably the most common form of partnership is the one where one person (the investor) puts up the down payment, and the other one, usually the occupant of the home, pays the mortgage. When the property is sold, the mortgage is paid off, the investor gets the down payment back, and the investor and the occupant split the profits on a previously agreed upon basis. A variation of this can be used on an existing home with an existing loan just as easily. Say that you want to expand the home but are not able to find enough cash from your own sources; it is feasible that you could offer someone a partnership deal to put up the necessary funds in exchange for a percentage of the profits when the enlarged home is sold.

> **Definition**
>
> *Equity* is that portion of value over the debt on any asset. It is also described as the net value of the asset.

When you step outside the realm of loans, and enter into partnerships, you need to understand that there are many forms of agreements between the parties, resulting in many different legal forms of ownership. Each arrangement has a different set of rules and regulations. These have been covered in detail in Chapter 3.

Residential Ownership

When it comes to housing, there are some traditional forms of ownership usually used by husband and wife. They can also be used by any other two owners without the necessity of forming a formal partnership. These relations are governed by law and do not require anything other than declaration on the deed of ownership. They are joint tenancy with the right of survivorship (JTWROS), and tenants in common. These rights and relationships are spelled out in law, but can be modified by written agreement between the parties. If modified, it is usually a smart move to adopt a form of partnership rather than the two ownership types above. Partnerships for residential ownership are the same as partnerships for commercial projects, and are covered below in the section on partnerships. I define a partnership loosely as an arrangement between the parties where funding and work responsibilities are pooled for mutual profit. The actual legal arrangement can take many different forms.

The True Cost of Partnership

That having been said, let us examine the cost of partnership, whatever the legal arrangement might be. (We shall look at the possible legal arrangements later on in the chapter.) There are many reasons to form a partnership; some of them are:

- To acquire more money for the deal
- To bolster the group's borrowing power (credit)
- To acquire additional skills

- To spread the risk
- To eliminate potential competition
- To acquire the best land (site)

The results of this "coming together" of individuals or companies are tangible factors for each party to the agreement. They include, but are not limited to, the following:

- The acquisition of a new profit opportunity
- The loss of autonomy
- Potential differing priorities of return on equity or net profits

The net result for everyone is compromise. The deal starts out with a series of written rules, and ends up being an endless series of discussions and compromises. It is rather like a successful marriage without the potential of divorce. To split up a joint venture, the asset must be liquidated, and that can be disastrous for both parties. The quest for profit dictates that compromise becomes the order of the day.

Your Money—My Time

Defining the role in any partnership depends on who is bringing what to the table; it also heavily depends on when the parties are going to join in the project. Loosely, a project goes through the following eight phases:

1. Identification of a need waiting to be fulfilled
2. Location of a specific property
3. Vetting the property
4. Conducting the feasibility study
5. Preliminary design and entitlements
6. Working drawings and financing
7. Construction and move in
8. Managing the finished asset.

The key point in the deal for the partnership/LLC is at what stage in the development process the investor comes into the deal, and at what price. The consulting partners are all contributing skills and time to earn a piece of the action, and all will join in the "joint and several" guarantee of the construction loan, but the investor can take several postures.

The Philosophy of Partnership

One of the great parts of real estate partnerships is the fact that all relationships are negotiable. You can make the deal into any arrangement that you can all agree upon. My take on it is that to make a deal work, the relationships and the profit and loss agreements must be fair and equitable or the deal may become unglued in the middle of the deal. No amount of legalese can force someone to do something that is onerous and contrary to his or her self interest, and anything that lands in litigation is a disaster. Litigation usually results in only the attorneys making money from a deal.

Borrowing

Most real estate purchases or development projects involve the use of leverage, so up to 80 percent of the costs are customarily borrowed from an experienced real estate lender. These lenders are, but are not limited to, the following organizations:

- Banks
- Savings and loans (S&Ls)
- Insurance companies
- Pension funds
- Real Estate Investment Trusts (REITs)
- Finance companies

These companies are considered to be traditional "conventional" lenders in our industry. Banks, S&Ls, and finance companies make loans on houses, and banks, insurance companies, pension funds, and REITs make loans on commercial property. Whether you are dealing with homes or commercial property, there are two classes of loans: interim and permanent. Interim loans generally carry the projects through the completion of construction; permanent loans are put into place when the projects are completed.

Interim Loans

Interim loans run the gamut from land loans to construction loans. They are designed to aid in the development of land and the construction of buildings. When a developer picks out a parcel of land to develop, he or she has to prepare the land for construction of buildings. In the case of housing, the infrastructure, streets, utilities, and services must be in place before houses can be built. The loans that are taken out for this process run from the traditional seller-carry-back land loan to gap (bridge) financing, and acquisition and development loans (A&D). An A&D loan is taken for the express purpose of funding the infrastructure prior to house construction. This is known as bridge financing. Once the infrastructure is in place, then the conventional construction loan takes place. A loan is funded to cover all costs of construction that pertain to that parcel of land dedicated to that specific building. All interim financing is interest-only or nonamortizing. All of the principal and interest is due in full at maturity.

Permanent Loans

This brings us to the subject of permanent financing. Permanent loans are, traditionally, loans that are amortizing over a specific period of time. The most common term of amortization has been 30 years, but in more recent times, since the 1980s, banks and other lenders are offering 15-year loans. Housing loans were always relatively simple. If you were buying or refinancing, the lender gave you a permanent loan. If you were renovating or building from scratch, the lender gave you a construction loan which was converted to a permanent loan at completion. This residential custom spawned the commercial Mini-perm loan.

Contracts and Consultants

Contracts in all their various forms, more than any other documents involved in the ownership and/or development process, determine the cash value of the investment. Houses and homes are easy to place a value on by the use of comparables and the market itself. In reality, when you put a price on a home and someone steps up and buys it, the price is determined by agreement. Unless something is highly unusual, residential appraisals will reflect the value as agreed upon by buyer and seller.

All project documents should be drafted with the express purpose of being enforceable, interrelated, self-referencing, and to avoid potential conflicts within the overall documentation structure. At a minimum, the set of documents required for the average home development project should include the following:

- The purchase agreement and joint escrow instructions
- Ownership documents such as articles, organization, or partnership agreements
- All governmental approval documents, including, but not limited to, the entitlement documentation applications as well as approvals
- Building permits and occupancy permits
- Construction loan documents
- Permanent loan documents
- General construction contracts and site improvement contracts
- Architectural and engineering contracts
- Utility agreements
- Any required environmental documentation

It sounds like a tall order and probably expensive. The truth of the matter is that these documents can vary all over the lot from simple one-page agreements for leasing out an apartment to a 200-page government lease for the Department of Energy (DOE). Depending on the project, the documentation will find its own level of complexity. Generally, the smaller and more rural the project, the more basic is the required documentation. Large sophisticated projects require complex and sophisticated documentation. There are common guidelines that run through all documents to make them both legal and enforceable.

The "Statute of Frauds," a federal law, states that, in essence: Real property contracts, to be enforceable, must be in writing, be of lawful intent, be executed by competent parties, and consideration must have passed between the parties.

From that as a starting point, all real property contracts come into being. The parent is the owner/developer, and the attorneys are the doctors/midwives, . It is the very proliferation of attorneys that will often dictate the level of documentation. If neither party to an agreement can afford an attorney, it will become a very simple and easily understood document.

The Purchase Agreement and Joint Escrow Instructions

While you will probably use your local board of realtors contract to buy houses, you might want to review this section when you decide to purchase land for development. There are basic areas that need to be addressed in most situations. When dealing with small parcels of land or unsophisticated sellers, it may be prudent to use a local Realtor's standard preprinted purchase form with an addendum addressing specific concerns for the site. In most instances, I recommend that a developer create a purchase agreement that can be used in all situations. That way, you, developer/buyer, will know the document well. Understanding a document and its built-in cross-references will enable you to more effectively negotiate the final document. The attorney's favorite trick for creating tools with which to manage a document is to create cross-referenced, linked conditions. This enables the insertion of conditions that are interlocked and, therefore, less obvious to the seller. This sounds devious but it is accepted practice for most legal documentation.

The basic information needed to be included in the document is as follows:

- The legal description of the land
- The size of the land and how it will be determined

Heads Up

Personally, I favor a document that tells the seller in plain English what I'm up to and lays out the schedule, the contingencies, and the price and terms I'm willing to pay for his or her accommodation. Without the wholehearted cooperation of the seller, it is very difficult to accomplish the entitlement process. Slipping one over on him or her in the document negotiation process will not go over well in the long run.

- The price
- Schedule of payments and close of escrow
- Seller's and buyer's representatives
- The designated escrow holder or title company
- Seller's scope of work and the permitted timeframes
- Buyer's scope of work and related timeframes
- Contingencies, and how the deposits are treated (refundable or not)
- Buyer's and seller's representations
- Buyer's and seller's recourse
- Default provisions
- Governing law and miscellaneous provisions

Any attorney worth his or her salt can flesh out an agreement to include many more items, but the above outlined provisions should get the job done.

Architectural and Engineering Contracts

This area of contract negotiation is a classic area of negotiation, centering on responsibility and cost. The architectural and engineering professions have created a standard document called the American Institute of Architecture (AIA) contract. The consultants will tell you that it is the industry standard, and, unfortunately, due to its acceptance by many unsophisticated owner/developers, it is. Do not execute it without specific modifications. Most areas of contention center on the price of services and the scope of work. I always take the position that a consultant should be "expert" in his or her field, or should not be hired. An expert should be able to assess the scope of work and quote a fixed price. Only if the owner makes a substantial and easily defined significant change in the scope of work should there be an extra charge. Avoid all hourly fees. Get firm written prices for all proposed extras, *before* authorizing the work. Make sure the contract states that you will not pay for any changes not authorized, in writing, in advance.

Make each consultant financially responsible for all mistakes in design, both the cost of correcting the design and the cost of any remedial construction work involved. If the consultant is inspecting work in progress during construction, make him or her jointly responsible with the contractor for the cost of any remedial work required to correct shoddy, unspecified, or unsafe construction, as well as any losses due to the delay in the project's scheduled completion date. Remember, if you are delayed when moving in, the interim cost of interest on the construction loan continues to climb.

Heads Up
Interest goes on until the loan is paid in full.

Building Permits and Occupancy Permits

Building permits involve filling out forms and paying the required fees, which vary from reasonable, in a pro-development municipality, and confiscatory in a "no-growth" municipality. The issuance of the permit itself occurs after the municipality's building department has examined and approved the project's working drawings. This is a costly and exhaustive experience, often involving redesign and the changing of the project's design characteristics to fit the department's interpretation of the governing ordinances. Fighting the building department's interpretations can be disastrous. Serious delays and increased costs will surely follow. Bureaucracy is no joke, and its practitioners have been perfecting the art of frustrating people's desires for many thousands of years. *Give them what they want!* When construction is completed in accordance with the approved plans and specs, the municipality's building inspection department issues a certificate of occupancy for each building.

General Construction and Site Improvement Contracts

Since there is so much money involved in the construction process, the contracts must be carefully drafted and administered. These documents can make or break a project. In general, the industry tries to use the AIA documents, but I strongly recommend against them. My reason is, as usual, they are drafted by architects, and therefore put the architect strongly in the driver's seat as the owner's representative. Even if you are a novice, you do not want to abdicate your owner's prerogatives to the architect, whose expertise is supposed to be in building design, not real estate investment. Make your own decisions, always! The architect should oversee and report to you, and you should make the decision. This is true whether you are developing a property from scratch, or rebuilding tenant spaces in an existing structure.

This set of contracts will determine the cost, the schedule, and the quality of the improvements. Selection of a reputable general contractor is the key to achieving a quality project. Good general contractors charge a profitable fee for their work and expect to earn that fee. The owner's role in this process is to find a good one, treat him or her fairly, pay on time, and enforce the terms of the contract, the plans, and the specifications. Key items in the contract to be negotiated are:

- Price
- Contingencies
- Payment terms: draws and terms of the draw
- Withholding
- Subcontractors

- Work rules
- Bonding for performance and completion
- Schedules
- Completion date
- Penalties and incentives
- Quality control
- Independent inspection

Here again the ubiquitous AIA document rears its ugly head. Try not to use one, but if you must, modify it to be responsible and performance-oriented. Make sure the responsible party pays for the mistakes, including loss of time, interest, and rental income. To have an enforceable penalty clause, there must be a corresponding incentive clause. It is a good idea. Do not begrudge the payment of incentive fees. Remember, the rent will start early and compensate the owners for the additional fees to be paid, and interest will be saved to offset the incentive pay. The penalties, if assessed, should offset the additional interest incurred by the delay.

General Contractors

Most people who invest in real estate use a general contractor to build anything. The "general" is the contractor with overall responsibility and financial accountability. He or she will give you a price, and you must make him or her build it as planned for that price. There are ways to accomplish this, whether using the traditional bid method, or the design-build method. First of all, ask the general to state in the contract that he or she has reviewed the plans and specifications in detail, and that he or she did not find any design deficiencies. Further, have him or her acknowledge that he or she is expert in the construction method contemplated in the plans, and is competent to review the plans and construct the building according to the plans and specs. Offer the contractor the opportunity to put any deficiencies in writing before the contract is executed, stating that this is the sole opportunity to change the scope of work and alter the price. Discrepancies discovered during the course of construction will be corrected at the expense of the contractor.

Heads Up
You must keep track of payments and lien wavers, or you will end up paying twice if there is a dispute.

Once the stage is set, then the balance of the contract should contain, at a minimum, the following clauses:

- Name of the owner, contractor, and engineer or architect.
- The location and description of the site, also shown in detail in Exhibit "A."

- A list of the contract documents and a detailed scope of work, as further detailed in Exhibit "B."
- The project schedule, including start and end dates, referencing a detailed schedule in Exhibit "C." Include incentive and penalty clauses as part of this section
- Spell out the contract price, and reference a detailed cost breakdown shown in Exhibit "D."
- Delineate the progress payment procedures, including samples of the paperwork required by the lender, attached as Exhibit "E."
- Specify when the final payment will be made, and under what conditions.
- Specify performance and completion bonds required, if any.
- Address the need for, and who pays for, temporary facilities such as power, storage, and security, and who is responsible for stored materials.
- Outline the insurance requirements for both owner and contractor, and do not permit any work to start until all certificates of insurance are in your hand.
- Outline the work rules requiring safety and drug laws. Put the responsibility on the general to enforce them, including the expense of delays due to shutdowns or noncompliance.
- Discuss the rights of assignment, and the owners' and contractors' responsibilities to each other.
- Outline the payment and lien procedures. Insist that there will be no progress payment until all lien waivers for the previous payment are attached to the new invoice. Include material suppliers as well. Make sure you include all suppliers and subcontractors who have filed a preliminary lien notice at the start of the work.
- Decide whether you will arbitrate a dispute or settle things in court. I recommend binding arbitration. It's faster and cheaper for all concerned.
- Provide for termination of the contract for cause. You will also have to allow the contractor to terminate in the event of nonpayment of contracted work.
- Add the usual boilerplate clauses, sign and date the agreement.

> **Heads Up**
>
> Try to get someone local, as code compliance, zoning regulations, etc., are administered by each individual municipality. The consultant's specialized local knowledge and reputation will save you both time and money in the end.

Subcontractors

If you choose to use a general contractor as a construction manager, instead of as a general contractor, you will have to sign contracts with all the subcontractors (subs) and suppliers. This is a good way to go, as it gives you more control and reduces the contractor's fees. It is a lot more paperwork, but you will find that you can learn a great deal about the construction process if you go through this exercise at least once. I prefer it to the general contract.

Architects and Engineers

These individuals are the most technical of any consultants you are going to hire. In view of this, you must research their backgrounds, and verify their expertise. Get recommendations from people you trust, get references, and check with the references. Look into their financial standing and make sure that they will be able to back up any professional liability incurred during your project. Insist on "errors and omissions" insurance.

When do you need them? If you are renovating or developing a house, the architect and engineer will be on board as soon as you tie up the property. You should do your research and selection during the time you are completing your market analysis. For simple home renovation projects, you are best off using a house planner or drafting service with the input of a good structural engineer. The principles of dealing with the house planner and the architect are similar, but the house planner is less complex and less expensive. My best recommendation for any housing project is stick to using a planner until the project becomes complex enough for an architect.

Heads Up

The architect's right to approve anything must be subject to your express, written approval; especially changes!

How to contract with them. The average architect will want you to execute a pre-printed AIA contract. I do not recommend this, but you will have to use it as a place to start. My normal practice is to amend a document by crossing out and initialing the offending language and adding an addendum to the agreement with my desired language. I have, over the years, developed a version of my own which few architects will sign. You will, most likely, have to use the AIA document. There are areas that you will need to amend, and they will include, at least, the following:

- *The scope of work.* This is usually an exhibit. Plan this very carefully, and be specific as to the work expected.
- *Reproductions and other expenses.* Include a basic list of the number of progress prints required, as well as a sufficient number of working drawing sets for permit submittal and for the general contractor. Insist that he or she provide you with sepia (reproducible drawing) of each finished drawing, so that you can order your own sets when necessary. It is considerably cheaper.

This is especially important when dealing with the contractor. You want your architect to be responsible for compliance, with you approving any changes in material or specification.

- Payment should be a flat fee, and extras or changes in scope should be agreed on in writing *before* the work is done, or do not pay for them.
- Insist on errors and omission insurance and liability insurance.

This item is crucial and it includes you, as well, if you have employees. If you deal with consultants only, make sure you have the certificates on file before they enter the site to do work. Include them in all the contracts.

Heads Up

Any consultant that goes onto your building site or into your building MUST have the proper liability and workers' compensation insurance. If he or she does not, and something happens, you WILL pay for it!

Other Consultants

There are a variety of other consultants that you will be encountering over the period of your involvement in real estate investment, and they require different arrangements. You will find that there are some who do not work with contracts, and they are, customarily, attorneys and accountants. Research and feasibility consultants, site research, such as surveyors, environmental consultants, and soils consultants like to work from short, memo-type agreements written as loosely as possible. There are ways to work with these people that will be to your advantage when disputes arise. Make sure the scope of the work is broadly stated, your requirements are met, and payment is subject to the successful conclusion of the work.

Heads Up

Whenever possible, get a fixed price from a consultant, put it in writing, and allow no extra charges unless you approve the change order in advance, in writing.

CHAPTER 14

Plans and Other Documents

he reality of real estate investment and development is paperwork, paperwork, and more paperwork. It enables the owner/investor to control any project and ensure the orderly work and collection of rents.

Paperwork falls into two categories: plans and contracts. Both are legal documents. All paperwork involved in a project is crucial to its success. Each document must be created with an eye for detail and enforceability. An investor/developer must look at the plans and legal documents with an eye not only to long-term enforceability, but also to cost control, schedule, and occupancy by the tenants or prospective buyers.

Heads Up

It is imperative that the paperwork be as correct, free of conflicts, and as clear and concise as possible. For this portion of the work The KISS principle should be your operating mantra; "Keep it simple, stupid!"

Plans and Specifications

While the plans and specifications are considered legal documents, the graphic, rather than the written nature of their form, has traditionally forced them to be handled separately from all the other legal documents and contracts. Plans and specifications for a project evolve in stages and each stage serves a crucial function. This section will follow a typical set of plans as it evolves into the final construction document phase, using drawings from residential and some commercial projects because they are at a scale that will make it easy for a newcomer to distinguish the illustration being referred to. Residential plans are used in the same way as commercial plans, for renovation and new construction.

Phase One: Schematic Design

This set of plans is the first step in defining the scope of the work, as well as the quality and the character of the project. It is essential in establishing the financial feasibility of the project. At a minimum it should include, from the civil engineer, a boundary survey ("survey") and topographic map ("topo"). These tools will then be used by the architect or planner to create the schematic design set of plans that will include the following:

- Preliminary grading plan
- Site plan
- An elevation
- A section
- Floor plate for each floor
- An outline specification
- A rendering

These tools will be used to establish feasibility, obtain required governmental approvals, and entice prospective tenants to execute leases in the proposed development.

Site plans. The preliminary grading plan and the site plan are the first two plans to be created. They should show finished grades to establish the building pad, the required parking layout, and the landscaped areas on the site, locating the buildings, the parking, and showing the location and extent of landscaping on the site. See Figure 14.1.

Figure 14.1—*Site Plan*

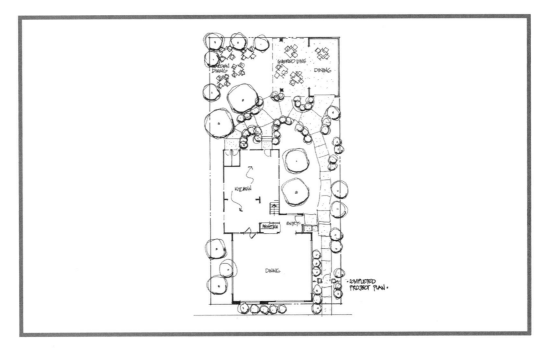

Elevations. The building's elevation plan will show preliminary details about the look of the project, the number of floors, the roof-line, the window heights, and the detail of the finish work. It will also establish the character of the building. The exterior of the building sets the image, the interior provides the livability, and the "finish" establishes the quality. In addition, the elevations will enable the governmental agencies that have jurisdiction over the project to determine the compatibility of the project with the surrounding area. From the site plan and the elevation, an artist can produce a "rendering" of the building depicting the artist's view of the future project. The intent of this (Figure 14.2) is to show the public how the building will look from the outside when completed.

Sections. Figure 14.3 is a cross section of the building, exposing the proposed structural system, the access (stairs and elevators), the utility accesses, the floor elevations, and preliminary details for exterior finish work. This particular plan will be a combination of input from three professionals: the architect for aesthetics, the engineer for structural design, and the contractor for cost analysis. The developer will be the final judge of what is planned.

Figure 14.2—*Elevation*

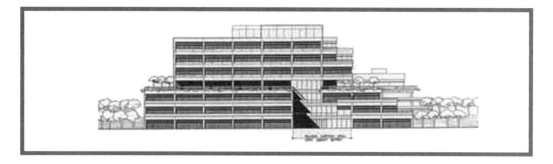

Figure 14.3—*Section*

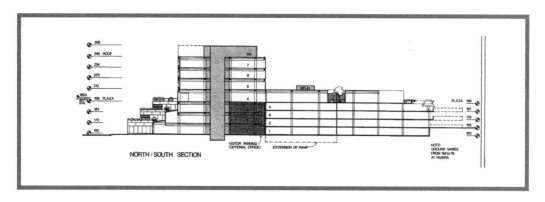

NORTH / SOUTH SECTION

Floor plans. The floor plan (Figure 14.4) depicts the floor space (the useable space) on each floor of the building.

Outline specifications. When the building design has been established, the preliminary specification or "specs" are written to establish the quality and detail expected of the building. This document is the key to establishing, early in the life of the project, exactly what the project will cost when constructed. This spec, together with the other preliminary plans, can be used to "bid" the project. No amount of retrofitting can make up for taking shortcuts in this process. Outline specifications cover the gamut of topics from soil compaction to any and all components of the building. Often, rather than specify a make or model of component, a performance specification is proposed so that competent subcontractors can propose proprietary packages such as air handling or other mechanical systems. In this event this type of bid becomes a bid as well as a "design/build" proposal.

Figure 14.4—*Floor Plan*

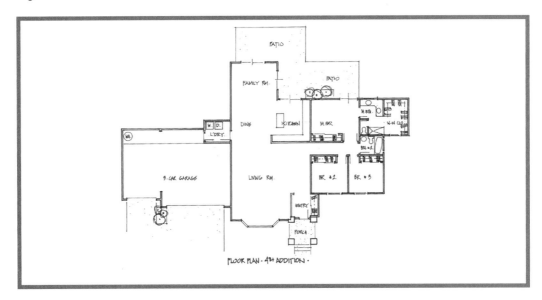

Figure 14.5—*Rendering*

Renderings. The rendering (Figure 14.5) is the most important piece of advertising and promotional material that will ever be created to represent the proposed project. Overdoing the rendering is a common failing of developers and planners alike. Sometimes the rendering will depict what owner/builders want rather than what they can afford to build.

The problem with overdoing this is obvious. The rendering is designed to show the public, the local governmental agency, and the prospective buyers, what the project will look like when completed. It had better be very close to the rendering, because both approvals and lease documents are going to be based upon the representations made in the plans and specs. Variations are permitted, but complete redesign necessitates a fresh start with both the governmental body and the tenants. They will hold the developer to the approved plans.

Phase Two: Working Drawings and Construction Documents

The working drawings, also known as the final plans and specifications, are produced to serve multiple functions. Primarily, they define the exact nature, size, shape, and texture of the building to be constructed. The governmental examination and approval of these documents (plans) is a necessary precondition to the issuance of a building permit. The "approved plans" will serve as a basis for the issuance of the building permit and a guideline for the inspection and certification of the structure and civil engineering work to be performed. Strict adherence to the approved plans is necessary for the governmental agency (the building department) to allow occupancy of the completed project. If the project is completed in accordance with the approved plans, an occupancy permit is issued, and the owner or tenant may occupy the building.

Plans and specs cover many areas, and can be simple, uncomplicated plans that contain all the data on several sheets, or run into hundreds of sheets of plans and volumes of specifications. In general, the necessary information must contain details for the site work, civil engineering, grading and paving, utility supply and distribution, detailed landscaping, and irrigation plans.

For the structures the minimum divisions of both plans and specifications must include the following:

- Foundation and soil preparation
- Structural design and details
- Floor plans for each floor
- Cross sections and connection details
- Finish schedules
- Detailed mechanical, electrical, and plumbing plans
- Any specialty trade details, such as elevators, escalators, etc.

The total cost of these documents, from preliminary plans through the completion of the working drawings, can vary from 5 to 10 percent of the total cost of construction.

Financial Plans, or the Numbers

Over the period of the last 25 years, I have had the best results with documents designed to serve the design/build/BID scenario, rather than the traditional fixed bid process. One of the most prevalent problems inherent in the development industry is maintaining a fixed budget. Operating for the last 25 years in a traditional joint venture format with all the capital paid in up front has forced me to ensure that all projects stay within the prescribed budgets. To date, this method of operation has not failed me.

The Logic of Accounting

Since real estate investment is a money-oriented endeavor, you need to keep score. That is done in two ways: traditional accounting (bookkeeping) and spreadsheets. Accounting systems are standardized the world over, and everyone connected with business knows what a profit-and-loss statement (P&L) and a balance sheet are, and what they can tell you. The limitations of traditional accounting are that they contain so little information needed to actually manage a piece of investment real estate. It is for this reason that developers, investors, and property managers have created spreadsheets to augment the financial picture and manage the properties. The combination of the two systems creates a complete picture of the investment from a financial point of view.

Traditional Accounting

These systems are all based on the double-entry bookkeeping system. They are available from a variety of sources and are completely computerized and very user-friendly. The double entry system is simple. It is based on the fact that each component or transaction has two parts to it. The breakdown is debits and credits. Debits are income, and credits are payments. Each transaction has two components; i.e., rent received from a tenant is both cash in the bank (a debit) and rent (a credit). It is in this way that, when the transaction is entered in tandem, the books are considered "balanced." This form of accounting is handy when summarizing all transactions into a snapshot in time.

Spreadsheets Are Your Most Useful Deal Tools

These tools, traditionally used in commercial projects, have been readily adapted for use in home construction and reconstruction. They can make a significant difference in any deal. Their purpose is to provide information at a glance, showing items like:

- Original budget
- Contracted costs
- Monthly expenditures
- Budget variances
- Total costs

These items are included in my primary spreadsheet for any type of project, residential or commercial.

Insurance

Insurance in any transaction is critical. There are two kinds of insurance that everyone must have when working on your property, including you: liability and workers' compensation insurance. There are other insurances necessary when dealing with specialized consultants, like errors and omission insurance, but everyone needs the two above to cover their potential liabilities.

Workers' compensation and general liability. Liability insurance insures you from injuries that happen to third parties. If someone trips and falls down your stairs, you're covered. Workers' compensation insurance, even if you do not have employees, covers you when anyone doing work on your property is hurt.

Other insurance. As an owner, you will need the following insurance to operate the building:

- If you are renovating or constructing a building, you will need "course-of-construction," fire and extended coverage, workers' compensation, and a liability umbrella insurance policy.
- As an owner operating a building, you will need fire and extended coverage, rent replacement insurance with a workers' compensation rider. I also always recommend an umbrella override policy.

The "additional insured's" option. Rather than have everyone connected with the project or management of a building carry redundant coverage, you can buy and maintain the master policy, naming all the other entities as "additional insured(s)" to your policy. The other companies in question can then pass along the savings to you and lower your insurance costs.

If you are renovating or building a new building, you will find that this option will save you many thousands of dollars.

CHAPTER 15

Loans

ost real property carries a mortgage due to the fact that leverage allows an owner to dramatically improve the yield on invested capital. No matter how much you borrow, all real property loans start out the same way: application, commitment, and funding. There are some fundamental differences between residential mortgages and commercial loans, which will be addressed here. Residential loans are relatively simple and tend to be handled informally. They are pretty much on a take-it-or-leave-it basis, whereas commercial loans are negotiated at the beginning and then granted or not.

Residential

Residential loans tend to be less structured until it is time to actually execute the loan documents, and then you might find out that the lender has changed the terms on you at the last minute. Usually you start out with a mortgage broker who gets a handwritten signed application from you and collects a check for the appraisal. This gets the ball rolling. To protect yourself from the usual practice of both lenders and mortgage brokers, always do the following when making a loan application:

- Make sure that you add language to the application that makes any fees and expenses contingent on the loan being "granted as applied for."
- Keep a legible copy of the signed application.
- When you are notified that the loan has been granted, request a letter from the lender or mortgage broker stating that the loan was "granted as applied for." This will serve as a commitment when attached to your original mortgage application.

Many times I have experienced a last-minute change in the terms and rates at the loan closing. At that time you are stuck; you have to close on the home and the mortgage loan or you are homeless. If you have in your possession a copy of the original application and the commitment letter you requested, you will have the lender and the mortgage broker over a barrel. They will have to amend the papers on the spot to reflect the original application.

The bait-and-switch. A popular change that the lender may pull at the time of closing is to require insurance and tax impounds. This is normal when you have a loan that is 70 to 80 percent of value. If, however, you are applying for a low-percentage loan, you can request in your application that the lender waive the tax and insurance impounds. Most lenders ignore this request, and, at closing, require you to re-execute the application, typed this time, and altered on the newly typed loan application. Do not be persuaded that you have to accept this. At a loan closing four years ago, I picked up a change on a 40 percent loan-to-value mortgage and made them change the documents on the spot. I merely pointed out that they made the commitment as applied for (as evidenced by the letter from the lender), I had paid the

Heads Up

Even though you are only contemplating a residential project, you should keep in mind that commercial loans are also addressed here. You might someday want to trade your paid-for home or your portfolio of rental homes for an apartment complex for a retirement income stream; the insight into the commercial loan process will be very helpful later.

fees as requested, and if they changed the commitment at the last minute they would be liable for breach of contract and damages. The upshot of this lesson is, make your application carefully and legibly at the outset, request the exact terms that you would like to have, and if the loan is committed, make sure you have a commitment letter for the loan "as applied for." By doing this, you should be able to avoid any last minute crisis.

Commercial Loans

Commercial real estate loans fall into two categories: new loans and refinancing. New loans are construction loans and first-time permanent loans. Everything else is a refinancing. All commercial loans begin with a written request to a mortgage banker or mortgage broker. When a lender expresses an interest in making the loan, the lender usually issues a "terms sheet" whose detailed terms are subject to the lender verifying that your representations regarding leases, financial condition, and income and expenses are accurate. Construction loans are often applied for directly with the lender, especially if you are an established borrower in the market.

The terms sheet. A terms sheet will be similar to the one shown in Table 15.1.

Table 15.1—*Lenders Term Sheet*

	Sample Terms Sheet Fast Money Lending Company	
1	Mortgage banker	XYZ Mortgage, Ltd.
2	Loan type	Fixed rate
3	Property	The Shopping Center
4	City, state	Podunk, USA
5	Quote date	9/14/2004
6	Loan amount	$16,200,000
7	LTV, debt service coverage	75% LTV / 1.25 DSC
8	Term	10 years
9	Amortization	30 years
10	Margin	1.61%
11	Treasury issue	10 year treasury

> ## Heads Up
> Do not stand for last-minute changes. If you have done as I instructed above you will prevail. I have done it several times.

Table 15.1—*Lenders Term Sheet*

	Sample Terms Sheet	
	Fast Money Lending Company, continued	
12	Current index rate	4.13%
13	Current interest rate	5.74%
14	Interest rate floor	5.40%
15	Loan fee	None
16	Interest calculation	Actual/360
17	Liability	Non-recourse, with standard carve-out liability
18	Assumable	Yes—with a 1% assumption fee
19	Prepayment penalty	Yield Maintenance/Flexpay
20	Lock-in period	3 years
21	Upfront standby deposit	.5% of the loan amount (refundable at closing)
22	Rate lock available	Yes—additional 1.5% deposit with remargining rights. 100% refundable at closing.
23	Rate lock cost	Included in the spread until 9/1/2005.
24	Tax and insurance impound	Required
25	Re-tenanting reserves	Required
26	Structural reserves	Required
27	Single purpose entity	Required—SPE Level III
28	Lock-box	Not Required
29	Legal opinion letter	Not Required
30	3rd party report deposit	$12,000—includes items with *
31	Physical condition report	Required *
32	Appraisal	Required *
33	Environmental Phase I	Required *
34	PML or seismic study	Required *
35	ALTA survey	Not required, unless required by title company.
36	Legal fees	None required, unless borrower changes standard CMO loan documents.
37	Processing/closing fee	$8,500
38	Other	
	Preliminary quote subject to credit/underwriting review and site inspection.	
	Spreads are held on quotes converted to completed applications within one business day.	

Referring to Table 15.1, take a walk through this document and interpret exactly what the lender is offering.

- Lines 1 through 6 contain the basic loan information.
- Line 7 says that the loan is to be a 75 percent loan to value (LTV) with a debt service coverage ratio (DSC) of 1.25. That means that the NIBDS must equal 125 percent of the proposed mortgage payment.
- Lines 8 and 9 are self-explanatory.
- Line 10, the margin refers to the percentage over the ten-year treasury notes' daily rate of interest at the time the rate is fixed.
- Lines 12 and 13 show that the current treasury rate is 4.13 percent and adding the margin, if the rate is fixed today, the loan rate of interest will be 5.74 percent.
- Line 14. The lowest rate the lender is willing to consider at the time of fixing the rate is 5.4 percent.
- Line 15. There is no commitment fee.
- Line 16. Interest is calculated on a daily basis, on the unpaid balance of the loan, on the basis of a 360 day year and a 30 day month.
- Line 17. No personal guarantees are required except on the "carve-outs'" (fraud and misrepresentation by the borrowers).
- Line 18. This states that the loan is assumable by a buyer with the payment of a 1 percent fee.
- Line 19 spells out the prepayment penalty, if any; in this case there will be a yield maintenance clause and a loan cancellation fee. You will get the details on this in the loan application document.
- Line 20. There is no prepayment allowed during the first three years of the loan.
- Line 21. To book the loan the borrower must pay a refundable fee of .5 percent.
- Line 22 indicates that to lock the rate, the borrower must put up, on the day the rate is locked, a fee of 1.5 percent which, together with the standby fee is refundable at closing.
- Lines 23 through 29 are self explanatory.
- Line 30 indicates that the borrower must tender, with the application, a $12,000 fee for the appraisal and any other third party reports required by the lender.
- Lines 31 through 38 are self-explanatory.
- The last two lines are lender boilerplate.

Now you know how to read a modern terms sheet. You should find that almost any lender's terms sheet will be similar, and you are free to negotiate any of the points up to the execution of the formal application. That's when the paperwork really starts.

The Application

Loan applications differ, but construction loans used to have a permanent loan to "take out" the construction lender, and this requires a "forward" commitment (approximately 18 to 24 months out) at the time the construction loan is granted. A typical home remodel or original construction loan will be a mini-perm type loan which starts out as a construction loan and is converted to a permanent or amortizing loan at the completion of the house. If you are building for sale to someone else, it would remain an interest-only loan until sale, and if you are going to occupy the home, it will be converted to a permanent loan.

A loan application will include, at the least, the following items:
- The application, or loan request, with specific conditions
- The plans and specifications of the project
- Financial projections
- A leasing exhibit showing current and projected leases
- Copies of all executed leases
- Financial statements of the borrower(s)

This application will, in general, contain the following clauses in letter form, addressed specifically to the lender:
- A specific file number and project reference
- A deadline date for the application
- Name and legal identity of the borrower
- The specifics on the proposed security, and proposed document (deed of trust, mortgage, etc.)
- Application Data Sheet, including information regarding principals of the borrowing entity, financial condition of the principals, management of the property, additional information on the property, existing debt on the property and authorization for credit inquiries by the lender is included on Exhibit "A," attached to the document
- A statement regarding any loan guarantees offered, if any, or a statement regarding the borrower's desire for a nonrecourse loan
- The terms and conditions of the proposed loan, including the following:
  - loan amount
  - interest rate

- payment terms
- impound accounts for taxes and insurance
- annual financials
- pre-payment terms
- a yield maintenance clause, if any
- assignment and transferability clauses
- secondary financing provisions
- lender's rights to approval of leases, fees, and costs
- The proposed application fee
- The commitment fee
- A condition precedent to closing, such as appraisal, environmental report, architect's and engineer's certification, seismic reports, etc.
- Broker's role and fees
- Breakdown of costs and who pays for what
- Proposed closing conditions such as:
  - Lender's inspection
  - Required leases
  - Documentation list
  - Appraisal
  - Change in interest based on prime at the time
  - Environmental documentation
  - Architectural and engineering report requirement
  - Tenant Estoppel Certificates
  - Miscellaneous provisions
  - Boilerplate clauses
  - Receipt by lender
  - Borrower's representations
  - Additional requirements
  - The date and the borrower's signature

> **Heads Up**
>
> The industry finally came to the rescue with the advent of the "mini-perm" loan, modeled on the residential construction/permanent loan. This was a construction loan that, for an additional fee (usually one point), could be converted into a fully amortizing short-term permanent loan. This new arrangement allowed a borrower more time to shop for a more sympathetic permanent loan.

Commitments. Once you have signed this application and included all the exhibits requested, you can attach the check and sit back and wait. Loan underwriting usually takes many weeks and is followed by formal approval by the lender's loan committee. After that, you will get a commitment letter reiterating the terms of the loan approved. Once granted, the commitment letter will contain, in addition to the terms spelled out in the executed application, at least the following caveats:

- Acceptance language and a restatement of the terms granted
- The date by which the borrower must accept and pay for the loan commitment
- Enumeration of fees, charges, and closing costs; who pays what and when
- The closing date usually stated as "on or before"
- Conditions of funding such as lender's approval of leases, the physical inspection of the buildings, collection of Estoppel Certificates, proof of taxes having been paid, and a minimum percentage occupancy at the time of closing
- A date and time of acceptance signature block

Heads Up

In the old days the construction lender was concerned about the "bankabilty" of the take-out lender, and insisted on specific language to ensure the take out. The mini-perm has put a stop to most of this nonsense.

Aspects of a commitment. You would think that with all this paper, you would be OK to go. The truth is, maybe not. In the case of a forward commitment, it has happened that, at the time of closing, lender's have declined to fund. If there is an exculpatory clause in their commitment that they can hang their hat on, you are out of luck, but sometimes lenders simply run into trouble and do not have the funds to close. They are liable, but it can be a nightmare trying to sue and collect. I have not heard of this happening in recent times, but be aware that this is a remote possibility, and keep track of your lender during that period up to closing. Be in contact with your mortgage banker. The banker is also liable as they have brokered the deal. Generally, if trouble surfaces the mortgage banker can find you a substitute loan at no further cost.

Funding and Documentation

Residential loans and commercial loans are handled in the same manner. The mortgage loan is a two-part document: the note and the deed of trust or, in the eastern United States, the mortgage.

When a loan funds, there are mounds of documents and procedures to be followed. In the case of the construction loan, the lender is aware of the contractor's potential lien rights, and wants to be assured that the loan will have "priority" of payment over any contractor's liens. This is accomplished by inspecting the site prior to closing to assure the lender and the title company that work has not yet started. Thus assured, the title company issues the lender a lender's policy of title insurance, in this case the aforementioned ALTA extended coverage policy, and all is well. The loan is then recorded. The loan documents are in two parts: the note and the security agreement, and a deed of trust or a mortgage, which will be recorded against the property at closing.

Note. The note is a relatively simple document that will contain the following information:
- Principal sum
- Date
- Maker and entity identification
- Address of the maker
- Holder
- Holder's address
- Interest rate
- Term
- Payments
- Definition of late payments and charges
- Default interest rate
- The promise to pay
- Partial payment provision
- Acceleration and pre-payment provisions
- The security description (Deed of Trust or Mortgage) attached as an exhibit
- Boilerplate regarding attorney's fees, governing law, venue, etc.
- The signature of the maker and the date

There may be more on your note, but these basics will surely be in any note.

Deed of trust or mortgage. This security agreement puts the world on notice that the owner of this property owes money to a specific lender and loosely outlines the terms. It is intended to preclude the owner from selling the property and ignoring the note obligation. The deed of trust or mortgage document will contain at least the following information:
- A cover sheet containing the recording information
- The documents, entitled Deed of Trust, or Mortgage
- The account number
- The borrower's name and mailing address
- The beneficiary's name and mailing address
- The trustee's name and mailing address
- The date
- The property's description: location, town, county and state, address and legal description attached as an exhibit
- The original loan amount on the note
- Recitals
- The terms and conditions, legal defense, attorney's fees, liens, payments, etc.

- Mutual agreements; damages, trespass, rights of assignment, partial reconveyance, personal guarantees, if any, surrender and satisfaction, and reconveyance
- Additional security, if any
- Default provisions and remedies in default
- Recording authority
- Successors in interest
- Rights of assignment by the beneficiary
- The borrower's signature and date of execution

The reassuring thing about these documents is that they are universal. Unless you are a very wealthy person, you will have little latitude in negotiating changes in your lender's documents. Be comforted that everyone else is in the same boat. Remember, it is their money, and you are trying to rent it. The terms are theirs, not yours. After all, you are the supplicant. Close your eyes and sign, then go out and make some money to repay the loan. Try to make enough so that you can keep some for yourself!

How to deal with loans in relation to your project is covered in Chapter 16, Dealing with Contractors.

Dealing with Contractors

I t matters little what you are doing with real estate—whether you're remodeling your home, expanding it, re-tenanting a commercial property, or developing a new property—sooner or later, you will be dealing with contractors. Licensed contractors are only one group of people who build buildings. It is legal for other people to build buildings as well; for instance, a homeowner can build his or her own home so long as it meets code and it is inspected by the building department. Handymen can work on your property as well.

This chapter leans heavily on controlling costs for new construction in a development deal, but it applies just as meaningfully to a renovation or tenant-improvement situation.

Licensing, Bonding, and Payment Enforcement

With all that is going on in the building industry, there is, and should be, people regulating the people doing the work. In most states, this agency is called the "Registrar of Contractors;" it is state-operated, and regulated by state laws. The way it works is that individual companies are licensed by the Registrar of Contractors to do the work. This involves an individual who "qualifies" for the license, having passed the test and posted a bond against faulty work or fraudulent practices. The companies are licensed, not the individuals doing the work. Individuals running their own companies, the one-man band types, are usually licensed as well.

One of the primary reasons for using licensed contractors is that they have been tested to determine that they have a minimum experience to do the work, and they are bonded at the time of licensing. To become licensed, each contractor, general and subcontractor alike, has to put up a bond or a cash payment to the recovery fund. If they do not do a professional job, they can be made to correct their work or lose their licenses. In addition, to a limited extent, the owner may recover damages against the registrar's recovery fund. This is only of use to homeowners for small amounts of money; commercial contracts have to rely on specific bonds purchased for a particular job. This system protects the owner and the contractor; it assures the homeowner or commercial owner that the people who are doing the work are regulated and meet minimum standards for competency, and it protects the contractor in the sense that the contractor has the right to enforce payment; only licensed contractors may lien a property for nonpayment for work performed. Contractors fall into two major categories, generals and subcontractors.

General Contractors

General contractors, or the "GC," are licensed generalists who deal with an entire project, and subcontractors are specialists who deal with only one part of the work. Some subcontractors may act as general contractors if the job at hand falls primarily under their specialty; for instance, a power plant project may be correctly generaled by the electrical contractor, and a dam project may be generaled by an earthmoving contractor. To serve as a general contractor, these companies must also be licensed as general contractors. In addition, general contractors may do some of the subcontractor work such as framing or concrete placement. As a rule, however, the general contractor earns his or her keep by overseeing the entire job, taking responsibility for budget, scheduling, and completion. His or her compensation is generally twofold: overhead or general conditions, and profit. The general conditions may include, but not be limited to, the following cost items:

- Mobilization {moving onto and off of the job site)
- Demolition
- Site supervision
- Layout
- Insurance
- Site security
- General cleanup
- Providing an on site office and communications
- Temporary power and water

Subcontractors

Subcontractors, or subs, provide all the specialty labor, and they include, but are not limited to, the following specialties:

- Earth movers and heavy equipment operators
- Concrete placement and finishers
- Carpenters
- Electricians
- Plumbers
- Mechanical contractors
- HVAC contractors
- Elevator and escalator installers
- Painters and finishers

As part of these subcontractor specialties, there are further divisions:

Heavy equipment operators. These folks drive the big machines: diggers, compactors, haulers, and lifters. They are also, quite frequently, general contractors in their own right on large land improvement projects. They also tend to be uniformly the most unionized of the trades.

Concrete placement and finishers. These subs form and pour the concrete for a diverse assortment of structures ranging from foundations to fire protection. Some of the concrete such as a foundation is merely formed and poured, and other structures such as walls and floors are also finished for architectural effect.

Carpenters. This trade has the following specialties within it:
- Framers are the people that work as a team, and they are responsible for erecting the structure of a new building and putting on the rough roofing and siding. They then move on to a new building. You will only need a framer if you are developing a building from scratch or adding space to an existing building.

- Finish carpenters take over from the framers and apply the finished siding and the interior. There are even specialists who deal only with doors and windows, and people who do hardwood floors and decorative millwork.
- Cabinetmakers and millwork specialists install the cabinets and add the fancy trim throughout the house that establishes the basic décor. There are even specialists within this grouping that make the cabinets and specialty items such as stair railings and trim.

Plumbers. Plumbers vary from steamfitters to general plumbers. They are most often broken down as follows:

- Steamfitters work in heavy industry and shipping. They handle heavy pressure piping, boilers, and steam generators as well.
- Site and underground pipe fitters install sewers and water systems up to the buildings.
- General plumbers do the plumbing for the buildings and hook up and install plumbing fixtures.

Electricians. Electrical work is also broken down into subspecialties.

- High voltage transmission and power plant work is a specialty that is in the "heavy construction" category.
- Site electrical work, distributing power within subdivisions, is a further specialty involving underground installation and working with transformers and distribution systems.
- General electricians deal with installing the basic electrical services in a building as well as the distribution of power throughout the buildings.
- The final specialty, which is a subspecialty of the general electrician, is the trim man or woman. He or she installs all the light fixtures and appliances in the finished building.

Painters and finishers. These professionals apply décor to the finished structures. There are several specialties that overlap with other trades, but deserve their own mention:

- Painters and wallpaper hangers
- Bath accessory installers
- Glass and mirror suppliers
- Cabinet shops making cultured marble walls and vanity tops
- Kitchen countertop makers, work in Formica, Corrian, Granite, and other stone
- Carpet layers

- Flooring installers use tongue-and-groove hardwood, vinyl tiles, ceramic tile, and stone
- Hardware specialists and locksmiths furnish locks and decorative hardware

Mechanical contractors. These people deal with specific mechanical systems, such as heating and cooling systems, elevators, and escalators.

Unlicensed Workers

Over 95 percent of people who work in the new construction industry are licensed, bonded, and insured, but in the remodeling end of the business, the overwhelming majority are unlicensed, not bonded, and not necessarily insured. Why this disparity in practice? In general, it boils down to contract law, state regulation, and industry practice. It is accepted in the contracting business that you seldom or never see unlicensed contractors working on a commercial structure or new housing project. However, the inverse is true in the housing industry. Most work done for homeowners involves remodeling and repair jobs, and is done by unlicensed contractors or handymen. The exceptions to this rule seem to be the plumber and the electrician; consumers are not comfortable with unlicensed plumbers and electricians. Consequently, these two trades are the highest paid in the remodeling industry. You can hire a carpenter for $15 to $25 per hour but you will pay $50/hour or more for an electrician and over $60/hour for a plumber.

Construction and Cost Control

By the start of construction of any project, the die is cast. If it is going to succeed, the right moves will already have been made. It can, however, still run afoul of problems if the construction process is not carefully monitored. The work to date sets the stage for the construction phase, and for the project to succeed, the following elements must have been successfully completed.

Prerequisites for new construction.
- The land has been properly selected for price, location, physical characteristics, and proper condition of the title.
- The market has been clearly established for the intended use, and the numbers show sufficient upside to warrant the investment and potential risks.
- The pre-leasing has progressed to the break-even point and the lender has given the go-ahead.
- The consultants, including the general contractor, have been retained with proper accountability and integrated into the design process.

- Sufficient money has been raised through equity and loans to assure the owners that the project can be completed without problems.
- The documentation is in place through the completion and the management phases.
- The construction loan is ready to fund, and the draw system is agreed upon between owner and lender.
- All utilities are available at the site, or at least scheduled to be available well in advance of the scheduled completion date.
- The necessary permits have been issued, and the project is 100 percent in compliance with the governing regulations.

If all of the above have been successfully completed, then the project is ready to start the construction phase. At this point, the meter starts ticking on the borrowed funds, and time truly is money. Examine the players at this point and monitor their responsibilities and backup. Who are they, and exactly what are they being paid to do? To whom do they report, and in what way are they accountable? Any project, to be successful, must control the costs and timing at this point. The process of producing the finished goods has now come to the final phase, delivering the finished building.

Control. How are all of these entities tied together, and how do they function so that the owner/developer retains control? The answer is contained in the documentation. The key to the enforceability of the documents rests with the expertise, financial strength, and responsibilities spelled out in the contracts. If the consultants have been properly selected, they will have sufficient credentials, net worth, and liquidity to back up their professional expertise with cash, should the need arise. If this is not the case, then they should not be retained in the first place. Most consultants also carry "errors and omissions" insurance (E&O) to cover them in the event of professional liability or malpractice. It is a good idea to select only those consultants that have this type of coverage, because their ability to procure and pay for this coverage speaks well for their financial condition and volume of work.

Budgets and "fat." The owner's primary tool in controlling costs is in his or her budgeting for the project. Everyone needs some "Kentucky windage" built into the budgeting system. Everyone knows that something always goes wrong and, generally, it is something that has fallen through the cracks, not necessarily attributable to anyone's incompetence or negligence. How do developers plan for this? It is best budgeted for at the time of the preparation of the quick and dirty pro forma. When this analysis is made, certain "fat" can be built into the projection for use at a later date. This is not necessarily an easy job, because the lender not only insists that there be a healthy contingency in the budget, but also demands control of what you pay out in each budget category.

Every owner/developer has a favorite spot to stash extra money in case of a rainy day. In Table 16.1 you will see a typical development budget for one of my 2004 projects with specific areas of "fat" identified for my future use. To actually use these amounts of money you will need to convince the lender that these monies are not needed within most specific cost allocations. By the time you need these funds, you should have established the maximum cost within these categories by contract, prior expenditure, or lack of need.

Table 16.1—*Budget with "Fat" Exposed*

Budget Fat	Item	Notes		Budget
	Land			
$113,500	Lot 5	61420	$16	$ 982,720
	Lot 6	52272	16	836,352
	Closing costs	WAG		7,500
	Total land			**$1,826,572**
	Soft Costs			
$5,000	Civil engineering	Contract		$20,000
$20,000	Architecture and landscape architect	Estimate	$4	101,440
	Insurance during construction	Estimate		45,000
	Soils and matl. testing	WAG		7,500
	Miscellaneous blueprints etc.			5,000
$25,000	Miscellaneous and contingency			25,000
	Building permits and hookup fees	In hard costs		
	Project management		6% of costs less land	150,000
$ 6,000	Appraisal and loan closing costs	Estimate		12,500
	Legal-finance			5,000
$ 5,000	Legal-leasing and REA			$ 5,000

Table 16.1—*Budget with "Fat" Exposed, continued*

Budget Fat	Item	Notes		Budget
	Soft Costs			
	Construction loan fee			$30,000
	Permanent loan fee			40,000
	Interest and lease-up reserve		2.5 M @ 8%	100,000
	Leasing commissions	$5 per sf	22,000	110,000
$50,000	Contingency reserve	WAG		50,000
	Total soft costs			**$706,440**
	Hard Costs			
	Off sites	Inc in land cost	$ —	
	Site preparation	$3.50 per sf		244,372
	Building shell			
	Anchor tenant—vanilla shell	$56 per sf	12,000	672,000
	Retail building grey shell	$47 per sf	10,000	460,000
	TI allowance	22/sf	10,000	220,000
	Nail salon	bid	1,200	33,600
	Super cleaners	Bid	1,800	64,600
	Tenant improvements lot 6 only	$22 per sf		220,000
	Sales tax	X .65	X Cost X .07	62,625
	Total construction			**$1,977,197**
$224,500	**Total project**	**$205.01**		**$4,510,209**

How to Bury the Fat and Fight Murphy's Law

Obvious cost categories in which to squirrel away money are the contingency and miscellaneous line items, as well as insurance and interest budgets. Once complete cost for these line items is established, lenders will allow the extra money budgeted to be moved into, and used as part of, the miscellaneous budget.

Within the construction contract itself, there should be a line item for contingencies. This line item can be a godsend to the owner and the GC. If this line item is incorporated into the contract amount by pre-arrangement, it can be used to correct oversights that are no one's fault. In addition, it can be used to improve the quality of the building or add to the interior improvements which can add real value to the finished product.

Representation, Expertise, and Accountability

A key factor in drafting the documents should be spelling out consultants' advertised background and their representations regarding their capabilities, experience, financial condition, and expertise. The owner has the right to rely on these representations. Clearly state the responsibilities and the fiduciary nature of the consultants' relationship to the owner. It is this unifying thread that should link all of the consultants, making them responsible to the owner, requiring them to look over each other's shoulders on the owner's behalf.

The architect's job assignment is, in reality, the most responsible of all the consultants in the process. He or she is charged with the responsibility of producing a quality building of sound design that meets the requirements of the intended use, and complies with all applicable codes and governmental regulations. He or she is responsible for the compliance of the project's design, up to the time the building permit is issued. Once the project construction gets underway, the architect then becomes responsible for the general contractor doing the job properly within the design parameters and the applicable building codes. If new regulations are promulgated after the design has been finalized, and the building permit issued, or new legislation is passed after the date the permit is issued, then the cost of compliance with these new requirements becomes the responsibility of the owner. However, implementation of rules or laws passed, but not yet in force, prior to or during the design process, such as the recent Americans with Disabilities Act (ADA), are the responsibility of the architect.

Definition

The *GC* is not presumed to be an architect or a structural, mechanical, or civil engineer.

Construction inspection for compliance with specifications and the quality of workmanship also falls under the architect's responsibility. Lenders require monthly certification that the construction is on time and in accordance with the approved plans and the applicable codes. If the design is in error, and correction is called for, it should be the responsibility of the architect to pay for the redesign and the remedial work. If the general contractor was part of the design team in a design-build contract, then the GC should share these costs with the architect in some prearranged manner.

The GC is presumed not only to be financially responsible, but also to be an expert in building construction and the current building codes.

The GC is responsible, within the scope of the plans and specifications, for execution of the required work within the code, as well as the quality and timing of all work under the construction contract. Late or shoddy work should be remedied at the contractor's expense. Timing is always a critical and costly issue in construction. The realistic approach dictates that "Force Majeure" or "acts of God" such as natural disasters, severe weather, strikes, etc., beyond the contractor's control, are the risk of the owner. All else is the responsibility of the GC, and the financial consequences attributed to this delay should be laid at his or her door. Since the meter is running on the interest clock, this cost of money can be tied directly to the schedule. To be enforceable, the contract clause must include a reward as well as a penalty. If the work is completed in advance of schedule, a bonus must be paid. If the work is delayed, a penalty can be enforced. The penalty is customarily assessed against the final payment of the traditional 10 percent holdback from the monthly construction draws.

The Monthly Draw and Interest

Every month during the life of a construction project there is a construction draw. Customarily, this draw is for a percentage of the total project, and is estimated by the contractor, approved by the architect, the lender's inspector, and the owner before being paid out by the lender. There are compelling arguments against this method of payment. First, it does not accurately reflect work in place. Second, it never reflects the cash value of the work previously paid for by the GC. And third, it allows the GC to get ahead of the subs and the owner, costing the owner too much interest on outstanding construction loan money.

Heads Up

Be sure to exclude from the monthly draw any materials stored on or off site, as these are properly the responsibility of the suppliers or the subs. They become the owner's property only when they are incorporated into the project.

A more precise method of payment, fair to all (the owner, the lender, the GC, and the subs) is payment by the invoice method. This method of payment requires that each sub, supplier, or consultant invoice for work completed during the current month.

The owner's insurance will be lower if this distinction is made, and there will be less "shrinkage" of stored materials as a result. Once the sub costs are tallied, the GC adds his or her work, overhead charges, and specific costs incurred, suitably backed by invoices from suppliers or payroll records, and the total cost of construction for the month is tallied. The owner then adds the soft costs invoiced for the current month, and the total is forwarded to the lender for payment. If this method is followed, the owner's expenditure for interest during construction, prior to occupancy, should drop by approximately half. This is a significant savings, and once the owners have occupied, this savings becomes permanent and money budgeted for this purpose may now be diverted to some other area to good effect.

Another point about payments is tied to the monthly lien releases.

This check-and-balance procedure ensures the owner and lender that suppliers and subs have been paid, lessening the possibility of liens resulting from nonpayment by the GC. Any supplier or sub not contracted directly by the owner is required by lien law to notify the owner and lender that he or she is doing work on the project. This "Preliminary Notice" is required by law to protect the lien rights of the supplier and the sub. At the same time, it puts the owner and lender on notice that this person is working on the project, thus enabling the owner and lender to track payments to avoid possible liens. The invoice method provides an excellent method of tracking these obligations. If there is any question as to whether suppliers or subs are being paid, payments to the GC may be made jointly to include the supplier or sub in question.

Heads Up

Each sub and supplier is required to submit, with the current invoice, a lien release for all prior work paid for by the owner. No further payment should be made until this is submitted and verified.

Other Resources

Several third party agents are usually employed to oversee the process on behalf of the owner and the lender. The testing engineer, usually required by both the lender and the building department, is an excellent consultant to check on various aspects of the construction. His or her role is primarily one of quality control, and the timely reporting of compliance or noncompliance can have a profound effect on the schedule, and by extrapolation, the total project cost. Once a quality control test is taken, it is presumed to be in compliance unless reported otherwise. Therefore, timely notice of noncompliance is essential for keeping the work on schedule. Having to backtrack to remove and replace prior work can cause severe delay, not to mention increased cost. The testing engineer should always work for the owner, at the direction of the owner and the architect. The building department and the lender will have some minimum requirements for inspection, but the owner and architect's best interests are served when inspections are thorough, random, and timely.

Likewise, the lender's construction draw certification agent, increasingly likely to be an outside consultant, is responsible only to the lender. The owner, however, can make this agent an ally by requiring that he or she be detailed and timely with the reports. Since the owner is paying for this service performed on behalf of the lender, he or she has the right to insist on having detailed inspections reported promptly. This way the owner can more accurately pay for the construction, and if these reports are completed in a timely manner, can make this payment in time to maximize any potential discounts from subcontractors and suppliers. If the GC knows that payment will be rendered promptly, he or she will not have to build into the budget the cost of interest on the payments that they are required to make to suppliers, to keep the work on schedule. This minimizes the impact of construction interest on all parties.

Best Building for the Buck

A common mistake made by developers is to try to save money on the budget. This can become a very shortsighted and ill-advised act. It does, however, depend on the project and the project's concept and goals. Obviously, if one is building a project for sale, such as a house, then reduced costs for subs and materials that do not affect quality will have little effect on the project. These savings will, in fact, raise the profits. In a project where rentals are the determining factor in establishing value and profit, money saved can be used to improve the project's final value by increased rent payments. If additional money is available from savings in certain areas, these funds may be used to improve the project's quality, to reduce long-term operating costs. In the case of commercial projects, the money can be used to allow tenants "over-standard" improvements, meaning those improvements that are above and beyond the landlord's standard tenant improvement allowance. Typically, the cost of over-standard improvements are, in reality, loaned to the tenant, and repaid with interest, fully amortized, over the base year period. They are not flagged anywhere as secondary income but customarily are evidenced by an increased rental rate. How does this improve value? Take, for example, over-standard tenant improvements of $20,000 installed for a tenant with a five-year lease. If the tenant agrees to pay for this at 12 percent per annum fully amortized, which is not unreasonable, the result is an additional annual rental payment of $5,340. This amount of money, capitalized at 8 percent, will yield a value of $66,750 that can be sold with the building. You will note that the net gain between cost and value is $46,750. This is a good deal by anyone's standard, and the increase in cash flow, by extrapolation, is real. It is not hard to visualize how some significant "fat" can be turned into gold by an astute owner/developer.

Get One Wholesale

CHAPTER 17

Site Selection Guidelines

I t doesn't matter whether you are buying a house, a building lot, an existing income-producing property, raw land for investment, or a parcel of land for development, the prudent approach is the best approach. Most of the following is intended for use when dealing with unimproved properties; however, all of the principles covered in this chapter apply to buying a house for investment. The steps outlined in this chapter are used by my companies, and have been developed over a 25-year period. They have served me well, and every step has a purpose and a risk-limiting value. Skip these steps at your own peril.

Heads Up

If you tone it down a little, apply some common sense, and use the realtor's preprinted forms with a few contingencies thrown in, the principles outlined in this chapter will also work for you when you are buying houses, building lots or raw land.

Start with Site Selection

Site/building/project selection may be initiated in many ways; you may be looking for a site for a specific use, looking for a viable use for property already owned, or simply looking to maximize the value of a parcel of land by converting it to its "highest and best use." The practical approach to site selection must incorporate many factors that influence the decision to acquire or prepare a site for subsequent development. How do the investors/developers pick their sites? While there are no rules as such, there are some factors that are common to all investors when looking for a site. First of all, the site should be in the path of growth, or along a highly used traffic arterial. Most cities or SMSAs grow in fairly predictable directions unless there are physical limitations such as rivers, lakes, or mountains; remember the diagram approach to analyzing your city or town as indicated in Figures 2.4 and 3.1.

Location

The old real estate adage of "location, location, and location" is today realistically redefined for commercial property as "Visibility, traffic count, and accessibility." For residential property, it is "accessibility to work, services, shopping, and recreation." Residential property must be accessible to major commute arterials, near vital services such as hospitals, schools, and churches, and convenient to shopping for the basic necessities. It is a plus if it is located near or, as an extension of, an established and popular residential neighborhood.

Limiting Financial Exposure

The purpose of this recommended approach is to limit your financial exposure as you progress through the deal. It works. I have done this successfully over 45 times in my career. It is the only way I develop income producing property, and it is a proven good deal for all concerned. As you review the following items of work, keep in mind why you are doing it this way. See how each step allows you to remove obstacles before you commit your funds.

Site Acquisition

Once the prospective property is identified it becomes the "subject site," and the next assignment is to get "control" of it. Having control of the site is, by definition, acquiring a "beneficial interest" in the site. Beneficial interest means having de facto rights of ownership, or the unequivocal right to acquire the site. This can be accomplished in various ways. The best possible way is to option the site for future purchase; the least prudent of which is immediate noncontingent purchase. The most common method of acquisition is the execution of a "purchase agreement" between the developer/buyer, and the seller, spelling out the terms of purchase and any contingencies thereto, with an escrow period sufficiently long to enable the buyer to evaluate the potential risks.

When drafting this document, there are some conservative rules that I recommend, using as a failsafe mechanism so that you as the buyer are able to limit your financial exposure at the front end of any project.

The Land Purchase Agreement

The purchase agreement is the most vital tool in the early stages of any project, as it lays out the project schedule and spells out to both buyer and seller who is responsible for what and when it is to be completed. This agreement will determine the lead time and cost of establishing the "feasibility" of the proposed development. At least, it should provide any prospective buyer with a period of time to perform what is known as "due diligence." The period in which this is scheduled to be performed is known as the "free look" period, so called, because the buyer may cancel the purchase contract anytime within this period and receive his or her money back. During this time a buyer can test, evaluate, and analyze the site to determine its viability as a potential commercial real estate investment. A sample "Agreement of Purchase and Sale and Joint Escrow Instructions" is included in a companion CD-ROM available from the author with working copies of the contracts and spreadsheets used in the development and management process (see Reference Material in the Appendix for ordering information).

Most homes are purchased with preprinted board of realtors forms; that does not present any problems other than reading them, as they are much longer than my form and deliberately printed in small type to encourage people to skip most of the form. If you read this chapter and then read the board of realtor's form, you can use it more intelligently to great profit. Simply fill out their form, crossing out clauses you do not like and add on the signature page "See Addendum attached hereto and made a part of this agreement." Write your business deal on the addendum in bullet point format, and start the addendum with the phrase "Notwithstanding anything to the contrary contained in the attached purchase agreement, the clauses enumerated below shall govern." Doing this negates anything in the preprinted form that conflicts with your addendum and puts your terms in charge of the deal.

Basic Clauses that Can Be Included

The purchase agreement should incorporate all the representations of the seller and the buyer, as well as the steps required to "vet" (evaluate) the project, and the general business terms and schedule of the proposed land purchase. The various approvals and evaluations necessary to successfully complete a commercial development project can be used as "contingencies" to preserve the buyer's earnest money deposit in the event that the site does not "shape up" during the evaluation process. By listing the "conditions precedent" necessary for development of the proposed purchase as contingencies to the buyer's completion of the purchase, the buyer can effectively limit the earnest money deposit exposure to being nonrefundable. The buyer should disclose to the seller what he or she intends to do with the land, stating that if that is not possible or feasible based on his or her market and site feasibility studies, then the purchase agreement will become voidable. It is important to have the option to void the transaction belong exclusively to the buyer, as the buyer may elect to proceed for some reason other than that initially intended for the transaction.

It is vital to represent to the seller that the purchase agreement is the beginning of the development process, not the beginning of a potential land speculation. It should clearly represent itself as the first step in a serious commercial development project. Most sellers will agree to contingencies if the buyer actively pursues the removal of these contingencies. They take great comfort in the fact that a principal/developer is willing to spend his or her own money to improve someone else's land.

Contingencies

While residential and commercial projects have different front-end concerns, the viability of each piece of land from a single house building lot to a 100-acre tract must be evaluated. Some specific types of contingencies common to purchase agreements in the investment/development industry are:

- Approval by the buyer of the preliminary title report
- The geotechnical investigation
- The zoning
- The boundary survey and topographic map
- The traffic impact study
- In the case of California, the environmental impact report (EIR or EIS)
- Approval by the appropriate governmental jurisdiction of the level one environmental assessment
- The lender's preliminary leasing requirements

- The archeological evaluation
- An endangered species survey
- The development plan
- Use permits, if required
- Finally, if possible, the actual building permits

This sounds like the seller is willing to be overly accommodating to the developer, but depending on the seller, and the buyer's experience and reputation, any or all of these conditions, and more, can be inserted into a contract as "conditions precedent" to the earnest money becoming nonrefundable, or at least the final closing of the site purchase. The price for this accommodation is, generally, that the buyer must pay "top dollar" for the site in question.

Most often, the seller will permit an examination of title, geotechnical and zoning, to be accomplished during the "free look" or "due diligence" period, but after that he or she usually wants to see some "hard cash" (nonrefundable money) at risk for delaying the closing any further. The customary method of converting the earnest money deposit into hard cash is to render the earnest money forfeitable after the expiration of the free look period in the event that the buyer does not close the escrow. It is common practice for the buyer to put up additional sums of money to delay the closing, as it enables the buyer to complete his or her laundry list prior to committing the large amount of capital necessary to purchase, develop, lease, and/or sell the land with or without the proposed development in place.

> ## Heads Up
> The purchase agreement is the most important risk-limiting document in the entire acquisition and investment process! Set your goals down in the agreement.

There are some realities that you need to take on board during this process. Remember them well:

- Do not close escrow (consumate the purchase) until you are ready to break ground if you are building.
- Do not close the escrow until all contingencies such as permits and financing are obtained.

This sounds simple, but it is not always possible. If this is not possible, then, at the very least:

- Do not close the escrow until acquiring the legal right (the entitlement) to build the project as conceived and evaluated. This right consists of having not less than the required zoning, site plan and architectural approval, and, if pertinent, special use permits, or in the case of residential and/or commercial subdivisions, preliminary plat approval.

How to Evaluate a Site

These general rules of acquisition aside, the factors that influence the buying decision are not less than:

- Market and economic demand for the proposed product
- Price per useable square foot of the proposed project
- The specific zoning
- The specific stipulations (stips) of the governing body (county or city)
- Geotechnical considerations, topography
- Exposure to the public (site configuration)
- Coverage available for development. (i.e., How many square feet can be built on the site?)

How do developers evaluate or "vet" the sites they choose? Using the new location criteria as a given, there is the gut instinct of the true investor/developer, as most sites cry out for a particular treatment. The technical or practical analysis is also vital, and is generally performed by the developer during the "free-look" period contained within the purchase agreement.

Finally, the clinical, "by the numbers" analysis must also pass muster, and, ultimately, the numbers will govern. If they pass all other tests, the total land cost per square foot of buildable leasable space will be the real deciding factor in the numbers analysis, as, without this, there is no hope of producing buildings at competitive prices. Most often, the price of the land will determine the feasibility of the project. To determine the land price per useable square foot, simply divide the land price by the number of net useable square feet in the proposed project. Accomplish as much front-end work as possible, the ultimate goal being a workable budget to enable the project to be built. This is a tall order, and investors/developers should try to eliminate most of the contingencies prior to investing a great deal of irretrievable capital. These front-end costs cannot be recaptured in the event the project has to be scrapped and the land resold, so keep these front-end expenditures to a minimum. Almost uniformly, developers want to see all the governmental approvals, except, perhaps, the final plats and building permits accomplished prior to closing on the land. Make sure that the purchase price is determined by a specific cost per square foot or per buildable unit as determined by an accurate ALTA survey! If possible, try to have the final purchase price determined by the total number of usable square feet or number of buildable units.

Heads Up

Until sufficient experience is accumulated, newcomers to the development business are strongly encouraged to hire experts to perform market demand and economic analysis of potential sites.

Usable and buildable square feet are determined by subtracting all areas that are restricted against building by easement, deed restrictions, or topography limitations. During the free-look phase of the project, the feasibility must be established to justify the purchase of the site. This all costs money, and, minimally, the following items need to be done to evaluate the site:

- Survey and topo
- Geotechnical evaluation
- Market survey and competition analysis
- Schematic design
- Pro forma evaluation

The Preliminary Title Report or Abstract

When referring to this precondition in the purchase agreement, there are some good ideas that can be incorporated into the language from a deal standpoint. Legal points should be supplied by the project's attorney.

DISCLAIMER: Nothing contained in this book or the companion CD-ROM constitutes the author's attempt to render legal advice, except "Trade honestly with all parties!"

The title should be conveyed in as broad a manner as possible. Ask your attorney for guidance in this matter. The exceptions noted in schedule "B" of the preliminary title report, or "the prelim," should reference certain recorded documents. Stipulate that the seller has not delivered a complete prelim for your evaluation unless the prelim is accompanied by legible copies of all documents referenced in the preliminary title report. Seek to have as much as a month to evaluate and approve the prelim. In no case agree to less than two weeks for the process. For states that do not use the title process, the prelim will be known as an abstract of title. Make sure that the title attorney evaluates each and every document with the developer's intended use in mind, understanding all the limitations and benefits that each document conveys.

Heads Up
Always purchase the extended coverage title insurance; it insures the buyer against all defects of title not appearing in the recorded documents. Tie this into the ALTA project boundary survey and topo and insist on the title company's written approval of the survey and topographic map as part of the extended coverage title policy.

The Well Driller Legend. The old urban legend of the driller appearing in the lobby of the high rise building, stating that he has purchased the sub surface rights and wants the lobby cleared so that he can drill for oil is not necessarily a fantasy. These things happen and are always financially ruinous! Do the homework, and do not approve the document until your attorney is 100 percent satisfied that the title will be sufficiently beneficial for the intended use. If not, back out, and find another site.

The site should always be inspected for conformance with the boundary survey and approved by the title company so that the buyer can get the extended coverage title policy at the close of escrow (COE), i.e., coverage for those problems that do not appear in the recorded documents. The boundary survey and the topographic map will be used by the project engineer and architect to determine the suitability of the land for the proposed use as well as the potential site plan and "coverage" (achievable density). Once again, if the site does not shape up, pass and find another. Throwing good money after bad is never a good idea.

Physical Evaluation of the Site

During the free-look period it is necessary to determine whether the geotechnical characteristics, topography, soil characteristics, and survey are adequate to support the proposed project. Most likely, there will be many government-imposed evaluations required. Geotechnical evaluations should be exhaustive, including, at a minimum:

- Seismic evaluation
- Topo or drainage impact
- Archeological evaluation
- Environmental, and endangered species evaluation-flora and fauna
- Potential vehicle emissions
- Traffic impact
- Visual impact
- Lighting and sound emissions
- Soil testing for load-bearing capacity

All of these considerations must be taken into account in a modern development.

The Environmental Impact Report (EIR or EIS)

In California, the EIR process includes, among other items, an environmental assessment, seismic evaluation, prior uses research including hazardous material contamination, both existing and potential, soil condition including load-bearing capacity, storm drainage characteristics before and after development, flora and fauna examination including the potential existence of "endangered species" on-site, traffic impact before and after, visual impact, economic impact to the area, visual or architectural impact, impact on existing "view corridors," and anything else the city or county planning staff can come up with.

In the state of Arizona the required evaluation is only prior uses and possible past contamination. Most states fall somewhere between the two extremes, and some states have no environmental evaluation at all. In reality, all states will soon have some form of environmental impact analysis, as it is the only responsible way to determine the actual impact of a proposed development. In the case of California, Washington, and the state of Arizona, however, it has been escalated beyond a legitimate tool of evaluation. It is now frequently used as a growth limiting device and as an opportunity to generate revenue for the governing authority.

Heads Up

The items on an EIR are a mouthful. You had better get used to it, because the EIR is going to spread to every area that people deem desirable to live. It is a viable growth-limiting tool, and is guaranteed to slow down any building project.

The Boundary Survey and Topographic Map

The boundary survey will verify the size and configuration of the land and should show all existing improvements or remnants thereof, recorded easements or restrictions, and anything that will show up on visual inspection and unrecorded documents. It will also provide buyer and seller with an exact square foot total to determine the final purchase price. The boundary survey, if done to ALTA or extended coverage criteria, will determine not only the exact size of the site, but also any restrictions such as easements, etc., that affect the buildability of the site.

The topographic map, or "topo," will determine the extent of potential site development (grading, cuts, and fills) needed to utilize the site for the intended use. For the most part, the analysis will boil down to the amount of buildable square footage or coverage available on-site. Coverage is dictated by zoning as well as physical limitations on the site. It is also constructed by decisions about the proposed building itself, i.e., the shape and the number of stories. The buildable square footage together with the required parking and landscaping will set the stage for the economic analysis. Each of these decisions will affect the feasibility of the site. See Figure 17.1.

One-, two-, and three-story buildings are the most common in suburbia. Two story buildings are considered to be less expensive per square foot, providing more room for on-site parking and landscaping; but even with the ADA requirements today, the two-story building, while not any less expensive, may still afford better building coverage. Three-story buildings are considered to be the least cost effective for suburban development and are used only as a last resort when the

Figure 17.1—*Boundary Survey and Topographic Map*

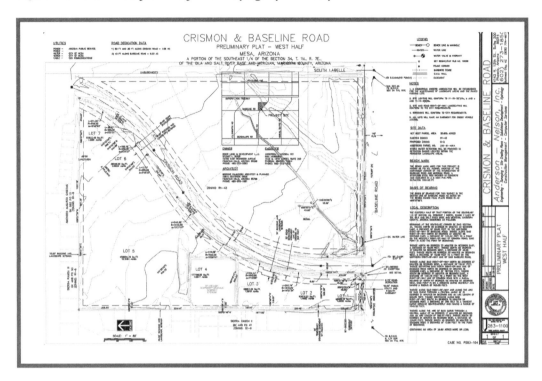

market will support the increased cost. Buildings of four to seven stories are considered to be low rise and appropriate for more dense suburban developments, usually accompanied by parking structures. In buildings over seven stories high, effective exterior-access fire fighting vanishes, and built-in, automated fire fighting capability is required, forcing the taller building to become an even taller highrise building to amortize the additional costs of this fire-fighting capability.

Parking requirements are most economically met by surface parking at a year 2000 cost of approximately $5,000 per car. When a car is stored in a structure, it adds a minimum of $15,000 per auto to the cost of parking. If the car is moved underground, it adds a minimum of $ 25,000 per car to the cost of parking.

Zoning, Entitlements, and Environmental Approvals

One of the trickiest areas of commercial development today is project "entitlement," or the right to proceed with the development of any site. This process starts with the zoning and ends with the issuance of a building permit. Some states are simple; if the site is correctly zoned for a certain use, then the developer needs only to apply for a building permit, and when it is approved, construction starts. Most states, however, starting with California, Washington, and now Arizona are using land use regulations as an effective growth-limiting tool and a serious money-raising opportunity for the affected community. In California, if a site is zoned correctly, the developer must also submit an environmental impact report or statement (EIR/EIS), as the case may be. This document usually costs from $250,000 to as much as several million dollars per site. If it is not approved by the regulating body, city, county, or state, then the project cannot proceed. The contingency of an approved EIR is imperative when purchasing land in states that require the EIR process.

This is a very real and substantial front-end cost, one that has driven many developers away from California and other states using these statutes. It is not uncommon to have purchased a site zoned for an approved use and then to be rejected by provisions in the EIR. What then? These costs are not refundable. Most developers are actively pursuing political agendas to keep close ties to the various political bodies in their area so that they do not run afoul of this process.

You can figure out if your project will get zoning or EIR approval through extensive conversation and negotiation with planning and zoning officials. Most problems can be accommodated, unless the government is bent on limiting growth at all costs. This is usually evidenced by the extensive use of inordinate "impact fees." Normal zoning contingencies involve a master plan change to accommodate a proposed project, a zoning change, as well as site plan and architectural approvals. Sometimes a special use permit may be required as well. Normally a seller will agree to delay closing, with suitable nonrefundable deposits, until these approvals are received. This process is not perceived by the seller as particularly risky, as these approvals enhance the value of the seller's land at the buyer's expense.

The Market Study

Probably the most vital feasibility tool is the market survey, including, at a minimum, the following criteria:
- Demographics
- Size, net in- or out-migration; population education levels
- Financial makeup and average wages, future health of the marketplace and competing geographical areas and their relative impact on the subject market
- Physical or topographical limits to growth, land and water, physical barriers, etc.
- Reasons for growth, general political climate (California vs. Arizona, and inevitable change, the "Washington factor")

- Shopping patterns (i.e., supply and demand of potential users within the defined "trade zone.")
- Market segments and locations, residential growth, transportation corridors, airports, industrial base, office and retail markets, sub-markets, and peripheral influences.
- Identification of the target market; let the brokers look for scarce or high economic use potentials. (i.e., What does the market need?)
- Location of the development resources such as brokers, title companies, contractors, architects, engineers, and designers.

At minimum, within a three- to-five mile radius of the proposed site, you must know the following:

- Supply and demand, absorption, and vacancy of the potential use.
- Know the competition; visit all of them, by category of use; which are successful, and why?
- Locate the high and low vacancy, by type of building. Between the highest absorption rate and the lowest supply lies the best opportunity.
- What category of competition is nearing obsolescence?
- What projects are planned? Check with the planning department.
- Are there potential uses not being addressed within the "trade zone?"
- Are these uses economically viable for building?

The SMSAs market must be examined to determine the basic characteristics of the market (i.e., static, shrinking, or expanding, and how it relates to the specific site in question). This will determine the most prudent type of project: urban high-rise, low-rise, suburban space, or mixed-use development. Specific project design can be tailored for any target market. In the absence of a clearly expanding market place such as occurred nationwide in the 1970s, I tend to look for the vacant niche in the market place, specialized sub-markets, medical, legal, intercept sites, or small towns, etc.

The basic tools for financial evaluation of a specific site with a specific proposed use, the pro forma "income and expense" and the "cost breakdown," should be prepared on a cash-on-cash basis first. Any other benefits will only enhance the transaction. This document should strive to be as realistic as possible, leaning, if at all, to the side of pessimism.

Preliminary Design

At this stage of the game, most investor/renovator/developers will have commissioned an engineer or architect or both to do a preliminary or schematic project design to determine the usability of the site. This tool will determine the overall building and site configuration showing total useable and buildable square feet or number of units, the parking and landscaping required, and any governmental stipulations attached to their approval of the development plan. The results of this preliminary design will enable the developer to do a "quick and dirty" set of numbers to see if the proposed project will be financially feasible.

The Pro Forma

The pro forma, defined as the financial objective of the venture, is usually a two-part document. Part one is dedicated to the projected income and expense (see Table 17.1), usually resulting in a net cash flow projection. Part two is a projected one-page cost breakdown (see Table 17.2). For a home building or a renovation project, there is no income evaluation, only an assumed or appraised sales price. If it is to be a rental unit, then you need a simplified version of Table 17.1

In table 17.1, I use the following constants:

- Land size 1.67 acres or 72,745.2 square feet
- Building size 20,000 square feet

Table 17.1—*The One-Page Income and Expense Projection*

Item	Notes	Preliminary Budget
Income		
Gross potential income (GPI)	20,000 sq.ft. @ $ 16/sq.ft./year NNN	$320,000
Less assumed vacancy	5% allowed	(16,000)
Effective gross income (EGI)		304,000
Expenses		
Operating expenses		
CAM charges	Estimated @ $5/sq.ft.	(100,000)
Less recapture from tenants	95%	95,000
Net operating expenses		5,000
Net Income Before Debt Service (NIBDS)		$299,000
Project valuation		
At 7.5 cap rate	NIBDS/s.075	$3,986,666
Mortgage value at completion of lease up		
Project valuation x .75 = $2,990,000		
Construction loan estimate $2,500,000		

Table 17.2—*The One-Page Cost Breakdown*

Item	Notes	Preliminary Budget
Land		
Land cost	1.67 ac @ $8/sq.ft.	$581,960
Closing costs	Estimate	9,500
Total land		**591,460**
Soft Costs		
A & E	Budgeted at $4/sq.ft.	$80,000
Survey/staking/testing	Budgeted—estimate	7,800
Leasing commissions	By contract $4/sq.ft.	80,000
Insurance/taxes/legal/acctg.	Estimated	10,500
Permits and fees	Budgeted	55,000
Construction loan points	1% on $4M	25,000
Permanent loan points	1% on	29,000
Interest during construction	8% on $2.5M 6 mos.	100,000
Miscellaneous and contingencies	Estimate (WAG)	25,000
Total soft costs		**$412,300**
Hard Costs		
Paving, curbs, and gutters	Including site work	
31,700 sq.ft. @ $4/sq.ft.	$126,800	
Landscaping	19,000 @ $2.50/sq.ft.	$38,000
Building shell	20,000 @ $48/sq.ft.	960,000
Tenant work (TI)	20,000 @ $30/sq.ft.	600,000
Taxes	.075X65% on TI + shell costs	76,050
Total hard costs		**$1,800,850**
Total Project Costs		**$2,587,290**
Valuation and ROI		
Valuation at completion from Table17.1		$3,986,666
Less project total cost		(2,587,290)
Gross profit		1,399,370
Residual equity required	Perm loan—costs	($402,630)
ROI		Infinite

Part two, the cost breakdown, is just that, but it also includes an analysis of the "cash on cash" rate of return or Net Income Before Debt Service (NIBDS) divided by total project cost generated by the income and expense projections. This breakdown is identical in any home building or renovation project.

What does the previous exercise tell you? It says that, on the first pass through the numbers, the project is not only feasible, but that it may likely "finance out." This term implies that you will have no residual investment in the building if you achieve your pro forma rents, and if you control your costs to be less than the potential permanent loan.

The cost breakdown can also be expanded to include any other form of analysis deemed relevant to the transaction, including, but not limited to, "after tax yield analysis" and the "discounted rate of return analysis."

Sum It All Up

The site selection process is like a merry-go-round; you can get on anywhere in the process.

- *Legal limitations.* What may be done on the site?
- *Physical constraints.* What can be placed economically on the site?
- *Market constraints.* What is feasible?
- *Financial constraints.* What do the numbers say?

Boil it all down and add your best guess. In the end, the numbers will determine the viability of the proposed venture. Remember the old adage, "figures never lie, but liars can figure." Do not lie to yourself when putting numbers on paper. Use the best numbers you can find. Consult the most authoritative sources you can locate and double-check all the projections. Finally, build into the budget some fat so that you are prepared for the unexpected or unforeseen. It always comes up. Murphy's Law is alive and well in the real estate development industry. My corollary to Murphy's law is, "O'Reilly's law," which takes the position that Murphy was an optimist.

The Go or No-Go Decision

If the site evaluation process has passed muster, the numbers look reasonable, and the project still looks feasible, then the developer/principal has to make the decision to

Heads Up

In my opinion, all other forms of evaluation, such as after tax analysis, discounted rates of return, etc. serve only to make the proposed project's rate of return look better, or to prop up a marginal deal. The pro forma must show a sound investment and stand up on a cash-on-cash basis, meeting the investment criteria of the proposed investors.

Heads Up

I have always had investors involved in my projects on the assumption that if I could not attract an investor or get the project financed, I should strongly consider abandoning it.

commit nonrefundable capital to take the project forward. The capital expenditures include, at the very least, the now nonrefundable earnest money deposit, architecture, engineering, leasing commissions, financing costs, zoning approvals, building permits, and construction commitments.

It is at this stage that the "Lone Ranger Decision" is made. If the buyer goes ahead on his or her own, then both the reward and the risk are his or hers alone. If the decision is made to attract partners to help with expertise and/or capital investment, then the ability to attract an investor/risk taker/partner is also another valuable check on the feasibility of the project.

There are always other points of view. Select yours and live with it. No matter what the decision at this point, if the project goes ahead, serious nonrefundable money is committed.

Who and What Is Available to Help You?

Before you get all upset and think that you cannot do this because you do not have the knowledge or training, read on and see who can help and what they can do for your deal. The cost of the professionals' help is, and can always be, built into the cost of the project/purchase/investment. Even seasoned professionals rely on these specialists, and they are worth the price of their time and effort.

The Players

The astute use of selected professionals can save you time and money, control front-end costs and can, properly guided, improve your project/purchase. Since fees amount to approximately 23 to 25 percent of the total cost of a project, select consultants carefully. Insist that they give some relief on the front-end costs prior to the go or no-go decision. Often consultants will do this in exchange for getting "market rate" fees rather than a negotiated fee. Try for it all. Boom times will not last forever, and most consultants would prefer long-term relationships with a developer rather than a one-time project. Almost without exception, a commercial development project will require the services of a marketing consultant, an architect or planner, an engineer, a broker, an attorney, a contractor (while not strictly a consultant, should be treated like one), and a property manager. Remember, if you do not ask, you will not receive. When I was starting out, I did not have the luxury of a capital pool. Therefore, I was forced to put together my first project in an innovative manner. In the process I acquired an attitude about the process that has stayed with me for 25 years.

In an effort to develop my first project, I decided to give away some of the ownership in exchange for services rendered to the project. The net result of that was that I was able to "front end" the project with little or no cash. In the process, I evolved a work pattern and ownership format that has served me well over the years.

Heads Up

I believe it is better to have part of a number of good deals, than 100 percent of any one deal.

Brokerage

The first step in the development process is finding a site. Typically, a commercial broker will present a prospective site to the developer. It is at this point that the potential project begins. Since brokers can earn up to 10 percent of the purchase price on a land purchase, they are usually eager to help establish the bona fides of the "subject parcel" to make it easier for their developer/buyer to make the decision to purchase. Most brokers specialize in specific areas such as residential land, office, retail, or industrial projects. As a general rule, the land specialist works hand-in-hand with the leasing specialist as a team.

There are many things a developer needs to know about a site, and the broker is uniquely situated to produce authoritative knowledge for the feasibility process. Most commercial brokers work in large companies that cover many bases within the brokerage community. Typically, a good commercial brokerage firm will have departments that specialize in land sales, leasing, investment sales, and property management.

Since the most vital aspect of any development process is the delivery of a fully-occupied building, the market survey becomes, perhaps, the crucial element in the feasibility analysis. Nothing has yet transpired on the project, no money has been spent; therefore, this is the perfect time to establish this parcel as a viable project by using the information stored within the broker's own company. While this does not constitute a formal market survey, it will suffice for most experienced developers.

How do you motivate the broker who already stands to make a solid 10 percent on the sale? He or she not only wants you to purchase the site but does not get paid until you close the escrow. My approach is to make the project more profitable to the broker by offering the brokerage company's team the opportunity to increase its fee income and to participate in the ownership of the project, should it proceed. This added factor on the ownership side will put the broker's knowledge and experience to work for the project at the beginning of the project where the design and marketing decisions will be made. This approach evolves into a 10 percent ownership, full leasing commissions, and the right to list the property for sale if the brokerage group meets the leasing criteria and schedule over the lifespan of the project.

Remember, at this point the broker has been given nothing other than an opportunity to make more money, and the developer has spent no money to date. The land broker immediately recruits a leasing or sales specialist from the company and, together, they become the initial project brokerage team or marketing team. Later, if the team is successful in meeting the project's absorption goals, they may add an investment property specialist to market the completed project.

The developer and the brokers establish the market feasibility by finding out the following market characteristics:

- Net annual absorption of product categories (housing, retail space, office, or industrial space).
- Direction of growth.
- Current rents achieved by new buildings and existing rental building stock.
- The location and effectiveness of competing projects.
- The location of this subject parcel in relation to the potential market.
- Finally, the team maps the potential sites that can compete with the subject parcel, and notes the price for each potential competitor.

At this point, the investor/developer has all the tools to make the decision regarding the subject parcel's potential to compete successfully within the market. He or she must determine:

- If the site is located properly and priced competitively in relation to the potential competition.
- If the site is configured to have the required frontage for signage and exposure.
- If the site is accessible to traffic.
- If the potential rents are enough to justify a new building.
- If the projected absorption of new space indicates that there is a need for new space.

Then the developer can feel comfortable placing the site in play by executing a purchase agreement with the seller.

The net result of this is that the developer has accomplished three things at the start of the process prior to having spent anything. The developer has:

- Found a viable site.
- Acquired a partner who can help make the project a success.
- Retained 90 percent ownership of the project.

The Architect

For the sake of this discussion, I will specify that the subject site is essentially a building project, rather than a land development project, when placed into escrow. This will necessitate the services of an architect rather than a planner or engineer. Sometimes, all three are used, but here we can assume that only an architect is needed. Within the profession, most companies specialize in certain types of buildings. If the developer is inexperienced in a particular type of building, it is vital that he or she choose an architect experienced in the building type required of the "subject parcel."

Most architectural contracts are based upon the cost of the building. This is dangerous for a developer, because it runs counter to the developer's interest if a building cost exceeds its budget. A typical developer negotiates a per square foot price for the project with an additional price for tenant improvement (TI) design. Sometimes a "space planner" is assigned this task, as it is an architectural specialty and not always found in an architect's practice. Once the price is established, the payment schedule is worked out.

It is in the developer's best interest to keep the front-end expenditures to a minimum, so, where possible, the architectural contract should always include the civil engineering. Once this is established, the price set, then the last chore becomes the payment schedule. Often a developer can persuade an architect to limit the early costs incurred prior to the go or no-go decision, to out-of-pocket items. Sometimes a piece of the action will be required to sweeten the pot. I have frequently given a 10 percent ownership position in a project to the architect. This keeps the early and usually risky financial exposure to a minimum for the developer and costs nothing at this point. The resulting project ownership would now reflect this addition; broker 10 percent, architect 10 percent, and the developer 80 percent.

The Engineer

Almost any project will need engineers:
- For buildings, a structural and a mechanical engineer
- For site work, a civil engineer and a soils engineer
- For quality control, a materials testing engineer

Most of these functions do not represent a significant early dollar expense, and with the exception of the soils engineer, can be added to the architect's contract for budgeting purposes. This is generally the case with the structural and mechanical engineers, except in the case of the "design/build" scenario. In the event that the project is a master-planned community or large subdivision, the civil engineer

Heads Up

Remember, until the project is a reality, participation costs nothing, and when a project becomes a reality, all parties with a participation in the project will have their net worth on the line and their attention fully focused.

should not be under the umbrella of the architect; in fact, the civil engineer replaces the architect and should be handled accordingly. The testing engineer and soils engineer at the front end of the project, as well as the compaction and concrete testing during construction, should always be under the control of the developer. This is a vital part of the quality control process for the project. Contracts for large land projects can be negotiated on a per unit basis, akin to a flat-fee approach, and, if necessary, participation should be considered as a sweetener to keep the preliminary costs to a minimum.

Everyone has so much to gain and lose that the net result is a very focused project team. This ownership structure will ensure that the project will take precedence with the individual consultants/partners over any other project where fees alone are at stake.

The Attorney

First of all, choose a firm that specializes in real estate law, or, at least, one that has an experienced real estate department. Brokers are often a good source of information on attorneys who are "deal makers" rather than "deal breakers." When planning a project, documentation will be a vital part of the developer's working tools. Their proper design and format will make the difference between success and failure if problems occur. Contract documents are the developer's major tools, and enable him or her to control the team, the consultants, and the tenants. The key documents are:

- The purchase agreement
- The project lease
- The exclusive leasing agreement
- The architectural and/or engineering contract
- The construction contract

Traditionally, attorneys have worked by the hour only. This is no longer the case. There are a great many attorneys, approximately one for every 350 people in the country, so a developer can afford to be choosey. Attorneys will negotiate flat fees for various documents. Put your agreement with the attorney in writing; keep it simple, one page or less. Specify that until the final documents are approved by the developer, there are to be no extra charges. Contract with your attorney for documentation only, not negotiation services; do your own negotiating! Remember, you are retaining an attorney for his legal knowledge, not for his business acumen. Do not let him or her make your business decisions for you. Never hire an attorney known to be a "deal breaker." When retaining an attorney, do not skimp on quality. Even an attorney who is not an expert in this field should have no trouble quoting a flat fee for each document. After all, attorneys, above all other consultants, should know what is needed to properly document a project. They are not reinventing the wheel.

The Contractor

The construction contract and the process of using a general contractor (GC) has been covered earlier, but, suffice it to say, that a developer wants the most building for the money budgeted. Having the contractor on board at the outset, after having him or her bid for a fixed profit, will ensure that there is another experienced team member available for the design process. It may also make sense to add the general contractor to the partner's list for an ownership interest, as the general contractor is a major factor in the project's cost and quality control. Once the contractor is a partner, you can rest assured that the prices will remain fixed. The resulting project ownership would now reflect this addition; broker 10 percent, architect 10 percent, contractor 10 percent, and the developer 70 percent. This leaves the developer with ample ownership interest remaining to attract an investor at a later date.

The Accountant

Since we are dealing with money and the making of a profit, we must always be in a position to know what is going on. The "numbers" are the primary tools of evaluation just as the contract documents are the primary tools of control. From the first one page "quick-and-dirty" pro forma through the management and resale of the project, the numbers should follow with ever-increasing detail from one stage to the next. All spreadsheets should be integrated into the accounting system, so that no matter what information is required, it can be accessed in both formats. This is very easily accomplished today, as most accounting systems allow import and export of data. Until you become proficient with this tool, it is highly recommended that you have a consulting accountant set up the system. Even though I have been doing this for years, I still have my accountant do a monthly check on the books and systems so that there are no errors. Working with investors' capital demands the highest level of fiduciary care.

Since you will need an accountant for tax purposes anyway, it should not be a significant cost to have one set up your system initially.

Team Efforts

The whole purpose of involving other professionals in your project/purchase is to enhance the deal. Job assignments must be specific, interlocking, and enforceable. This issue has been covered throughout this book in the chapters covering paperwork and contracts. Always be aware that there is a difference between responsibility and authority.

Wealth—The Long-Term Objective

CHAPTER 18

Selling Property and Beyond

How do we wrap this up? We have discussed purchasing, developing, and managing residential income property. The highlights are:

- How to make tax-free money on your own home.
- Investing in houses for profit.
- How to buy and renovate housing and rental properties.
- How to develop real estate.
- Managing income property for profit.

The last point to go over is the disposition of assets when you are ready to sell, and then, what's beyond the sale. The thrust of this book is to guide you to the accumulation of some serious amounts of money with a view to minimizing your downside. I will deal with them in this order:

- How to dispose of property in the best way
- How to minimize or defer the tax burden
- What to do over the long pull

If you remember what you went through when you were getting ready to purchase or develop a piece of property, you must now realize that someone who has read this book may be looking at your property to buy. Fair's fair, after all. Since a fair deal is one that satisfies both parties, then you are charged with maximizing your sale price and, at the same time, giving the buyer a fair deal. The system for selling property differs when you are selling single family housing and commercial property, so we will separate the two.

Common Elements

As seen earlier in the book, there are common elements to all real property deals. As far as acquisition, disposition, and retention, it matters little whether you're dealing in houses or commercial properties. The common points are, but are not limited to:

- Taxes
- Exchanges
- Leverage
- Portfolio building

Taxes

We have discussed taxes, and, just as a reminder in capsule form, here's a reiteration of what I know based on my experience to date.

Disclaimer: The information here does not constitute tax advice. I am not qualified to give you tax advice. Consult your attorney or tax professional regarding these issues.

1. You can sell your personal residence after 24 months of continuous occupation, tax-free; you can do it over and over again.
2. If you buy and sell real property, you will pay ordinary income on investment properties held for less than one year, and capital gain on investment property held over 12 months.
3. If you build or refurbish houses or any other property specifically for resale, your profits will be classified as ordinary income.

4. If you refinance property, the proceeds are generally tax free until the properties sell.

5. You can defer taxes on investment property sales by doing a 1031 tax deferred exchange. The properties must be "like for like." Consult your attorney and tax professional for specific guidelines.

Leverage

With all that in mind, you can create an impressive portfolio by leveraging your profits with new loans, re-investing the proceeds into new properties. This is how empires are built. One word of caution, go to your local news library and look up the name "Zekendorf." Read his story and remember it well. It is a classic case of how not to leverage your empire.

Portfolio building. When you are using your profits to increase your holdings, here are some fail-safe rules to live by so that you do not put your entire pile in jeopardy.

- Keep each property separate in ownership; create an LLC for each one.
- Keep the monies from each property separate; make each deal pay its own way.
- Do not cross-collateralize multiple properties.
- Take advantage of insurance that can cover the whole portfolio using common elements of ownership to make the insurance effective.
- Pay attention to all of the properties, all of the time. Changing markets can sneak up on you; remember 1989–1990.

Residential portfolio growth. If you think that commercial income property may have significantly better return than residential property, read this section with care, as we will examine both approaches and compare them.

We will use the scenario of buying two renovatable houses each year; you keep one and sell the other. Live on what you make on the one you sell, and keep the other one in your portfolio. How does this work? Let's set up a scenario for the purpose of analyzing the possibilities. We will make the following assumptions:

- You have completed one live-in renovation project and have made $100,000 profit, tax free.
- We will use the $100,000 to set up the business.
- You will tackle two projects at a time, and these will be in the $100,000 to $300,000 price range.

To analyze this, we will need to make some reasonable assumptions about the market. You will be working in an older established neighborhood that is experiencing a renaissance. The old homes are selling for $120,000 on large lots, and the upper limit of the market is around $350,000. This is not a far-out scenario; you can find locations like this if you look.

The renovation budget might look something like Table 18.1.

Table 18.1—*Renovation Cost Breakdown*

Item	Notes	Cost
Acquisition price	1,750 sq. ft. 3/2/2car ($68/sq. ft.)	$120,000
Landscape	Minor planting and cleanup	5,000
Painting	Inside and out	5,000
Add rooms	600 sq. ft. @ $60/sq. ft.	36,000
New carpet	210 yds. @ $15/yd.	3,150
Appliances and fixtures	Kitchen and baths	10,000
Loan fees	80% loan one point 100K	1,000
Interest	9% for six months	4,500
Misc. overhead		5,000
Total costs		(189,650)
Proposed sale price	After commission and marketing costs	265,000
Gross profit	Sale less cost	$75,350

If you assume for the sake of this scenario that both your projects during this particular year were approximately the same in size and profitability, then you will have a year wherein you have made approximately $150,000 if you sell both houses. If we assume you are a prudent and parsimonious person, and you have a desire to build a portfolio for your future, you sell one and keep one, renting out the keeper. You live on the $75,000 produced from the house you sold. Let's look at the impact, Table 18.2, of keeping the one house.

By keeping this property, you are effectively letting someone else increase your equity. If you rent this house out for a net of $1,265.00 monthly, anything else is gravy. In a neighborhood where homes are valued at the above prices, it is not at all unreasonable to assume that you can achieve this level of rental income.

If we look at the effect of this game plan, selling one and keeping one, you have accomplished the following during your first year of operation:

Table 18.2—*Leverage Analysis*

Item	Notes	Values
Appraised value	At completion	$265,000
Mortgage value	As an investment property assume 75% of value	198,750
Your cost	Look carefully	189,650
New financing	$190,000 30 years @ 7% .0799 K	
Monthly mortgage	Above at APR .0799	$1,265

- Made $75,000 cash
- Created $75,000 in capital gain
- Recovered your working capital from both houses
- Launched your long-term goal of financial independence

Going a step further, assume that you are able to keep doing this every year for ten years; what then have you accomplished? You have supported yourself for ten years and accumulated ten rental properties. Not too bad! If there has been no increase in the value of these homes over the ten years, and the tenants have repaid none of your principal, then Table 18.3 calculates your new net worth:

If these assumptions are accurate you have accumulated $750,000 in net worth over the ten-year period. However, when you factor in a conservative, noncompounded, annual appreciation factor of 5 percent per year on the houses, the amortization of the original debt, the values look like Table 18.4.

I bet you're impressed!

Table 18.3—*New Net Worth*

Item	Value
Ten houses worth $265,000 each	$2,650,000
Less mortgage debt of 10 x $190,000	(1,900,000)
Net value	$750,000

Table 18.4—*Appreciated Value*

House Number	Original Value	5%/yr.	Mortgage Balance	Net Value After Mortgage Balance
1	$265,000	$132,500	($163,020)	$234,480
2	265,000	119,250	(166,630)	217,622
3	265,000	106,000	(170,050)	200,953
4	265,000	92,750	(173,090)	184,664
5	265,000	79,500	(176,130)	168,375
6	265,000	66,250	(178,790)	152,466
7	265,000	53,000	(181,450)	136,557
8	265,000	39,750	(183,730)	121,028
9	265,000	26,500	(186,010)	105,49
10	265,000	13,250	(188,100)	90,160
Total net value and new net worth				**$1,611,804**
Total increase in value		$728,750	($1,767,000)	

Commercial deals. If you contrast that residential scenario with only one commercial deal purchased and properly managed, you get a ten-year spreadsheet that looks something like Table 18.5.

You can plainly see that the capitalized value in year one is $2,337,000, and by year ten, it is up to $3,625,454. This is a net gain through ownership and good stewardship of $1,288,454.

This leads me to believe that housing does not have to take a back seat to commercial, or vice versa. If you look at the potential of having developed a commercial property, then you have the added bonus of the initial developer's profit as well as the potential increase in value over a ten-year period.

Selling

Your entire purpose for going through all this work is to finally take your profit. You do this by selling what you have created or enhanced. What you do with the proceeds is up to you. There are several attractive choices, but first, get it sold.

Table 18.5—*Ten-Year Income Projection*

Ten-Year Cash Flow Projection					
Income	**Year 1**	**Year 2**	**Year 3**	**Year 4**	**Year 5**
Rents	$225,400	$236,670	$248,504	$260,929	$273,975
Less 5% vacancy	−11,270	−11,834	−12,425	−13,046	−13,699
Gross potential income	$214,130	$224,837	$236,078	$247,882	$260,276
Expenses					
$4.75/ sq. ft. x 16,000 sq. ft.	$76,000	$79,800	$83,790	$87,980	$92,378
Less recapture from tenants	−72,200	−75,810	−79,601	−83,581	−87,760
Net expenses	3,800	3,990	4,190	4,399	4,619
NIBDS	210,330	220,847	231,889	243,483	255,657
Value @ 9% cap rate	2,337,000	2,453,850	2,576,543	2,705,370	2,840,638
ROI on cash $460,000	21%	23%	26%	28%	31%
Additional annual capital gain	$576,087	$692,937	$815,630	$944,457	$1,079,725
ROI on cap gain if sold	125%	151%	177%	205%	235%
Income	**Year 6**	**Year 7**	**Year 8**	**Year 9**	**Year 10**
Rents	$287,674	$302,058	$317,160	$333,018	$349,669
Less 5% vacancy	−14,384	−15,103	−15,858	−16,651	−17,483
Gross potential income	$273,290	$286,955	$301,302	$316,368	$332,186
Expenses					
$4.75/sq. ft. x 16,000 sq. ft.	$96,997	$101,847	$106,940	$112,287	$117,901
Less recapture from tenants	−92,148	−96,755	−101,593	−106,672	−112,006
Net expenses	4,850	5,092	5,347	5,614	5,895
NIBDS	268,440	281,862	295,955	310,753	326,291
Value @ 9% cap rate	2,982,670	3,131,804	3,288,394	3,452,813	3,625,454
ROI on cash $460,000	33%	36%	39%	43%	46%
Additional annual capital gain	$1,221,757	$1,370,891	$1,527,481	$1,691,900	$1,864,541

Houses

Getting residential or commercial property ready to sell is roughly similar. You must target your potential buyer and sell to that buyer. Both residential and commercial require presentation and representation, but with commercial property there is added paperwork that has to do with the income portion of the real estate. Homes are sold as buildings, but income property is sold as an income stream with the building tossed in as a bonus.

Homes are set up for sale by targeting a specific buyer. Why is this important? The answer is relatively simple and logical. All salesmanship boils down to presentation. If you have positioned the home correctly or at least in the ballpark, there will be one specific buyer that you should appeal to more than others. I'm not referring to a specific person, rather a type of buyer such as a young family, an empty nester couple, or a single person. There are features in your home that might appeal to a variety of buyers, but the sum of all the features should appeal to one group more than others. The size of the home, the proximity to schools, and transportation are factors that appeal to families. The proximity to entertainment and shopping would appeal to single adults and empty nesters that have more time and discretionary money than young families. You need to push all the buttons, but your realtor can advise you how to "spin" your home's features to appeal to a specific target audience.

Sell the neighborhood with the home. What you also have to offer is your neighborhood, and its features that can help attract the buyer. Lots of children imply a good place to raise kids, and a place where the buyer's kids can find new friends and have a good time. Similarly, a home in a community with recreational facilities like exercise rooms, tennis courts, and swimming pools will appeal to active single adults. When you start to create the sales pitch, you will want to create a flyer for the property. Your realtor will create a flyer that is consistent with the standard in your area for handouts, but you might want to consider spending a few hundred dollars to create a better one with more pictures, a floor plan, and a list of newly remodeled features. You should always offer a home warranty that includes all mechanical equipment and appliances. The average cost is somewhere around $350. The nicer the brochure, the better your home will hold up in the buyers' minds when they are doing their comparison shopping.

The listing. An integral part of any sale is listing your home with a realtor. This is normally done by executing a listing agreement. These documents are relatively uniform in any area, and can be executed without much concern. Your attention should, however, focus on the business points of the agreement, and address the performance part in the agreement. Remember, all agreements must be in writing to be enforceable and executed by both parties. Issues you should specifically address are, but are not limited to, the following items:

- Is this an agency listing or an exclusive right to sell?
- The broker's obligation to publish in the MLS directory, and cooperate with other brokers in the system.
- Your broker's commitment to split the commission; you will pay 50/50 with any cooperating broker.
- How long will the listing be effective?
- Your right to cancel the listing any time for your broker's non performance
- Advertising and open house obligations.

Promotion. What value are open houses? They give your home exposure, and they also provide the broker with a steady stream of potential clients for your home, as well as other listings for the broker. I encourage you to have open houses on weekends when there are a lot of people out looking, but don't overdo it. Most important is to have a box on the sign out front full of brochures on your home. People driving by who like what they see can take a flier with them, and if they like what they see in front of your house, they can arrange to see the home. This is more important than open houses. Make sure that you have the fliers under your control, and that you keep the box full. The broker should supply the fliers, but you should make sure they do not run out.

Should you hire an agent? Some people think that paying a brokerage commission to sell a home is too big an expense, and in certain areas of high desirability, that might be the case. Unless your home is in a highly desirable area, it is very difficult to sell your home on your own. The only people that are aware of homes for sale by owners (FSBO) are those that drive by. If you decide to sell your home yourself, you also need to consider the contract of sale and what you should do if a broker brings you an offer from one of his or her clients. You need to use a lawyer for the sales agreement, and if a broker brings you a deal, you should consider paying a one half commission to the broker bringing you the buyer.

Commercial Property

By now you can see where I'm going with this chapter. There is life after a sale. Selling a piece of commercial income property is a little more complicated than residential because of the documentation, but the philosophy is the same. Make it easy for the buyer to decide to buy. The major thrust of preparing to sell an income property is have all the homework done for the buyer so that the free-look period is as short as possible. This leaves new financing as the only substantive contingency.

Meeting the buyer's objectives. This is a rather straightforward process and it includes, but is not limited to, the following:

- Background
- The investment scenario: the competition and how your building fits in
- Run the numbers
- Back them up
- Separate the above and below the line items
- Tax history
- The physical plant

You need to prepare the background history of the building, couching it in the context of the current market, delineating its niche within that market, providing a positive narrative on how the building fits into that niche and how it got there (purchased and massaged into position, or developed for that niche). This will provide the selling broker with a story to tell, and at the same time, position the building in the buyer's mind. It makes the job easier for the broker and the buyer.

You already have your spreadsheets prepared, so you have to pick a point in time, such as the beginning of the current year, and project the numbers forward five or ten years, depending on the type of property you are selling. Five years should be sufficient for most, unless you have some large tenants scheduled for some significant increases in rent between years five and ten. The rationale for creating the five- and ten-year income and expense projections is to demonstrate to a prospective buyer that his or her ROI will start to grow significantly in a short period of time. This demonstrates that the asking price is, therefore, reasonable. Make sure your income and expense data sheets do not include any below-the-line items. The current ownership's income tax records are not relevant to the buyer and should not be exposed to the buyer. You should have a current third party physical inspection of the building and its major systems completed and ready to show. Make sure that you take care of any identified deferred maintenance items. Now you are ready to put the property on the market. The upshot of this preparation for sale is that you have effectively short-circuited the buyer's review and approval time; it helps the process along and controls the timeframe.

Setting the price. Residential prices are set by market comparables and appraisal, and commercial properties are valued by income stream; the selling price is a function of two factors, the properly documented and proven NIBDS of the investment property and the market for real property investments. The NIBDS is a given if your numbers are in line and easy to substantiate. The market is a little harder to determine, and your take on it may differ from the buyers. The more empirical the data backing up your position, the easier time the buyer/investor will have meeting your asking price. Items to factor in are, but are not limited to, the following:

- The market, the MSA
- Cap rates and the competition
- Current investment alternatives
- Potential financing for the buyer
- Timing

How these items string together to become a reasonable pricing structure is as follows. The income property market is a function of rate of return, supply and demand, comparable sales data, and competing investments like REITS, stocks, and bonds. In addition, the big item is the actual anticipated cash-on-cash potential dictated by the current loan market. This will determine how much the buyer must invest, and what his or her leveraged cash-on-cash ROI is likely to be.

Who gets the listing? Another important item is who lists the property for sale. If you have become a broker, it is still unlikely that you have become an income property specialist. Selling income property is not like buying or leasing. It is a specialized field, and the broker's buyer contacts are a very real and important part of the process. Good investment property brokers have acquired a reputation with buyers coast to coast, and their recommendation to a prospective buyer can go a long way to getting your property closed. This is not a good time to attempt to wring one last commission out of the deal.

It is your responsibility to provide the raw material for a proper sales package, and it is the broker's responsibility to assemble it and pay for the brochure or sales package. It should include at least the following items:

- Eyewash; photos and graphics
- Floor plans and as-builts
- Short-form spreadsheet of income and expense, with major tenants featured *without any lease details*.
- Comparables and market data

From this material the broker can assemble a viable sales package. Detailed information should be available to the buyer only after there has been an offer and acceptance and the buyer and buyer's broker have executed a nondisclosure agreement. You should have all the pertinent leases, contracts, spreadsheets, etc., duplicated and ready to turn over as soon as escrow has opened.

Documentation. The required documentation will include at least the following items:

- As-built surveys.
- A set of building plans, including tenant improvements.

- Warranties still in force.
- Hazardous materials report.
- Level one environmental report.
- Tenant leases and floor plans.
- Maintenance and management agreements.
- Operating costs and income and expense data for at least one year prior.
- Any pertinent business between the landlord and any of the tenants that might survive closing such as ongoing lease renewal negotiations, etc.

Now What?

If you have done all this, and someone steps up and buys your property, you are faced with the same dilemma as any income property owner: Do you pay the tax and shut down, or do you exchange into another property and continue to amass your portfolio?

Rather than wait until the property sells, you must have your future mapped out in detail prior to listing the property for sale. You have basically three options:

1. Sell and pay the tax
2. Exchange into another property
3. Keep the property, refinance, and buy another

The options for commercial are the same as they are for residential sales. Your objectives will most likely be shaped by your experience with any particular deal. The aggressive approach is to sell and exchange into larger properties or multiple properties. I personally favor keeping a good property you know and have worked on, and refinancing it to provide cash to buy or develop another property. The only caution I can give you on this approach is to make sure of your tenants. You must have tenants that will not wipe out your cash flow by moving on. If that is a potential problem down the road, then set up reserves to carry you through. Make sure that any property you keep will not fall prey to locational obsolescence.

Now you know everything I know about making money in real estate, so you are at least as well equipped as I am to make a living at it. All you need is practice, perseverance, and a little luck.

Have at it with my best wishes. Please feel free to drop me an e-mail (slrider@riderland.com) if you need to vent or if you have a question about what you have read in this book. While I get a great many e-mails, so far I have been able to keep up with them. If you need working copies of any of the documents and spreadsheets in this book, you can purchase a CD-ROM simply by logging onto my web site at http://riderland.com/cdrom.html.

Appendix

Reference Materials

Throughout this and my other books, I discuss various contracts and financial tools that form the basis for an organized approach to real estate investing, not only in houses, but also in the broader real estate market. These tools are available to you on a CD-ROM that can be purchased by logging onto my web site at http://riderland.com/cdrom.html .

The contents of the CD-ROM contain usable versions of the following documents and spreadsheets, divided into two folders: Documents and Spreadsheets.

Documents

- General Partnership Agreement
- Limited Liability Company and Articles of Organization
- Exclusive Sales Agreement
- Exclusive Leasing Agreement
- Development Services Agreement
- General Construction Contract
- Subcontract
- Leasing Plan
- Mortgage Application
- Commercial Lease: Divided into three parts: Main Body, General Provisions, and Exhibits
- Purchase Agreement

Spreadsheets

- Monthly Requisition
- Income and Expense: Quick and Dirty
- Costs: Quick and Dirty
- Costs: Detailed
- Five-Year Cash Flow
- Five-Year Income and Expense
- Operating Worksheet, including CAM and Allocations
- Tenant Information
- Bar Chart Schedule

Disclaimer

All documents included on this CD-ROM are intended to be used only as a guide to suggested topics for inclusion in commercial real estate transactions, and no representation is made as to their sufficiency or legality in your state, or their appropriateness for your proposed project. All legal documents should be reviewed by your attorney prior to use.

Glossary

Absolute net. Income with no expense deductions.

Absorption. The rate at which available space is leased.

Acceleration. To call a note early and force a premature payoff.

Accessibility. The ability of a person or vehicle to gain access to a property or a building.

Acknowledgment. A document attesting to the fact that the tenant has taken possession, is occupying a premises, and is paying rent.

ADA. Americans with Disabilities Act—ensures access to all buildings for all handicapped people, enacted 1998.

Agency. The legal representation of another party; does not imply the ability to "bind" them to a transaction.

Agent. One who represents another.

Agreement. A written contract between parties involving real property.

AIDT. All-Inclusive Deed of Trust, a recorder lien wrapping an existing First Deed of Trust.

ALTA survey. A survey that includes the results of a physical inspection of the property.

ALTA title insurance. Insurance against any and all documented or undocumented flaws in the title to a property.

Amortization. The prepayment of principal over time, creating level payments.

Anchor tenant. A tenant with sufficient net worth to enable financing for a project.

Appraisal. A formal document that gives an "expert's" opinion of value.

Arbitration. The binding settlement of disputes between parties by a third party selected by the parties in dispute.

Architect. A licensed designer of buildings.

Article. A section in a legal contract.

Assessment district. An area, usually contiguous; multiple properties included in a special assessment.

Assessments. A special lien for a specific improvement benefiting two or more properties.

Asset. Something with a positive worth definable in currency.

Bankable. A loan commitment that can be borrowed against, easily financed.

Bench appraisal. An estimate of value informally given by an appraiser.

Beneficial title. As good as ownership rights to real property.

Bid. A binding commitment to build for a specific price.

Boilerplate. Required clauses in a contract.

Bonds. Publicly sold financial instruments, generally guaranteed by a municipality.

Boundary survey. A map showing the boundaries, direction, and geographic orientation of a parcel of land.

Break-even. Where income equals expenses.

Bridge loan. A loan to tide one over until another can be funded.

Broker. A licensed real estate agent who can employ other agents.

Building department. A city function to evaluate and approve proposed building projects within a community.

Buy-sell agreement. A contract between the interim and permanent lenders and the borrower to pay off the interim loan.

Buyer. An entity purchasing a piece of real property.

Call the loan. Accelerating a loan's due date.

CAM. Common area maintenance.

CAM charges. Costs of CAM passed on to the tenants.

Cap rate. Abbreviation; see capitalization rate.

Capital. Cash, money, funds available for investment.

Capitalization rate. The process of valuing an income stream by assessing a numerical factor to the probability of risk.

Carry-back financing. Financing given by a seller to a buyer.

Carry-back loan. A loan made by the seller to the buyer to finance part of the purchase price of real estate.

Cash. Money, gelt, spendable dinero, the absolute required commodity in any real estate deal.

Cash flow. Income less expenses.

Cash-on-cash. Net income (NIBDS) income divided by total project cost.

Category. A use designation for a piece of real property, a zoning definition.

Ceiling height. The height of the ceiling above the finished floor (FF).

City council. The governing body of the city, always elected.

Clause. An article in a contract dealing with a specific subject.

Co-housing. Housing sharing common features or amenities.

Co-op. Residential units in a high-rise building, individually owned, does not include the land, which is held by a co-op association.

Collateral. Land or other saleable assets pledged against the timely repayment of a debt.

Commercial. Nonresidential or residential on a large scale.

Commercial real estate. Real estate not single-family oriented; the practice of development of investment property.

Commitment. A contract to lend money.

Compaction. The degree of compression of soil, expressed in terms of its bearing capacity, or as a percentage of ideal requirements.

Construction. The building of buildings or other improvements to the land.

Contingency. An event that will preclude consummation of a contract.

Continuing guarantee. A guarantee that survives a closing event.

Contract. A legal, binding agreement between two or more parties.

Contractor. One who is licensed to build buildings and make other improvements to the land.

Contribution. A donation toward the whole, an offering.

Convertible. A construction loan that may be converted to a permanent or mini-permanent loan.

Corporation. A form of company ownership where the stockholders' liability is limited to the loss of their investment.

Corridor. Land accessed by a traffic arterial, a linear description of a zone.

Costs. The amount of money required to do something.

County Board of Supervisors. The elected governing body of a county.

Coverage. The amount of building allowed on a given site area, generally defined as square feet per acre.

Criteria. A list of requirements for an event or item.

Critical path schedule. A sequence of events, the execution of which depends on the successful completion of a prior event.

Cross-collateralization. Assets liened as a result of a loan on other assets.

Debt coverage. The amount of total net income before debt service (NIBDS) over the amount of a loan payment expressed as a percentage of total income, i.e., "a 50 percent loan to value."

Debt coverage ratio. The total net income before debt service (NIBDS) divided by the amount of the debt payment.

Debt service. The mortgage payment.

Deed of trust. A recorded lien on real property, generally a mortgage.

Default. When one party fails to live up to the terms of a contract.

Deflation. When money increases in value.

Demised. The legal definition of a premises.

Demographics. The statistical sampling of a population; information pertaining to a specific population.

Depreciation. The systematic accounting of building obsolescence through time.

Depreciation allowance. The legal amount allowed for annual depreciation.

Depreciation schedule. The unequal depreciation allowance over a period of time.

Depth. The dimension of a premises measured from the front door to the rear windows.

Design-build. The construction contract wherein a contractor agrees to deliver a finished building within a certain price range, without the benefit of final plans and specs.

Design review. The municipality's review of a project's proposed design.

Developable. The ability to build on a piece of land.

Developer. One who creates commercial real estate for a living, the principal, the owner.

Developer's risk. The period of time during which the developer's cash is at risk.

Development. The production of income-producing real estate.

Disclosure. The process of revealing all the pro and con features involved in a project.

Distressed. A property whose value has decreased due to loss of tenants, economic obsolescence, or both.

DOE. The U.S. Department of Energy.

Down payment. Cash invested to buy something with a balance due, a percentage of the price.

Downsizing. The reduction of a workforce or leased premises.

Due date. The date on which a loan must be fully repaid.

Due diligence. The process of discovery of all the pertinent facts about a piece of real property.

Early call. An acceleration of a loan's due date usually for cause.

Earnest money. Money given as a deposit against the purchase price for real property.

Easements. Portions of real property reserved for use by the public or third parties, generally restricted as to buildings thereon.

EIR. Environmental Impact Report or EIS.

EIS. Environmental Impact Statement or EIR.

Elevation. Height above sea level or graphic depiction of a building's facade above ground.

Encumbered property. Property with liens recorded against the title.

Endangered species. A life form designated by the government as threatened with extinction and protected by law.

End game. Exit strategy, the time to divest and reinvest.

Entitlement. A legal use (benefit) that goes with the land.

Environmental. Dealing with the physical environment surrounding any given property. Pertaining to the physical world.

Equity. The value evidenced by ownership.

Errors and Omissions (E&O) Insurance. A policy designed to protect architects' and engineers' clients from malpractice or error.

Escrow. A real estate sales and purchasing facilitator.

Escrow instructions. Executed instructions to the escrow agent from both buyer and seller in a real property transaction.

Exchange. The process of trading one piece of real property for another to avoid immediate taxation of profits.

Exclusive. The right to represent a property without worry about another agent's preemption of the listing position/commission.

Executed. A document that has been signed.

Executory. A document ready for execution.

Exhibits. Documents attached to a contract detailing specific issues.

Exit strategy. How and when to dispose of an investment.

Expenses. Costs of operation of a project.

Expert. One paid to do a specific chore and acknowledged as competent and highly experienced in the field.

Fat. Budgetary surplus, contingency monies.

Feasibility. The likelihood of sucessfull execution of a planned action.

Feasibility study. The process of evaluating a deal.

Fee. The land or a payment for services rendered.

Fee simple absolute. The unequivocal, unencumbered ownership of land.

Fee title. The land; clean ownership rights to land.

Fees. Money charged for services rendered.

Fiduciary. An enforceable, legal obligation undertaken by an agent or partner to another person or entity.

First deed of trust. A recorded, primary lien on real property, second only to the local taxes assessed.

Flipping. The practice of reselling land before having purchased it.

Floor plan. The layout of tenant improvements in a specific location.

Floor plate. The layout of a building floor prior to tenant improvements.

Force Majeure. Acts of God or natural disasters.

***Fortune* 500.** A designation by *Fortune* magazine of the 500 largest companies in the United States.

Free look. The time period in a real property contract during which the buyer's deposit is fully refundable.

Free trade zone. A legal tax-free zone for import, export, and manufacture of goods.

Gap loan. The loan that covers the gap between equity and permanent financing; usually a land loan, or a seller carry-back loan.

General partner. A partner who is "jointly and severally" liable for all debts of a partnership.

General plan. A map showing the distribution of zoning categories in a designated area, i.e., township, city, or county.

General provisions. Boilerplate clauses in a legal document.

Geotechnical. Pertaining to geology, seismology, and soils condition.

Gross lease. A lease which includes all costs of operation.

Gross potential income (GPI). The entire income before deductions or offsets.

Guarantee. A promise to pay, if another does not.

Hard costs. Construction costs.

Hazardous materials. Materials defined by the government as hazardous to human beings and animals.

Hazardous waste. Waste decreed by the U.S. government to be a hazard to human and animal health and well being.

Health department. A government agency charged with protecting the health of the citizens.

Home. A dwelling for one family, synonymous with house.

House. A home, a dwelling for a single family.

HVAC. Heating, ventilation, and air conditioning.

Improvement bonds. Bonds sold to the public to pay for improvements to real estate.

Improvements. Construction, additions to land.

Industrial building. Single and multi-tenant manufacturing or warehouse buildings.

Inflation. When money decreases in value.

Institution. A financial entity, usually a bank, a savings bank, a life insurance company, or a trust.

Interest. Rent paid on capital or money borrowed.

Interim loan. Temporary or construction financing.

Investment. Capital, money devoted to equity, or ownership of real property.

Investment grade. A property worthy of investment for the long term.

Investor. One who risks capital in a venture.

Joint and several. All parties are liable for the total amount of all unsecured obligations.

Joint venture. A project undertaken by two or more entities.

KISS. Keep it simple, stupid!

Land. Real property, or the fee, the site, the plot, the dirt.

Land lease. A contract for the use of land without the transfer of ownership; it conveys a beneficial ownership.

Landlord. The owner, the lessor.

Landscaping. Plantings added to a piece of real property.

Late fees. Fees charged when rent or mortgages are paid later than contracted for.

Leasable. Able to be leased (rented) for money.

Lease. A written contract enabling the use of an item or premises for money.

Leasehold interest. The legal right to occupy or possess real property. Not ownership rights, but enforceable and transferable.

Legal notice. Notice recognized by the courts as having been duly received, by the party being notified.

Lessor. The owner or landlord.

Leverage. The principle of increasing one's yield through borrowing money.

Liability. A legal obligation.

Lien. A recorded legal obligation, a flaw in the title to a piece of property; a legal notice of an obligation of the land owner.

Like kind. A piece of real property defined by the IRS as being equivalent to another for tax purposes.

Limited liability company (LLC). A form of ownership with the limitation of liability of a corporation and the tax benefits of a partnership.

Limited partner. A partner whose risk is limited to the loss of his or her investment.

Limited partnership. A form of ownership where the general partner assumes the liabilities and the limited partners can lose only their investment.

Lineal foot. A linear or lateral measurement.

Liquidity. The relative speed of converting an asset to cash.

Loan package. A collection of documents that constitutes a complete loan application; the loan request, collateral description and appraisal, financial statements and projections, and sample documentation.

Location. The relative position of a parcel of land within a designated zone (city, town, etc.).

Lot line. Property boundary.

Majority in interest. Ownership totaling over 50 percent.

Market. The free, legal exchange of money, real property rights and entitlements between parties.

Master plan. A plan for the whole project.

Master-planned development. A planned development, usually a large residential community.

MBA shop. A company employing masters of business graduates in the 1980s, generally credited with causing the great recession of 1988–1991.

Mediation. A process of negotiating a nonbinding settlement between opposing parties.

Meets and bounds. A legal description of real property using geographical coordinates.

Member. A person or entity in a limited liability company.

Modified gross. A lease that includes only some of the operating expenses.

Modified net. A lease that includes at least one expense of operation.

Mortgage. A recorded loan on real property.

Mortgage payment. Principal and interest payments calculated to amortize the principal over the term of the loan.

Municipality. An aggregation of population acting as one political entity.

Negative. Below zero, in the minus column, in debt, without positive value.

Net income (NI). The receipt of money over a designated period of time, money left over after all bills are paid.

Net lease. A lease that does not include operating expenses.

NIBDS. Net Income Before Debt Service is deducted.

NNN. This stands for net/net/net, meaning rent that does not include operating expenses.

Non recourse. A loan without personal guarantees.

Note. A contract for repayment of a loan.

Numbers. Financial projections, accounting documents, or the pro forma.

0-lot line. The ability to build right up to the property boundary.

Occupancy permit. A legal document entitling occupancy of a building.

Offset. The right to pay expenses and deduct the cost from rent or other monies due.

Option. A right to purchase, a beneficial interest, generally transferable.

Ordinance. A law passed by a community regulating land use.

Over standard. Improvements other than those offered as standard.

Owner. An entity which, or who, takes title to a piece of real estate.

Parcel. A piece of land.

Parcel number. A legal description of property within a county, generally assigned by the tax assessor (APN).

Percent. A portion of a whole divided by the whole.

Percentage. A portion of less than the whole.

Permanent loan. A loan for ten or more years, whose payments include principal and interest, i.e., amortized, a take-out loan.

Planning commission. A government body charged with the oversight and approval of building projects, generally elected.

Planning and zoning department. A governmental agency devoted to examination and evaluation of building projects.

Point(s). One percent of the principal; money paid to secure a loan, either interim or permanent.

Preliminary lien notice. A legal notice that a supplier or contractor is starting work on a property that could result in a lien if unpaid.

Principal. The owner, or the balance of a loan.

Private placement. The limited solicitation of equity capital. Also, the legal securing of investment capital from others without public solicitation.

Pro forma. Projections of cost and income.

Pro rata. A percentage share allotment.

Property description. A legal definition of a piece of real property.

Punch List. A list of unfinished or defective work.

Purchase agreement. A contract to buy and sell real property.

Quadrant. A one-quarter portion of any whole that is divided into four parts. Generally divided north to south and east to west.

Range and township. A form of property description common to the western United States.

Rate of return (ROR). An annual or cumulative percent return on monies.

Real estate industry. Inclusive term denoting all individuals and entities, all property, skills, disciplines, and functions involved in the production of CRE.

Realtor™. A licensed salesperson or broker engaged in the sale of homes.

Realty. Real property, generally defined as a house and land.

Recession. A period of economic downturn.

Recourse. The ability to enforce repayment of a loan or obligation.

Real Estate Investment Trust (REIT). An owner of many projects, usually publicly owned.

Remedies. Negotiated or adjudicated compensation for defaults.

Rendering. A perspective graphic representation of a proposed project.

Restrictions. A list of uses denied for a particular site.

Return. A positive return on capital or effort [work] expended.

Return on investment (ROI). Cash back from an investment, return of capital; expressed as a percentage of the money invested.

Right of offset. The ability to offset expenses against monies owed.

Risk. An estimate of the likelihood of an event taking place, i.e., quantifying an investment's potential.

Risk capital. Money invested in a nonguaranteed venture.

Roll over. The ability to convert an interim loan to a permanent loan.

Saleable. The marketability of an item.

Schedule. A timed sequence of events.

Schematic. A preliminary, rough graphic representation of a project.

Section. A graphic "slice" through a building or 640 acres.

Seismic. Pertaining to the earth's stability.

Seller. An entity selling a piece of real property.

Service the debt. Paying the mortgage or note.

Setback. The distance from the property line in which nothing may be constructed.

Shell. The outside of a building without Tenant Improvements.

Single family. A dwelling for one-family unit.

Site. Subject parcel, the land, the dirt, a location, or the fee.

Site plan. A graphic depiction of site improvements and buildings on a parcel of land.

Soft costs. Costs of a project other than land and construction.

Soils analysis. The examination of soils for load-bearing capacity and consistency.

Special assessments. Specific liens for specific benefits to real property.

Specific density. The relative compaction of soil.

Specifications. The specific description of an item as to use, dimension, construction, and quality; also called specs.

Speculation. The risking of capital for potential inordinate gain due to possible increased demand for a commodity.

Speculator. One who buys and resells unimproved land for a profit.

Square foot. One foot by one foot area; 1' x 1' = 1 square foot.

Standard survey. A survey showing the physical boundary of a parcel of land with any recorded easements shown.

Stipulations. A list of items to be done prior to improving or entitling a piece of real property.

Stockholder. One who owns stock in a corporation.

Structural. Pertaining to the building's support skeleton.

Structure. A building or constructed edifice, the skeletal support for a building.

Subcontractor. A contractor employed by another contractor or supplier rather than by the owner.

Subordinated. Status of a lien, junior in position to another lien, i.e., "subordinate to."

Subordinated land lease. A land lease that is junior to financing in the event of default; the loan can foreclose out the land lease.

Supply and demand. A prime determination of price; the greater the demand the higher the price and vice versa.

Survey. The act of gathering data for the graphic legal description of a piece of land.

Take-out loan. A permanent loan designed to pay off the interim or construction loan.

Tax write off. The depreciation allowance.

Terms. The conditions of a transaction.

Title. Ownership rights to real property or a document outlining the condition of a property's legal encumbrances.

Title insurance. Insurance issued to protect the buyer or lender in the event of flaws to the ownership of real property.

Title report. A written report regarding liens and claims recorded and not recorded on real property.

Topographic map. A graphic description of the grades (contours and elevations) of a piece of land.

Total costs. The all-inclusive number, nothing excluded, includes land, hard and soft costs.

Township. A map section used to locate land.

Tri-party agreement. A contract, a buy-sell agreement, between the construction and permanent lenders and the borrower.

Unsubordinated land lease. A land lease which has a higher lien priority than the loan.

Index